THE HIKE

and every damn
thing else!

DON SHAW has been a full-time writer for film, stage, radio and TV since 1968, and before that a teacher of the deaf. He won his first award in 1968 and went on to become one of the top TV writers, winning awards both at home and internationally. He was the creator of the BBC drama series *Dangerfield*, and has been Visiting Professor in Drama at Derby University for many years.

His first book, *The Hike* was self-published and at Christmas 2004 outsold *The Da Vinci Code* in Derbyshire

Married with three children, Don lives in Mickleover, near Derby.

DON SHAW

THE HIKE
and every damn
thing else!

DB
PUBLISHING

First published in Great Britain in 2008 by

The Breedon Books Publishing Company Limited

Breedon House, 3 The Parker Centre, Derby, DE21 4SZ.

This edition published in Great Britain in 2012 by The Derby Books

Publishing Company Limited, 3 The Parker Centre, Derby, DE21 4SZ.

ISBN   978-1-78091-175-5

CONTENTS

DEDICATION
To all the hikers who love the Peak District, its peace and beauty
throughout the seasons.

ACKNOWLEDGEMENTS
Once again I am grateful to David Allard of Buxton, Peter Scragg, Sir
Richard Fitzherbert of Tissington Hall and many others for their help.
A special mention for my close hiking friend who seeks, as always,
anonymity. He knows who he is as he's the only constant hiker who
complains about its length. I also thank countrybookshop.co.uk of
Bakewell for awarding me the prize for the best local book of last
year, *The Hike and the art of Onedownmanship*. A special thanks to
WH Smiths and Waterstones bookshops of Derby for making that book
such a success. May it be repeated.

JANUARY

'*What* did you say?' Freddy shouted through gritted teeth against the icy blast. 'You are going to run in *what* race?'

'The Dovedale Dash!' Whereas Freddy kept his chin tucked inside his storm jacket, Phil's stuck out as he leaned into the wind, cutting the kind of heroic figure we used to see on Soviet propaganda posters. 'It's next month,' he yelled. 'You start by running down the side of Thorpe Cloud!'

Freddy's response was to bang gloved hands together to generate warmth as well as show delight and gratitude. 'Old age pensioner commits suicide. Falls off mountain into river. Exquisite! Well, it's your funeral!' And then added, with a grin at me, 'I'm pleased to say.'

Phil retaliated by brandishing his stick. 'There's no part of the race where I will fall off a mountain. I just run down a hillside.'

'And keep going – faster and faster,' cried Freddy. 'Gruppenführer crashes out of control. Legs a blur, say witnesses. Last words as life blood seeps into River Dove, – "keep the hike going." Oh, we will. We'll go downhill. Think of it, Don. When he's gone all hikes downhill!'

'How can you have downhill hikes?' Phil laughed scornfully.

'Oh dear, all you need are two cars. The first is parked at the bottom. We then drive to the top and set off strolling down to the bottom. Then we get in the...'

'I know, I'm not stupid.' Phil cut in mildly. Freddy's taunts were irritating, but something he'd learned to put up with. And if Freddy's quips at his expense might amuse him, he tried not to admit it. Using both hands, he crammed his beret close to the right-hand side of his head – too high or too upright it didn't look military – then added, 'If you did the Dovedale Dash you'd realise how fit you were. And what made you fit? Hiking!'

Freddy hooted, at which a sheep in a gateway stepped timidly backwards. We began to climb the steep road from the hamlet of Hope to the village of Alstonefield. Five years had passed since hike leader Phil, ex-National Service Para sergeant, had called on Jean, Freddy's wife ('Black Wednesday' as Freddy called it), and talked her into passing him into his care. Freddy had tried to hide in the shed.

Little had changed. Freddy still went about the village slating Phil, saying hiking was second only to the rack as a means of torture. But he went all the same. The hike was still our weekly trip into Utopia. Nothing bad happened there, we liked to think. On good weather days the sights, sounds and smells of the countryside filtered into the inner being, reinforcing that emotive trigger we call nostalgia – useful in lightening dark moments such as rush hour on Derby's inner ring road.

Phil had spent breakfast in his conservatory scanning *New Scientist* for anything that promised ways of stemming the rusting process known as ageing. Relishing the rattle of wind against windows, he had answered Freddy's phone call as he piled cholesterol-free butter on one of Aunt Mabel's farmhouse muffins. 'Freddy, there's nothing in the rules that says you have to enjoy it. It's how you'll feel *after* the hike.'

'It's not after,' Freddy had protested. 'It's feeling how bad I am *before* and *during* that I do not like!'

It made no difference, it never did, but Freddy would not be Freddy without making some kind of complaint. As usual, wife Jean had packed him off with lunchbox, thermos and woollen gloves neatly packed inside his rucksack. On cold days like this she had recently taken to cooking him a Cornish pasty, made to Freddy's exacting standards, with no vacuum between crust and meat. It lay in his rucksack, wrapped in layers of kitchen foil, still warm from the baking. He also carried with him her latest creation, Indian sweet chutney. The sweet agony of waiting for lunch break was all that kept him going this bitterly cold day. Another incentive was the possibility of re-encountering Jenny, the border collie, who had once led our trio a long and merry dance – until we discovered a message tied to her back that asked the finder to save her life by reading out the printed words. The magic had worked. Jennie had looked crestfallen, but then obeyed the command and ran home. Freddy, lover of anything eccentric – and possessing a sense of humour that few could understand – sorely missed her. Had she died? Around her home at Stanshope, a mile west of Mill Dale, he kept his eyes open, especially on days such as this: anything to alleviate the misery of the hike.

The third – and sometimes the most satisfying – aid to maintaining Freddy's morale was 'Phil baiting'.

Opportunities were plentiful; there was no need to provoke our leader into making outrageous proclamations because they poured forth unsolicited and at frequent intervals. He continued to lose himself in a self-spun world of schemes aimed at lengthening his lifespan. In between times, Phil worked on the business of 'time stretching'. This activity was aimed at slowing down his body clock. He said it was the perception of time that mattered, not Greenwich Mean Time. A night spent camping between hikes had been a typical product of this theory, and Freddy had failed to sabotage it, in the process ending up in a far worse plight himself. Thus there was little chance that Freddy would co-operate in the furtherance of any more of his Gruppenführer's overnight operations. Time stretching could be like pulling at an elastic band, he said, only for it to snap back in the most painful manner.

It was Phil's prophet-like pronouncements, often made high on hilltops and dealing with the great matter of immortality, that maintained Freddy's morale on the hike, in the process eliciting from him some of his more trenchant witticisms.

One of Freddy's best 'wheezes' had taken place on Phil's 66th birthday, when our hero had announced that his chronological age was meaningless as he was biologically no more than 55 years old. Freddy had sent him a birthday card made up from a flyer advertising a James Bond movie. He had cut out Daniel Craig's photograph and replaced it with Phil's. On top was superimposed the colourful and dramatic title 'The Man With The Golden Bus Pass'. A copy of it had been handed around the village, causing great mirth. Phil was not amused, not even by my card, which had a picture of Don Quixote tilting his lance at a zimmer frame. Fortunately Phil never took real offence because – as Freddy pointed out over a pint in the Red Lion – 'If he got really upset he might lose me from the hike altogether, and then he'd be useless. What good's a führer without a gruppen?' Freddy was right. The ex-Para sergeant enjoyed his command. And Freddy enjoyed sniping at Phil. As typified by the Cold War between the West and the Soviet Union, a polarisation of forces can keep things neatly in balance. As today.

Near the hilltop we approached a renovated farm cottage. At an upstairs window a naked female stared out at us, her brilliant red lipstick contrasting with the milky white of her body. We had grown used to the exhibitionist. It was a tailor's dummy. On its head sat a maroon and feathery concoction, a hat that would not be out of context on Ladies' Day at Royal Ascot – but on a Peak hillside?

Whenever we passed by, we found the model always wore a new hat. It was a mystery that would eventually be solved, but not today. In the absence of any commercial sign outside the cottage, Freddy's imagination had created scenarios that would fit.

The first time he spotted the bared dummy he said she was a 'flasher', but close up saw her without breasts, so decided she was a hermaphroditic 'Miss Havisham', changing hats in a desperate attempt to win back her AWOL bridegroom. There were other diversions that kept Freddy entertained, including the fiendish face stuck on a pole by an irate farmer to keep hikers away, and also a regularly refuelled, but never driven, Rolls-Royce. Freddy's sense of humour was such that the resurfacing of any of these oddities – plus a spot of 'Phil baiting' – kept him on the hike, ticking over, year in, year out.

The wind held back as we approached the brow of the hill but, on reaching the crest, renewed its attack. We passed the donkey sanctuary in the sloping grass field to our right, but there was not an animal to be seen. And the large metal shape of a donkey, which had proudly advertised the place on our last visit, now swung loose, creaking in the wind, giving an air of abandonment, a feeling which stayed with me as we entered Alstonefield. In the last two years second-home buying had put paid to the village post office. Even its replacement, the café, had gone. Where once carts rattled and neighbours chatted the absence of domestic noise gave the wind a melancholy sound.

We walked past small, empty cottages, drawn towards the sole place that exuded warmth and hospitality, that oasis in summer and magnet in winter, The George on the village green.

Normally we sat outside for lunch, but Freddy had other ideas and scurried on ahead to press his nose against the small panelled window and stare wide-eyed into the snug. There the copper and brass around the room gleamed in the light of the coal fire. He turned as Phil and I approached. 'Gruppenführer…'

'No.' Phil spoke firmly and plonked himself on the wooden bench at the side of the green, opened his rucksack and took out his blue plastic lunchbox.

'But it's New Year!' Freddy appealed to me. 'Don, we always mark the occasion! We always call in at a field dressing station for repair at New Year!'

'No, Freddy, no.' Phil intervened before I could answer and slipped off the thin elastic band that kept the lid clamped to the box. He had to show firm leadership, especially in winter when Freddy had demonstrated more than once that he lacked the resolve that it took to leave a pub's warmth for an afternoon of cold hiking.

A Muscovy duck waddled towards us from the green, a sharp eye on the main attraction, Phil's lunchbox.

Freddy looked back into the snug. 'Look at that. Warmth, beer, pleasure. Stevens, I draw your attention to rule 33a...'

'Appendix B.' Phil quoted the rule that cancelled all other rules, his own invention, for his own use, employed to counter Freddy's self-invented rules, usually aimed at improving his own lot, based – Phil said – on his three vices of 'warmth, alcohol and immobility', comforts strictly at variance with the virtues of the hike as he, himself, conceived them – 'freezing, sober and hard slogging'. Freddy said it was crazy, out of Kafka, frequently laughed incredulously about it and told Phil he had to be nuts if he thought he could get away with it. But he did – always.

Freddy pointed to the large painting of St George and the Dragon fixed over the pub entrance. 'Gruppenführer,' he said firmly, 'I want to go in here for a drink and get warm. That is my right. As agreed.'

Freddy was correct. The bribe Phil had used to lure him into hiking in the first place had been the promise of a pub visit. On the fourth hike Freddy had one too many and fell into a heap of slurry. Pub visits were out, declared Phil. Freddy, outraged, had declared he would hike no more. When Jean pushed him out on cold, wet days 'for the good of his health' he told her it was the HSBC bank to visit for his financial documents if he failed to return. 'Off you go' she would say, laughing under her frizzy mop of ginger hair. 'You can have a pint of Boddingtons when you get back.' On hot days the promise was usually a Magnum ice cream.

But soon Phil had to relent somewhat in the face of a peeved and humiliated Freddy (if too goaded he might just cut and run) by offering a new rule, 24d, which would allow a maximum of one pint 'whenever there was no time pressure or when the heat was oppressive.' Freddy said that Phil always brought 'time pressure' to the hike and the navigator was more oppressive than the heat. 'A new rule, another fascist edict,' he moaned, forcing Jean – at last – to admit that Freddy had a case and, keen to keep him hiking, she suggested a compromise. She invited Phil to drop in for coffee and partake of a slice of her freshly baked Bakewell tart, a treat designed to soothe troubled waters. Phil accepted and, calmed into a mellow mood, offered to provide Freddy with a drink at least once a month, 'time in pub not to exceed 20 minutes'.

'What a good compromise,' said Jean, with a big smile. 'I'm sure Freddy's happy with that. Aren't you?'

Freddy sighed, put upon yet again. When Phil had gone he said he wanted the cancellation of unilaterally imposed rules and the cessation of his wife's adoration of the Gruppenführer, comparing it to Unity Mitford's worship of Adolf Hitler. He also wanted assurance that a lunchtime pint would not be regarded as a debt which had to be repaid in some trial of Herculean endurance. Today, outside the George, the latter fears arose as Phil suddenly put the lid back on his lunchbox. 'Fine,' he said. 'One pint and no more than 15 minutes.'

Freddy stared at Phil. 'Beg your pardon?'

'Fine. Inside.' Phil packed away his lunchbox. 'Twenty minutes max, you deserve it.' Phil picked up his rucksack.

'Deserve what?' Freddy and I exchanged perplexed glances.

'You said "mark", not "celebrate", New Year. Well come on, you've lost a minute.' Phil walked to the pub entrance, then turned. 'Freddy, you know I don't like New Year! I never "celebrate" it! So thank you!' He raised his eyebrows in a winning smile. 'Boddingtons?'

'Oh.' Freddy said suspiciously, picking up his rucksack. 'I don't have to crawl up Thorpe Cloud on my hands and knees, then?'

'No. I told you! It's your turn to buy a round, by the way.'

It was true that Phil hated New Year, which he called 'that annual nail in my coffin'. Since the great camping debacle at Kinder Scout – Phil swore it could not possibly have been as long as three years ago – his complaint about time and the need for it to be expanded had become more urgent. He complained that his brain had developed a black hole through which weeks poured with the speed of days. The grim conclusion, he maintained, was that his lifespan had been reduced by one third. He'd already lost a third through sleep. He believed that it was the brain chemical, dopamine – or rather the lack of it due to ageing – that was to blame. Freddy's quote of some years ago – from Wordsworth, inevitably – had stayed with him, niggling and resurfacing each day.

'We'll talk of sunshine and of song and summer days. When we were young, sweet childish days, that were as long as twenty days are now.' As we stood around the snug fire, clutching our beers and warming backsides, Freddy cocked an eye at Phil and spoke dryly. 'Just to warn you that I am not entering the Dovedale Dash just for this pint – for which I have paid myself, by the way.'

'Freddy, you don't have to do anything you don't want to!'

Freddy uttered a slow 'Hmmm', his laser probe piercing Phil's brain. 'Is it Canada again? Not even if you pay me thousands am I going in those Rockies with a raving loony. You'd even scare the bears!' Freddy raised the glass to his lips then froze, 'Oh – hold on. Hold on. I know what it is!' He pointed a finger at Phil's chest. 'That Cape Kennedy job. It's us going into space with you, isn't it!'

The 'NASA for nutters caper', as Freddy termed it, had flowered in Phil's brain 20 years earlier when he had shaken the hand of Jim Irwin, the driver of the Apollo 'moon buggy', after his talk at Repton School. It was that physical contact with someone who had stood – and driven – on the moon that had seeded a rare orchid in Phil's garden of dreams. It would be time-stretching with a vengeance. Years later, when John Glenn shot back into space, the first senior citizen to achieve this feat, Phil had envied him greatly, never thinking for a moment that he would get the chance to go up there himself.

Of course any such hope was pure fantasy – until 2005. Then, amazingly, NASA stated that the search had begun for 'suitable' oldies to go into deep space. Older people would live out their natural lives before the effects of radiation poisoning could kill them, not the case with young astronauts. Phil sent off for three application forms, one for each of us, to my consternation and Freddy's horror. No way, he said, was he going to subject himself to G-forces that would rip out his fillings. He informed Phil that Jean had him booked driving a camper van around the Dordogne and wouldn't want him hanging out around Jupiter.

Phil appeared to accept our excuses and concentrated on shaping his image as a space cowboy by chewing gum and playing 'Top Gun' video games. By the end of the first month nothing had been heard from NASA Mission Directorate, Washington DC. Phil actually took comfort from this, assuming that all the failures would by now have been notified.

Phil waited for a customer to leave the snug before speaking, addressing us both. 'Look,' he said. 'I've filled in your applications.'

'You've...!' Freddy's mouth gaped.

'Don't worry. It's only the preliminary. I did it because it would be great if we could go together. There's plenty of time to pull out.' He became urgent. 'Think about it! You don't know what you'll be missing, Freddy.'

'Oh but I do! Trapped with you in a space capsule? Watching you run for light years on a keep-fit treadmill like a demented hamster?'

'Oh, alright then. I'll go alone.' Phil spoke in clipped tones, raising his chin in dignified martyrdom.

'That's the style,' Freddy said encouragingly. He raised his glass. 'We salute our Gruppenführer's ride to the stars. May he go far – very far.'

'Thank you,' said Phil graciously, completely missing the innuendo.

Freddy took another sip of Boddingtons, leaving a thin trace of white foam on his upper lip. He continued in top form, helping to obliterate the morning's misery. 'Spaceship arrives on Mars. Bobble-hatted pensioner declares "One step for mankind, a giant cock-up for me, I forgot to cancel the newspapers".'

While we warmed ourselves, Richard Grandjean, landlord of the George, made one of his rare sallies from kitchen to snug, bringing with him a pleasant odour of Lancashire hotpot. Beaming brightly, his domed forehead glistening from the kitchen heat, he wiped his hands on a blue striped apron, a trifle nervously since he brought unexpected and cataclysmic news. 'Just to tell you chaps that Sue and me, well, we're retiring in March.'

A pause – and then three groans of 'Oh no.'

'Yes,' said Richard, sadly.

'Twenty-five years you've been here.' Phil said it more as a fact than a question.

'And the rest,' said Richard. 'Over 40. Well, got to get back. Soup to make. Chaps, have a drink on me.' He disappeared, still wiping his hands.

Phil was motionless, appalled. 'He's been here *40* years?' I came here with Ruth 20 years ago – couldn't have been more than that – and I'm sure he'd only just arrived! That's impossible – over *40*?' Disbelief turned to despair. 'That's over 20 years I've lost...' He exhaled, eyes wide. 'Hell's teeth,' he whispered.

'Gruppenführer,' Freddy tried to sound reassuring. 'You haven't lost 20 years. They were his years not yours.'

Phil screwed up his face at him. 'I know! But it's my perception of it! You still don't understand Freddy! It shows I've slipped out of the normal feeling for it! Every day I get up at eight, have breakfast and then it's 12 o'clock! What have I done – nothing!' The jar of beer quivered in the tight clutch of Phil's hand. 'How many more times do I have to keep telling you, time does not exist outside our body clocks! I've been saying that for the last three years!'

'No, five,' I said. 'Five years...' I tailed off at Phil's glassy stare.

'Five?' Phil's voice had gone faint. He seemed to sway a little, his eyes clouding over. Freddy put a considerate hand on Phil's shoulder, as you might a trauma victim. 'Never mind, old chap.'

'But I do! That's it! I do mind!' Phil gave out an explosive 'Ugh!'

'Look,' said Freddy, gently. 'You'll stretch time with your Dovedale Dash. You might only be in a coma for a day, and when you come round you'll think it's been a whole year. Think how great you'll feel when you find it's not true.' He accompanied his homily with a smile and little nods of the head.

Phil put on a faint, dry smile. 'Do you know something Freddy, it's a good job that Francis Drake didn't have you as counsellor. He'd have stayed at home still playing bowls.'

'It's a good job he didn't have you as navigator,' retorted Freddy. 'Round the world? Three years for you, a lifetime for him!' He grinned happily and toasted Phil again. 'Happy New Year, Gruppenführer.'

'Don't,' Phil said sternly, reminded for the second time in 10 minutes of the one date in the calendar that undermined his spirits more than any other. New Year celebrations, he annually maintained, should be banned and the people who promoted them bound to a gun carriage and given 40 lashes. He said he had considered starting up a web site to be called 'Black New Year'. It would be a post board for men in similar straits whose concept of time had similarly robbed them of one-third of their retirement. Freddy suggested he called his site *www.gruppengripe.co.uk*.

Phil had an additional anxiety at New Year stemming from the activities of his wife Ruth and her women friends. Each year Ruth, Jean and Liz, plus five others, took it in turns to host a party (how anyone could celebrate the end of an old year, which they'd survived, to welcome a new one that held no such promise, he failed to comprehend). His dread of 31 December arose from these females never failing to transmogrify themselves into brides of Dracula. Each year the midnight bong not only resonated with the mark of his mortality, but was the cue for these creatures – sober and gentle all year as they wheeled around Tescos – to turn into leering predators, in turn falling upon his mouth with ravenous intent. Inevitably, being the middle of winter, at least one would have a heavy cold. It was appalling.

Worse, it threatened the hike. Since the first occasion, after which he was forced to miss one through a chest ailment, he fashioned for himself a small TCP spray out of a perfume bottle. After all the sloppy kissing he always nipped into the bathroom to disinfect his nasal passages and the back of his throat. He even brought it with him on the hike in case he found himself, as now, in the unhealthy warmth of a pub bar where dodging sneezes would prove awkward.

Phil stared into the fire and breathed in deeply as if to give strength to what he had to say. He turned to face us, 'Look,' he said with determination, 'there's no reason why all three of us couldn't go with NASA. All you have to…'

Freddy cried out 'You see!' choking on his beer. 'It *was* the payback! This miserable pint is for NASA! You are amazing Stevens. You are absolutely amazing. Your trickery would outmachiavelli Machiavelli.'

'No, listen.' Phil was adamant and fully open, 'It's for you, not me! You know your heart can stand it. You've had hypothermia and heat stroke and survived every time! Think about the time-stretching! Also remember when you get back from Mars it's later on Earth! Think how many years you'll have had for the price of one!'

'But I won't have experienced them, which is what you're always on about! And I don't fancy going to my doom!' Freddy said that he still had a bad memory as a child of being sick on board a whirligig at Little Eaton's 'Tittlecock Fair'. He doubted hurtling into space propelled by tons of rocket fuel would be any less disturbing. And he would hate having to drink weightless fluids through a straw. He pointed out another problem basic to life extension; he would not have the pension to cover it. 'Gruppenführer, I'd rather be dead than poverty-stricken.'

Phil shrugged, replaced his empty glass on the bar counter and picked up his rucksack, about to exit.

'Hold on!' Freddy said, 'What about Richard's drink on the house?'

'Next time,' snapped Phil and marched out of the door. Freddy sighed, gestured in dejection and traipsed out after him, head down against the cold wind. We walked through the village towards the hamlet of Mill Dale. A sign opposite the church warned of parking under the heavy branches of a beech tree. 'You see,' Phil said, through a tight mouth against the cold. 'Look at that. Fear of being sued. And a council chopped six conker trees down just because a kid broke his arm falling off one. What kind of society is this?' Phil adjusted his red beret to an inch above his eyes, looking peeved.

Freddy raised his head to peer at Phil, 'Hah, but think of the mayhem you'd have caused staying at work after 60 as you wanted to do.'

'What's that got to do with conker trees?'

'You had to retire at 60. You were chopped down before you could cause loss of life and limb.'

Phil grunted. He could never get Freddy to be serious about anything. Phil had worked as an air traffic controller, tasked with keeping aircraft safely apart from each other. Retirement was at 60. Phil had tried to stay on, writing to the Civil Aviation Authority stating that he honed his brain each day in a variety of ways, from crossword solving to – as he obsequiously put it – 'memorising whole tracts of CAA literature'.

The authority was unimpressed. Phil had to go. Freddy had applauded their action and declared the world was now a safer place.

We passed the churchyard. Over the stone wall, as per ritual, I glanced at a headstone labelled 'Mottram', an ancestor of mine. Further on, under an overhang of small trees, was the grave of 'Old Mary,' whose funeral two and a half years ago we had seen turn into a rousing wake in the George. The autumnal flowers of remembrance on the grave were now as faded as the writing on the attached memorial cards.

Phil walked on. He never looks into churchyards if he can help it. When we came to the steepest part of the narrow walled lane, the cold wind at our backs, he stopped suddenly. 'Okay, forget NASA. But I know you two could do the Dovedale Dash if you tried.'

We stopped and stared. Freddy groaned loudly. 'Oh lors,' he said. 'Who will rid me of this turbulent madman?'

'Alright!' snapped Phil. 'I'll beg no more. But just don't try to stop me doing it. I am not going to drop dead, or drown or get injured. May I remind you that the doc said I had the heart and lungs of a 35-year-old?'

'Yes, the trouble is he wants them back,' said Freddy. 'You've had them long enough. Oh, and that doctor is now in recovery in a Buxton health spa – wouldn't set much store by *his* opinion.'

Phil tutted, but hid his grin. I laughed. It was Freddy at his best. It made up for the cold day.

Freddy continued lightly. 'Stevens, you are in your 68th year. Do you remember when we came across the Dovedale Dash? We were worried about putting one foot in front of another on that hillside, and the next minute these madmen came hurtling past us, not one looking where to plonk the next foot, suicidal all of them. And you stood there, radiant, chin tilted like Moses? Now, do you recall your brief participation in that Shrovetide football? Your ancient body interfaced with a pack of young farmers? You ended up flattened, out cold. Just tell me this – how will you keep your balance at your age running down that hillside? You know the ground underfoot? You should, we've walked it often enough. It's loose rocks, mud and water. Those runners are fell runners, all young guys, and even they get injured. It will take mountain rescue all they've got to scrape up your bits and pieces. You might as well throw yourself off Beachy Head.'

Phil frowned, grunted and quickly shook his head. Muttering indecipherably, he marched on ahead, past the miniature Wesleyan chapel down the steep lane to approach Maureen and Donald's tiny shop. But the refuelled – without being driven – Rolls-Royce, which had stood at the side of the cottage, was no longer there. The little hatch in the wall opened and a woman popped her head out to look at us. 'Morning,' she said, brightly.

It wasn't Maureen. We questioned her.

'Oh Maureen and Donald retired at Christmas. I've bought it now.'

First Richard and now Maureen. And the Rolls-Royce as well as the donkey sanctuary – all gone. Things of this nature would be overlooked in the hurly-burly of city life but were of great importance out in the Peak, which we perceived as our idyll. That was the whole point. Nothing should change – should it? Logic had nothing to do with it.

We turned left to follow the Dove upstream towards the river bailiff's house. Phil, at last, came out of his dudgeon. He spoke stiffly, 'Alright, there's no Dovedale Dash for you two. And I did have a treat in store – but I've changed my mind. You don't deserve it.'

'Thank God,' Freddy said. 'What type of pain exactly?'

'Not painful at all. Something very special.' Phil wore a smug smile.

'Time-stretcher, of course?' asked Freddy.

'Oh yes. Par excellence. The best, you've no idea.'

'There has to be pain. Mark it out of 10.'

'Zero Freddy! I told you! You see? Who was the boy who cried wolf too often? See what he might miss?' Phil kept the smile on his face as he strode ahead. Freddy's concern for his personal welfare kept him at Phil's pace, though it was difficult keeping up with him as there was not room for three abreast on the narrow pavement following the river.

Freddy was determined that Phil revealed the nature of the threat. 'I suppose this is something that would have totally changed our lives?' he said, looking up from the gutter. 'It would hurt, though, wouldn't it? "No pain no gain" your motto?'

'Absolutely not, this time. Pure fun. Ah well, pity. It's your bad luck, not mine.' Phil walked with an even faster stride.

Freddy started to pant with the quick pace. 'Come on Gruppenführer. There's nothing you ever suggest that doesn't hurt. It must entail *some* physical effort?'

'No. None.' Phil smirked. He was now at light infantry pace. 'It's something that you could never do. It would have sent your spirits flying high. Pity, but there we are.' He marched on, leaving Freddy struggling.

'By the way,' shouted Phil with a turn of the head. 'We are not stopping at Harold Barker's for whisky.' He referred to the gauntlet we ran every Christmas and New Year. Harold, should he spot us, would be certain to invite us in out of the cold and fill us with Scotch, anathema to Phil and delight for Freddy, whose extrication from the warm house would have to be by winch and pulley.

We reached the packhorse bridge, the subject of many a watercolour artist. Just beyond was the river bailiff's house, outside which a man, wearing a padded jacket, dug over the vegetable garden with a fork.

He was not Harold. We questioned him. 'Oh, Mr Barker. He's retired. Yes, just retired. New Year's Eve. I'm the new bailiff.'

That night Freddy called on me, with Montague. We ambled around the village in the cold glow of a frozen moon, slowed down somewhat by the dog's arthritic leg. 'All those friends gone,' said Freddy, his breath steaming. 'In one day.' He brightened up as we got on to the subject of the Dovedale Dash. 'It would be even better, you know, if Phil didn't die because that's a wish too far. Best he gets a permanent injury. Maybe he'll fall on his head and forget who we are. Loss of memory! That's it!' In his enthusiasm Freddy hurled part of an immense 50-year-old Leeds University scarf around his mouth and neck, leaving the rest dangling down to his waist. His voice was muffled as he continued. 'You remember me Phil? Your task in life was to torture me? You used to be a hiker, remember? You hated it.' He gathered the loose length of scarf and chucked it across his left shoulder. 'And I saved you from it.' Freddy laughed out loud and punched the air. 'Yes! We *will* have all downhill hikes. Luxury hiking! Freedom! Gruppenführer your days are numbered!'

* * * * *

Freddy kept a wary eye open for Phil's treat. On average Phil would introduce a new scheme for arranging immortality or 'time-stretching' without giving too many details. After a few days he would then suggest we met for a drink in the pub, which was code for 'I hope that after a few pints the alcohol-induced anaesthesia will soften the blow I am about to land.' But this time it was different. A fortnight had passed – two hikes and three days to be exact – and still Phil had not come within a breath of detailing the delight he had in store for us. It aroused Freddy's curiosity and alarm in equal measure. Phil would never plant a time bomb and abandon it. It was reasonable to conclude that something serious was afoot.

Freddy waited until the Friday evening, our usual meeting in the Red Lion. Before Phil arrived he confided in me, 'At a rough guess this will be the most painful…' He broke off as Phil came up unexpectedly, 'Oh Gruppenführer, before you buy me a drink – your turn by the way – just tell us so we can all relax. What is this treat exactly? I need to know.'

Two hours later, the great inglenook fire that had been dancing with flame was a dull red layer atop a mound of white ash. We had shot down the Government for its continual knee-bending to Eurocracy and damned everything from teenage behaviour to the penal system. It was time, Freddy said, for Phil to make a clean breast of it. He scraped his chair over the red quarry tiles to get nearer the fire. 'Come on, Phil. Stop messing. Don and I need to know in case we have to update wills and get affairs in order.'

'Hmmm.' Phil grinned, luxuriating in Freddy's frustration.

'Oh sod it,' said Freddy and drank from the tankard the landlord kept under the bar counter for his private use. 'Whatever it is, I'm not doing it.'

Phil meditated a moment before speaking. 'Just accept that I am the one who has to undergo pain. All you do is have the fun of it.'

'There is no fun, ever, in any of your capers, none.' Freddy glanced at his watch. 'Look at the time.' He tried to relax and spoke in a friendly tone. 'Phil. Come on. Let's have it.'

Phil grinned. 'I will tell you. But there's no point if I fail the first test. Things have got to happen, first.'

'Oh God,' said Freddy. 'Like you having an energy transplant, hopefully from somebody who was a croquet player or a zombie.'

'No. I have to have a medical examination, not operation.'

'Hah. Will they be looking for screws loose, upstairs, you know?' Freddy tapped a finger against his head.

'No.' Phil took a deep breath. 'You see, you keep doing it! If you'd taken me seriously I'd have told you by now.'

Freddy stared gloomily at Phil. 'Just tell me one thing – be honest – does it involve hiking?'

'No.'

'But it does involve some torture of the human body, limbs mainly. I know, fingernails pulled out if I don't go up Kinder again.'

'No.'

'Free-fall parachuting. Me strapped to your back? Over the Cairngorms, followed by a 30-mile route march?'

'No, that's for later. I'll tell you after I've had the exam.'

The next day Freddy was in Tescos when he spotted Ruth by the organic vegetable racks. He went up to her and after a few pleasantries remarked that Phil looked even fitter than ever and no doubt had some new 'health card' tucked up his sleeve? Ruth either had been sworn to secrecy or was ignorant of her husband's latest plan of action. 'No, don't know of any. Is he still being a pain?' she asked with a grin.

'Pain? Phil? Good grief, no. If it weren't for him I'd be a couch potato.'

Ruth gave a tiny shriek.

* * * * *

It was a fortnight later, a Tuesday afternoon, 4.25pm to be exact. Freddy sat in the corner of his bedroom window. It gave him a good sightline down the hill on the left. If he leaned forward he could see into the village on his right. The low sun forced him to shield his eyes as he looked for signs of the jogger who was punctilious with the times he passed by the house each day, 9.15am and 4.15pm. Freddy gave up after waiting another five minutes.

'Hmm,' he murmured to himself. 'Interesting.' Freddy consulted his 'spy notes'. According to his surveillance, Phil had missed three jogging sessions in the last fortnight – and always when the weather was fine. Now why was that? Phil professed to love running on sunny, cold days, saying the oxygen content in the air was much greater and so helped him run faster. So why had he missed them and only exercised on wet or misty days? It didn't make sense.

There followed a damp and foggy 48-hour period in which Phil jogged his normal routine. The next day the clouds disappeared as a high pressure zone came in with a light north-easterly. The sky was gloriously blue and the forecast was similar weather for the next day or two.

Freddy rang Phil at 9am.

'Yes Freddy?'

'Just wondering. Nice day. Fancy a walk with Montague?'

'Er…no, can't make it today. Ruth's got something on. Dragging me along.'

'Oh. Okay. See you soon. Bye.' Freddy put down the phone, went into the hallway and put on his hiking jacket and scarf and went out to his ancient Land Rover, which started up with its customary rattle, sounding like stones churning in a tin drum. He set off through the village to park in a secluded gap between the church and the school, giving him a good view of Phil's house without much chance of himself being seen.

The pink-washed walls of the small 18th-century half-timbered building glowed in the bright low sun. Freddy switched on Classic FM. Having recently heard an evening's concert without commercials, he had grown to tolerate the daytime breaks.

After waiting a quarter of an hour he saw the kitchen side door open and Phil step outside, wearing a short brown leather jacket and a blue jockey cap, apparel which Freddy had not seen on him before. Phil also carried a blue holdall. Freddy watched him get into his dark green Volvo.

The car, with running sidelights, slipped out of the drive and turned towards open countryside. Freddy hurriedly started up the Land Rover and followed, his right foot flat on the floor as the old engine struggled to build speed. The Volvo left the village and disappeared from view around a bend. Shortly afterwards came a crossroads. Freddy hurriedly looked left, then right, just in time to see the Volvo make a left turn a quarter of a mile ahead. When Freddy reached the spot he found a private road which led up to a group of sectional buildings, at one time a farm.

In front was the old concrete farmyard, now used as a car park. There were six or seven cars parked and one or two vans. Freddy drew up in the lane outside, unseen at the point where evergreen shrubbery obscured the view of the lane from the car park. He got out of his vehicle, leaving the engine running. Standing on tiptoe he saw something that alarmed him.

He could see Phil standing by his Volvo, in conversation with a middle-aged man who wore a sheepskin-lined leather jacket. The man brought his right arm up above his shoulder and then smoothly down an imaginary incline as if in demonstration. An engine started up, the noise suggesting that it came from behind the buildings. It sounded like an air-cooled engine, and Freddy knew precisely what it powered. He retreated to the Land Rover, quickly reversed and, with his heart bumping in fear, set off for home as fast as his ancient banger would allow.

FEBRUARY

A fiendish lash of sleet whipped through the dale, forcing the crowd to huddle together, faces either shielded by hoods or averted from the blast. Freddy, with screwed up eyes, blinked at the hillside opposite, determined not to miss one inch of Phil's downfall in this human equivalent of banger racing. Two paramedics wearing 'high vis' clothing stood by the Stepping Stones, giving witness to the danger facing the Dash runners at the foot of such a steep drop.

'Them's as die'll be the lucky ones,' chuckled Freddy as he tucked into a tub of sticky ginger cake, held in a square of kitchen paper. He used a small plastic spoon so it would last longer.

'Naah, Phil won't die,' I said facetiously. 'Madmen always survive. Look at Hitler. How many attempts were there to kill him? They never did.'

Freddy licked his sticky-edged spoon, still relishing the idea of Phil doing a Humpty Dumpty. 'But he came a cropper at the Shrovetide game,' he chuckled. 'Went home with a bag of frozen peas on his head. It doesn't matter how fit he is. He's still an old guy with old bones and joints. How can he race down that hillside over there without coming to some sort of grief?'

Freddy chortled happily at the prospect and peered once again at the hilltop. 'It doesn't have to be serious, Phil,' he crooned. 'Just a little ankle strain will suffice, there's a good fellow.'

High up and out of sight, in a field close to Thorpe village, lines of runners waited for the gun, Phil among them. The first part of the race, the steep drop to the riverside, he knew was risky, but he had told me that it depended on how fast you ran. 'You keep the legs going quickly, then you won't fall over,' he said.

It had tickled Freddy no end. 'He hasn't a cat in hell's chance. The faster his legs go the further he'll fall. Oh the calamity. Oh the beauty. I can't wait.'

But Freddy's sense of humour, which sustained him in his cold vigil by the Stepping Stones, had not been in evidence when Phil used the last two hikes as training exercises for the Dash, racing up and down every hill we encountered. It had driven Freddy to distraction. 'I'm on strike Stevens, hike's finished!' was his cry of protest, echoing down the dales. It made no difference. He kept hiking. He had no choice. Jean would see to that.

Phil was further galvanised by an article in *The Times* which reported the latest 'immortality wheeze,' as Freddy put it, that strawberries eaten together with blueberries made a potent chemical brew which would help keep body rusting at bay. On the physical front Phil's arsenal now included a complicated contraption of doubtful Scandinavian provenance, won in an internet auction. Unfortunately its handbook was missing and so Phil had invented exercises which, he claimed, stretched every part of his body. The machine took up a large part of the garage. 'Looks like a Turner prize entry,' said Freddy, viewing it for the first time.

He said that its twisting tubular shapes and inter-locking mechanisms suggested the title 'Incest'. He likened Phil's exercises on the machine to the kind of body contortions put on as entertainment in the days of the old music hall. Two days before the Dovedale Dash (D-Day as Freddy called it), Phil was tucked deep into this machine when Ruth poked her head into the garage. She said she needed her car and would Phil please take his 'thing' out of the way? In trying to make a quick exit, Phil accidentally pressed the wrong button. His left thigh, already bent upwards, found itself in the region of his left armpit. His right arm, in trying to push down his leg, became trapped and a bar gently levered his chin backwards, squeezing his face into the colour of beetroot, which brought forth a strangled 'Aaaargh!' The more he struggled the tighter the grip of the devil's machina. Ruth fluttered about, screeching in laughter as she tried to free him, but in so doing she trapped his left arm. She was gagging as she phoned Freddy. 'He's wrapped up in himself (rasping deep breath) eeergh!...he's got this hang up...eeergh!'

Freddy arrived and quickly worked out the sequence, right arm first then left, followed by a general unravelling and accompanied by Ruth's minor hysterics. 'I don't know why I'm releasing you,' Freddy said. 'You should remain the man in the iron cage. Don't you think so Ruth?'

Ruth clapped her hands together, shouting 'Oh yes, yes. Imprison the bastard!' so enthusiastically that Freddy wondered, he told me later, if Ruth suffered at the hands of the Gruppenführer as much as he did. On his release Phil threw out a fluttering hand in exasperation at the general lack of appreciation and went indoors to drink a litre of filtered water and massage sharp smelling oil into his thigh. It smelt very much, Freddy said, like the Elliman's Athletic Rub of his schooldays, reminding him of painful, compulsory cross-country runs. Freddy told me that he thought Ruth had married Phil because he made her laugh without even trying.

The crowd had now swelled to about a hundred, plus a couple of local press photographers, all wrapped up against the intense cold. Freddy's dress was highly individualistic. He retained as warm-wear his seemingly endless scarf, designed originally to combat the damp cold of university digs half a century ago. Pinned around his shoulders was a waist-length, black cloak, similar to the police cape that was standard uniform into the latter part of the 20th century. A Sherlock Holmes-style deerstalker hat completed a capricious appearance that Jean had worked hard to prevent. Freddy had bought his first deerstalker on the day of his release from the sulphur mines, prompted by Freddy Mercury's song *I Want To Break Free*. Jean, on seeing it, had whipped it smartly off his head and spirited it away to the Scouts' jumble sale. 'No, Freddy, but no. You look ridiculous.'

Freddy had to be devious with the latest edition. He kept it hidden inside his archaic Land Rover, to be brought out only on cold hike days and whenever Jean was not in the offing. He could not get away without shaving, however. She saw to that; you can't hide a beard. But behind the 'weirdo' image, as Phil called it, was a deliberate logic governing both Freddy's appearance and behaviour. It had started on retirement, he told me. (He kept it from Phil, knowing it would be beyond him.) Having spent a lifetime in soulless manufacturing, he could now devote himself to (a) discovering the meaning of life and (b) offering himself as a figure of mystery. Originally he valued the latter aim more as entertainment, but it also had a serious secondary purpose that had risen in importance as he grew older. He decided there was a need to cast off the mental straitjacket imposed on him by the consumerist society in which he lived. He hoped that his peculiarities would help objective (b) to support objective (a). Having come, as he said, to a sticky end as technical manager of a glue factory, he offered the ensuing analogy of a free-fall skydiver who could look down on the world below, choosing an interesting territory on which he would land, and there convert the inhabitants to a more meaningful way of life.

Phil neatly turned the metaphor to mundane advantage, reminding Freddy that parachuting was for people whose aim was to survive the drop, which meant landing somewhere flat, without features and hopefully without people.

But Freddy was thinking ahead. 'If I have to stand outside the crowd to understand what's going on I have to *be* different.' To this end he invented the art of 'onedownmanship', a creation that puzzled Phil but had me in stitches. Its intention was that it would render its victims so bewildered, and they would suffer such a loss of ego, that a seismic shift would take place in the mind. It was supposed to work by pricking the bubble of self-inflated people whose vision was limited by their proud demonstration of material wealth. He said 'each pinprick would help create a popular buzz, like Jung's *Collective Unconscious*.'

'Like bees intercommunicate,' I suggested. Freddy agreed, saying it would bring his victims, albeit subconsciously, to join him in the great quest for the 'meaning of life'. Freddy often meditated upon future victims during the 'pain hours' of the hike, the one at the start and the one after lunch, when there was no tempting sweetener on the horizon. The first use of onedownmanship had been an exercise that Freddy called 'Operation Molar', a lightning attack on his dentist neighbour who, despite possessing a garage, always parked his immaculate Porsche 911 on the driveway, in full public view. Prior to retirement Freddy's company car, a BMW Series Five, had sat on the adjacent driveway, but only because Freddy lacked a garage.

It was a contrast that had prompted the dentist to smile smugly, particularly if he caught Freddy casting a glance at the Porsche. But the dentist's ego was about to sustain a sharp knock when Freddy gave up his company car on retirement and sought a replacement to initiate his first attempt at onedownmanship. He had intended to secure a truly awful car, that old communist relic, a Trabant. But Jean had refused to entertain the idea of 'the worst car ever made' standing on her driveway. 'Imagine what the neighbours would think, Freddy.' Freddy could hardly tell her that this was precisely the intention.

Then he struck lucky. A blizzard ended a hike. Freddy persuaded Jean that a four-wheel drive vehicle would not only ensure passage to and from the Peak, but it would also assist whenever the hill outside the house became icebound. And so he bought a Series 2 Land Rover, which in Phil's view – and to Freddy's delight – was 'a complete load of crap'.

The dentist was thunderstruck by the sudden appearance of a filthy, battered, 50-year-old Land Rover standing alongside his Porsche.

Whereas Freddy's company BMW had been something of a competitor – easily outclassed by the Porsche, of course – the Land Rover, admittedly a cult vehicle, was such a heap that there simply was no competition. After the dentist had suffered the trauma of seeing it for the first time, Freddy noted with deep pleasure that the German beauty was not kept quite as clean as hitherto.

And the dentist himself, he observed, was not quite as neat and smug looking. The day after the attack Freddy swore that he ranged about, looking wild-eyed and dishevelled. On the Richter scale of mental disturbance, Freddy had put it at 9.0. The success of the operation in terms of creating a 'collective buzz' would take years to assess, he said, as suitable victims were few and far between. I was not to hear of any more onedownmanship operations until high summer.

Still no sign of the Dash runners. Freddy grimaced, knitting his sleet-coated eyebrows together. 'I don't know, Phil does all this to live longer, but all the time he's in danger of living shorter. You know why it's called *fell* running, don't you? It's the past tense of what they did, they fell. That's what I'm here for, to see him fall. The joy!'

I laughed, but closed my mouth as a whack of wind and sleet had me tottering. Freddy threw his scarf one more turn around his neck and pulled down the earflaps of his deerstalker a notch tighter, securely fastening the strap beneath his chin. Then he brought out a silver hip flask containing whisky. 'To Phil. Let's hope the injury isn't too trivial!' He laughed with a frozen jaw, making me realise just how much he relied on humour in the face of life's adversity. I scanned other faces. How much real *schadenfreude* was there among these onlookers, awaiting the runners, about to hurl themselves into the icy river below?

'They're here,' someone shouted.

And indeed they were, or rather an individual flying downhill – literally – so fast that his long striding legs seemed to pedal on air. He was a quarter of the way down the hillside when the main pack came into view.

And there was Phil, in a small band detached from the main group, jogging cautiously down, eyes rooted to the ground.

'Oh dear,' said a disappointed Freddy. 'He's looking where he's going.' The front runner, a ferret-eyed 30-year-old built like whipcord, bounded down on to the riverside and ran rapidly over the Stepping Stones. Then more runners arrived and a queue began at the first stone, one or two stumbling and falling into the river. Others, trying to make up time, jumped into the water and waded laboriously across, Phil among them. He wore the jockey cap that Freddy had spotted on his surveillance operation and a white vest emblazoned with the words 'Ist Batt Red Devils'. Sensibly – and this was a surprise – he wore thermal red leggings, stretching from ankle to waist. His state of the art Adidas Micropacer running shoes were a sound investment in terms of foot comfort and safety. Around his wrist was an athlete's stopwatch. And strapped to his waist was the latest in running technology, a lightweight 'talking pedometer'.

'Hell's teeth,' said Freddy. 'Geriatric action man.'

But, despite his 67 years, Phil – Freddy later admitted – appeared to be moving without any sign of distress.

'Come on the red devil,' I found myself shouting. But Phil gave no sign of having heard, so intent was he on balancing his way across the river.

'You have to admire the silly old sod,' said Freddy as he clapped his hands in ironic admiration as Phil climbed on to the footpath on the far side, then turned southwards to squelch along with the general pack. Freddy and I moved off with the crowd. 'Uninjured,' groaned Freddy. 'You're right, Don. Madmen have all the luck. Us, the good and the sane, none.'

Later, as we arrived by car at the finishing line, Freddy cheered up when an exhausted Phil, hands on knees, complained that his running shoes had been sucked off in a specially prepared farmyard trap, knee deep in mud.

'They cost a fortune,' Freddy said. 'Now perhaps you'll pack in these mad things and behave like a normal 67-year-old human being.'

But if he hoped that Phil's strenuous efforts might lead to a cancelled hike the following day, he was to be disappointed.

* * * * *

Freddy rang Phil at 8am, loftily announcing his grave situation. 'I report facts. Because of my support for you in that madness yesterday, four of my fingers and two-thirds of my toes may now have be cut off through frostbite. I had to stand there for two hours, in 20 below freezing...'

'Freddy,' Phil cut in. 'It wasn't 20 below or anything like.'

'No matter. The action's now for £2 million. You had the victory of the will to keep you going, your SS training, but what did I have?'

'Freddy, after yesterday you deserve a treat. How would you like to see some gliders? You'd enjoy that, wouldn't you?'

Freddy picked me up in his Land Rover, angst-ridden. 'Phil's taking us to see gliders.' He hesitated, 'I didn't tell you, but he's been having flying lessons – for our "special treat." Bound to be that.'

'Flying? Phil? Well he was an air traffic controller.' I digested the news. 'Wow, well, well. Maybe he thinks he'll have a hard time getting us up to Mars,' I said. 'Or braving bears in Canada. So this is the fall back.'

'No!' Freddy was animated. 'He's going to fly us to Canada himself! Don't you get it? This glider stuff's just to throw us off the scent!'

'Phil? Fly us across the Atlantic?' I sounded extremely doubtful.

'In a light aircraft, it's possible. I checked. Temporary large fuel tanks.'

I had a thought. 'Do you think that medical he's taking is a pilot's one?'

'Of course!' It dawned on Freddy. 'Yes! Why don't we knobble him – dope him, so he fails? It's a matter of life or death – our deaths.'

Phil stood outside his house, ready for us as we arrived. 'Just heard,' he said excitedly, as he got in the car. 'They reckon anybody who's 55 now could become immortal. I'm biologically 55. That's me!'

'But only if you live long enough,' said Freddy.

Phil gave him a slow, tired look. 'Yes, Freddy,' he said, sighed and flopped into the seat.

We motored past Haddon Hall, one of the finest – and one of the most atmospheric – mediaeval and Tudor houses in England. On the approach to Bakewell, the low sun broke through a thin veil of cloud and poked its nose into the car, nudging us with a tinge of warmth. 'You should get some nice views today Freddy,' called Phil from the back seat.

'Oh good,' Freddy said dryly. 'Unless that blizzard wipes it out. I hope you've brought your spade and rope. I do not wish for a repeat of the Middleton Top expedition.'

'Don't worry. We'll be fine,' said Phil. 'That snow won't get to us till tonight. Enjoy the views Freddy. You see I'm not all Philistine.' Freddy shook his head. 'Oh yes you are. You're plotting something painful. Your eyes have gone bloody. They always do when you're scheming to get me. And your neck bulges. I read you like an X-ray.'

As we donned our hiking gear outside the Traveller's Rest, a public house in Brough at the extreme western end of the Hope valley, Freddy looked upwards at the pub sign. 'The Traveller's Rest? You dare bring me to launch myself into a day of pain under that sign? Let me tell you that turtles rest and enjoy life and live longer than you ever will. Non-hiking turtles, Gruppenführer! Learn from nature!'

Phil, who was keen to show he had recovered from the previous day's exertions, was unimpressed. 'I slept well. I don't need to rest.'

'But I do. Why can't you go back to being an insomniac? Life was so wonderful then.' Freddy had greeted that period of Phil's weariness on the hike with joy and gratitude. It was proof, he said, that 'even fascists had human failings'. Until Phil had found a way back to full vigour every hike had been relatively short and flat. But then Phil had come across Autogenics, a mental exercise which, he claimed, had cured his sleeplessness.

As he tied up his bootlaces, Freddy recalled the moment when we met the most unwelcome man in England, a practitioner of Autogenics. 'Of all the bus shelters in all the world he had to drop into ours.' Freddy stamped his feet to settle them into his boots. 'It's criminal,' he said. 'I was a flat, happy hiker, then that happened.'

Phil stayed cheerful. 'But you'll have my special treat to make up for it. Not today's. Something special. Another day.'

'So, Gruppenführer,' Freddy said, looking at me significantly. 'Is this special treat the one you said we didn't deserve?'

'Yes,' Phil said. 'But you've been more deserving of late. You will go to the ball.' Thinking he was being funny, Phil jauntily stuck his thumbs through the straps of his rucksack and strode off happily.

Freddy trudged behind muttering to himself. 'The optimism of the Führer, and what happened? He took all of Germany down with him at the end, flames purifying his curse. That's my fate too – cursed by his deputy's insanity.'

Freddy lapsed into silence as we crossed the river by a footbridge and joined Brough Lane for the long slow plod up towards Abney Moor.

We both noticed that Phil kept glancing upwards into the clear blue sky.

Then he pointed a finger ahead, 'That edge there, that's where they take off. Hucklow's one of the best places in the world for lift. They've got waves of air coming up from the slopes below, and they're in sync with the prevailing wind. Do you know gliders can go cross-country for 70 miles? If they're really good they can get up to 23,000 feet. The only problem with that is the Manchester CTA – control area.' Phil was at his most animated since we had started our weekly hikes. 'I worked at Manchester once.' He flung an arm in the air. 'If a glider contravened our airspace we'd just shoot it down. Great fun gliders, though. And cheap to run.' He tugged at his red beret. 'Unlikely to get much lift today though. No thermals.'

A stone went skittering past Phil. Freddy had suffered enough and kicked it. 'What have I done now?' said Phil, astonished.

'That's it,' Freddy said, abruptly. 'Take me home.'

Phil appealed to me, 'What did I say Don?'

Freddy took off his rucksack and sat down on a rock. 'That's it,' he said foraging for his thermos. Phil enquired at me again. I shrugged in response.

'Freddy,' said Phil. 'I…'

'No need,' broke in Freddy lightly, 'I've got your number. You're rumbled. End of story.' He took out his old Argos thermos.

'What's he talking about, Don?' Phil chuckled, but hesitantly.

'Stevens. I know the enemy strategy. This glider stuff is a cover. Your intention is to take me up in an aeroplane of the engine powered variety.'

Phil stood still, his head raised in a frown, the grey wispy hairs under the sides of his red beret fluttering in the light breeze. He said nothing.

Freddy poured himself a cup of coffee. 'No need to spread more disinformation. I followed you to the airfield that day.'

Phil lowered his head, about to say something, but instead sat down on a shelf of rock. 'Go on,' he said tersely.

'All this time you've been having secret flying lessons. And what for? We all know. To subject me to fear and agony. I have all the evidence for the court. Loads of it.' Freddy pointed his banana at Phil.

'Hmm,' Phil pouted his lips. 'I see. Carry on.'

'I had you sussed out, alright. I sat upstairs at the window on fine days. You didn't jog on fine days. Only wet. Why? Because they go flying on fine days. And that's where you were, flying. Plotting my downfall.'

I took my rucksack off and sat down for this unscheduled coffee break.

'You see m'lud,' said Freddy, airily addressing an invisible judge. 'There is precedent. The accused took me camping nearly three years ago, in order to train me to hang food on trees, this to prevent bears eating campers' food in the Canadian wild. But that failed as a plot, because I refused to go. But, the accused thought of another way, this time using the liking that my wife has for light aircraft. His plot was to secure a pilot's licence and then suggest to her that he fly me as passenger, first to Scotland, where I would be subjected to painful outdoors training, after which I would be flown first to the Faroe Islands, the next day Iceland, the third day Greenland. From there I would be taken to Hudson Bay. The following day the accused, being criminally insane, would then fly me to the Rocky Mountains, where I would be subjected to painful hikes. My wife, already hypnotised by the accused, would force me to go. To my death.' He challenged Phil. 'Do you deny the charge?'

Phil, peeling a banana, gazed into the sky. A silvery glider, with long and tapering wings, sailed slowly above the slopes of Bleak Knoll. He raised a hand, shading his eyes. 'It's a K7 I think. Look, two o'clock high. It won't go far today, not with the lack of thermals.'

Freddy chortled scornfully. 'Two o'clock high. Bandits at nine o'clock. Angels one seven. You'll be wearing goggles and a silver scarf next, claiming you shot down the Red Baron.'

'Freddy,' said Phil patiently. 'General aviation is not military.'

'Stevens, you haven't entered your plea yet. Guilty, or not guilty?'

Phil chuckled, lifting his arms, appealing to me. 'Look, I don't go around trying to kill...'

'Guilty or not guilty?' Freddy cut in, his face set in determination.

'Freddy, I promise. You won't do anything you don't want to do.'

'Unless Jean tells me to do it. And we know how that comes about...'

'Freddy.' Phil broke in. 'Freddy, Freddy, Freddy. Look, don't let's talk about silly things. Let's talk about your meaning search. Have you found out yet? Who was right, Wittgenstein or Russell? Can a hippopotamus be in my conservatory, or not?'

'You are not getting out of it.' Freddy drank some coffee.

Phil paused and made up his mind. 'Okay, fair enough,' he said, putting up his hands. 'It's true I didn't want you to know I was having flying lessons because you'd think just that. You'd suspect the worst.'

Freddy smiled ironically and shook his head slowly, 'Stevens, you are the most brazen and devious of all Gruppenführers in the whole world. I'd go so far as to say that Lucifer lit your candle.'

Phil jumped up. 'Right,' he said abruptly, 'unofficial break over. I thought I was giving you a treat. But, there we are. Can't be helped. Soldier on.' Phil stomped off with a dignified air, head erect and trying to fasten his rucksack by feel as he walked. He stumbled, looking silly.

Freddy and I exchanged big grins.

Towards lunchtime we climbed towards the launch site, Freddy lagging behind. 'Rule 67,' he called out. 'No hiker shall be forced to follow an unestablished route. The action's now for £5 million.'

'No. Three! Last one was two! Anyway, Appendix B!' Phil shouted back at Freddy.

Reaching the plateau we were just in time to watch a group of men push and pull a glider into a line-up position, after which a winch cable was attached. Even Freddy came out of his dudgeon, hypnotised by the ritual. First, the slack was taken up and then the winching machine, positioned further down the runway, began to turn, at first slowly but soon rapidly. The glider jerked slightly, then slithered forward to skid quickly over the grass. Take-off was sudden. At a height of 1,000 feet it cast loose its cable and began to circle. At one point I thought it was motionless, reminding me of a hovering kestrel. And then it settled for a few descending turns and landed after no more than a few minutes aloft. Freddy eased his neck after the strain of staring upwards. 'Stevens, how many gliders take passengers?'

'Hardly any. Usually one seat. They have to have two-seat trainers, one for an instructor, else you couldn't learn. Don't worry.' Phil laughed and sat down on his bum warmer. 'There is no chance of you getting in a glider with me, now, next week or any week in the future.'

'There we are then. You are meaning to get me up in a plane. Well, you won't.' Freddy popped a chocolate into his mouth, a stress buster. 'Not ever. Never. Over my dead body.' The rest of what he said was lost in a chocolatey mumble. Now he had pronounced judgement, he was physically less stressed. He sat down on a flattish rock and took out his lunch. To his delight he found sticky ginger cake for 'afters'. And then a thought struck him. He looked darkly at Phil. 'You've already been talking to Jean, haven't you?'

Two and a half hours later Freddy dropped me off at home, having ridden a roller coaster of emotion. But the dark cloud had descended again. 'It's a pound to a penny that he's going to get round Jean,' he said gloomily. 'There should be an anti-Phil pill you could take, one that kills the pain, mental and physical. There must be millions like me, all over the world, all beset by mad Gruppenführers. Why can't the EEC pass a law? They pass it on everything else!' He paused. 'We all know Phil. It doesn't matter what he says. It's what he *does* that matters.'

Freddy and I met later that evening, for a Montague walk. We trudged down the lane, to the hesitant hoot of an owl. 'I've got another theory,' he said. 'Could it just be possible that he's turned to gliding because he can't afford powered aircraft?'

I hesitated, and was about to speak, but Freddy continued. 'I know it costs about five to six thousand in lessons to get a licence. But he's not going to have a lot left over to keep up powered flying on his pension, is he.'

I paused, having bad news to impart. Freddy frowned at me. 'What?' He sounded wary. 'What is it? Do you know something I don't?'

I hesitated once again before speaking, not wanting to cast Freddy back into gloom. 'Well,' I paused. 'He did tell me he was left money by his mother.'

'How much?'

I paused again. 'Something like £60,000.'

Freddy stared at me, '£60,000?' He broke off at my nodding, lowered his head, bent down and slowly unhitched Montague from his lead and watched him walk past the forge and into the wood. Eventually he spoke in a clipped tone. 'Well, I suppose it's the end of life as I know it.' Freddy unexpectedly gave a short bark of a laugh. 'Oh crumbs,' he chuckled helplessly. 'Why am I chosen?' He imitated Jean, using the tone of voice and formal address she reserves for reprimand or domestic orders.

'Frederick, you can't let Phil down. He's doing all this for you. You must go. Frederick! Don't walk off, I'm talking to you!'

I laughed. Freddy's grin faded. 'But when I get up to those pearly gates there'll be some questions asked,' he stressed. 'Definitely.'

On his return home he hunted out a pack of tarot cards that someone had given him so long ago he couldn't remember who it was. He found them in the shed, a tatty pack crammed in a tin box together with dominoes, some cigarette cards and military cap badges he'd saved as a child. He took the cards upstairs to his room, sat down and shuffled the pack before spreading them in a fan shape across his desk. He paused, made a wish, then drew a card and turned it over. It was 'the Fool'. Freddy booted up the computer and went swiftly to Google. He typed in 'tarot cards' and up came the colourful list.

It was all nonsense of course – he poured scorn on himself, but desperate people will try anything. It might offer a lifeline, or lead to one, or at the least put him in a better frame of mind. He'd tried it once before *in extremis*, the time when Phil had tried to drag him into hiking. It hadn't helped, but it was a positive action, a chance, a line cast in the water. When the chips are down and escape routes cut off, why not? A 'fool' will look at anything... the search engine clicked and Freddy was into 'Divination and explanation'.

It was scary: it promised 'Beginnings, most probably of journeys... unexpected happenings... important decisions to be made... ill-advised risks... a bad time for commitments... may also consistently seek changes in environment or job.' Freddy collected the cards. So he was a fool for looking at them. Impetuously, he tried again. This time the card was 'Death'. Freddy's first reaction was one of dread, but then he recalled that it did not necessarily mean someone was about to pop their clogs. He looked up its 'Divination'. Well, at least he wasn't going to die, but what he read confirmed his fate: 'Major changes... the end of a phase in life which has served its purpose... abrupt and complete change of life and patterns of behaviour.' Freddy switched off the computer. What could be more appropriate? What was flying with Phil if not a major change or the 'end of a phase' in life, if not life itself?

The next morning Freddy walked into the beech wood with Montague. Pale sunlight flickered through the branches, but there were enough leaves still on the twigs to display brilliant splashes and daubs of greens, yellows, oranges and purples. And then a patch of blue sky spread from within the frame to suffuse the colours into a painting that might have come from the great impressionists. It was revelatory, magic out of nothing. Freddy remained still. He only moved when cloud crossed under the sun, and the picture was no more.

Phil had a phone call from Graham Goodall, the man who had once rescued Freddy from hypothermia and who possessed 50 Trabant cars. He had bad news: 'The planning authority's ordered me to get rid of all the Trabbies.'

'What!' Having sounded appalled and offered his commiserations, Phil committed us to a visit on the next hike to see if we could be of any help. After calling me he rang Freddy to tell him the news.

Refusing to listen, Freddy cut in with his own announcement. 'For your information,' he intoned, 'I have seen a soothsayer who tells me never, ever to venture forth into a light aeroplane. Therefore, I have given Jean instructions not to allow you within a hundred yards of our front door, from which extends a flight exclusion zone of 50 miles, radiating out to all points of the compass. So Thursday's hike will not include me if aeroplanes feature on any navigational heading the route takes.'

Phil laughed out loud.

'Gruppenführer, it's not funny. You are the navigator and...'

'Freddy, it's the way you tell 'em. Terrific.'

'It is not terrific. It is terrifying, because you have only one directive on this earth from that dark angel that sent you, which is to plague me. No! Listen! What are your current four co-existent, life-enhancing obsessions? One, hiking, two, time-stretching, three, flying, four, scaring me. And what is common to all four? Canada.'

'Codswallop. Listen...'

But Freddy kept up his grand indictment. 'There is no doubt you'll try to wheedle your way round Jean and drag me into it. That's why I've set the exclusion zone, for my protection. I tell you for the last time, definitively and absolutely, that under no circumstances will I be dragged into a light aircraft by a mad ex-air traffic controller.'

'Freddy, I promise I will never allow any mad ex-air traffic controller to drag you into a light aircraft.'

'No, *you*,' said Freddy. 'You are the mad ex-air traffic controller. You are the dangerously mad ex-air traffic controller.'

'Freddy. Do not worry. We have a more pressing problem. Your saviour Graham's in trouble and we've got to help him. He just rang.'

There was a pause. 'Graham? You mean Graham Goodall?'

Phil stood in the conservatory and compressed his stomach, thigh, arm and chest muscles, feeling the knot of strength flowing from the abdominal region. He felt as fit as a rock. Then he relaxed and sat down to eat. It was a week since the last hike, the day after which he had been given the result of blood tests, which gave him a 'less than nine per cent chance of dying of a heart attack in the next 10 years.' The doctor had told him that his score on the 'Framlingham scale' was 'brilliant for his age'.

Phil's rush of adrenalin had steamed ahead. New exercises were employed. Phil was seen all over the village dashing around like a lunatic.

On the Friday night Phil turned up at the Red Lion, declaring himself happier than any millionaire. He would soon have his pilot's licence, he said. He would have his wings stitched on to his leather jacket. And he would buy a pilot's watch with three dials. He bought two rounds of Boddingtons best in a mood of generosity. It made Freddy very suspicious.

On this hike morning, thrilled by the wind and rain rattling the windows, Phil tucked into a Derbyshire breakfast of Saddleback bacon, sausage, eggs from heather grazed hens, rounding off with a honey coated muffin. He reached out for the coffee pot and sighed in blissful satisfaction.

An hour later I pulled up, with Freddy, outside Phil's house. He appeared with his rucksack, locked the door and jogged through the driving rain to open the car boot and dump his gear. He carried an unopened letter in his hand, which he opened and read as soon as he was inside the car. Within seconds he popped it back in its envelope and stared straight ahead. I glanced at Freddy and then back at Phil. 'You ok?' I asked.

'Fine. Let's go,' Phil said tersely.

'Bad news?' asked Freddy.

'No.' Phil quickly changed the subject. 'Right, the day's itinerary.' He said the morning's walk would be through Lathkill Dale, starting at Youlgreave. The route would take us past Graham's house in the afternoon, where we would spend half an hour with him before moving on. He reckoned we might be free of rain by late morning.

Freddy said he was nuts. 'It's as cold and as wet as it was when I nearly died. It's me who's mad coming out in this.'

'Hah,' said Phil, 'but you're doing it for Graham.'

Ironically, given similar weather on both occasions, it had been Graham who had saved Freddy from hypothermia – Graham, dressed as an East German military guard, driving a Trabant patrol vehicle with an AK47 rifle attached. He had whisked a frozen Freddy to his house for massage and a slow thaw in front of the fire. And he had brought the hike car back to life as well. Our thanks were eternal. Any help that Graham required was always forthcoming.

Forty minutes later I drove northwards along the stone-walled road that links Ashbourne to Buxton across the high ground of the White Peak.

The wind on the plateau was at gale strength at times, blasting the nearside of the car in gusts, causing it to skip and dance in lateral movements that, although small in magnitude, prompted howls from Freddy in the back seat. Phil, master of the elements and sitting in the front passenger seat, chuckled in enjoyment.

'You're insane!' shouted Freddy against the noise of the gale. 'We could have talked to Graham about his problems on the phone. What are we doing risking life and limb? We're not emergency services!'

It wasn't until we turned right at Newhaven heading into the wind, causing fewer car tremors, that his terror subsided.

Ten minutes later we approached the large sloping square of hard ground at Middleton, the surrounding trees softening the greyness of the stone walls and houses, one of which had a 19th-century date carved over its portal. I never arrive here without thinking of the crew of the bomber aircraft that crashed nearby during World War Two and who are commemorated in a memorial on the upper side of the square.

We parked outside Graham's house and entered the yard, heads ducked against the wind and rain. Graham had heard our arrival and stood in the open doorway, pipe in mouth. Moving quickly I had the vague impression that the yard was tidier than I'd ever seen it. The familiar squat Trabant cars and the bust of Queen Victoria welcomed us as usual. A garden gnome gave further greeting by the doorstep. The sign on the back door still read 'Jesus Christ. He's the real thing.' I could hear the hostile hiss of geese, Graham's mobile burglar alarms. And then I was inside the hall, cloaked in warm air.

'Go in and sit by the fire.' Graham ushered us through the house. 'Now then, Feldschlossen! We must celebrate!'

'No thanks, we're hiking, Graham.' Phil ran a hand over his wet forehead. 'Coffee would be nice, though.'

Graham looked incredulous. 'You're not hiking in this lot are you? Don't forget it was like this when I came across Freddy at death's door.'

Freddy smiled at Phil. 'You see, Gruppenführer, here is a sane man of the Peak. You should listen, absorb and contemplate wisdom.'

Graham chuckled and went into the kitchen.

'It won't last,' Phil said, irritably. 'I've told you. It's a front moving through and it will be gone in an hour.'

'This is what I have to put up with, Graham,' called out Freddy. 'The incredible optimism of the incredible sadist.'

This brought a booming laugh from Graham. As we waited for the kettle to boil, Freddy stared out of the window and noted that the rain had eased considerably. 'Good grief,' he said. 'Stevens, there are few times I salute you, but give credit where credit's due. I think it's stopped raining.' Then, for no apparent reason, Freddy disappeared out of the house via the back door.

He returned minutes later to smell the aroma of coffee mingled with the perfume of Clan aromatic tobacco and – occasionally – a whiff of burning pine from the fire. He gave no response to my enquiring look, awaiting his moment.

'So my friends,' Graham said, puffing his briar pipe and handing out the first of the coffee mugs, each picturing a Trabbie on its side. 'What am I to do? I've nowhere to store the cars. And I can't sell them easily. There's only a few of us in this world who admire simple machinery.'

I thought of Freddy's onedownmanship attack on his Porsche-owning neighbour. And then I realised that in Graham he had a soulmate: 'onedownmen' the pair of them.

'Why don't you put them in the back garden?' It was Freddy who spoke. The logs on the fire crackled sharply in the short silence that followed.

'How do you mean?' asked Graham, taking the pipe from his mouth.

Freddy had it all thought out. 'The whole of your back garden is rough grass,' he said. 'And it's surrounded on all sides by thick bushes which don't lose leaves in winter. I paced it out and I reckon you've got more than 1,600 square feet, which is equivalent to at least 40 Trabbies. If you parked them side by side in rows you'd get them all in and nobody would see them. Problem solved.'

Freddy picked up his mug of coffee and took a sip, waiting for a reaction. Graham enthusiastically puffed out wreaths of smoke, which curled upwards to float sideways between the oak beams. Then he took his pipe from his mouth and jabbed it at Freddy. 'I like it. I like it a lot. Why didn't I think of it?' He began to laugh, bringing forth chuckles from the three of us.

Later, we said our goodbyes and set off down the rough lane towards the river. Although the rain had ceased, Phil pulled the anorak hood over his head and walked slowly as if deep in thought. Both Freddy and I overtook him, such was his slowness, then turned round to enquire.

'You alright?' It was Freddy who spoke.

'What?' Phil looked up, hardly registering the question. 'Yup,' was all he said, terse and dismissive. What had happened to bring about this sharp change of mood?

We entered Bradford Dale, crossing the river, and passed by the overgrown and moss-covered sheep wash pens, each separated from the next by stone walls. For centuries the sheep would go down the lane in a smelly state, be washed in the pens and then be driven back up the hillside, after which the villagers would entertain themselves with drink, dancing and song. I made what I thought was a funny reference to this, but it brought no reaction from Phil, who remained preoccupied with whatever thought was troubling him.

We walked past the old fishing pools divided by weirs of varying heights and gazed into the water which, though clean and translucent, had a stillness that belied its hidden currents. Although a relatively short dale, it is rich in rare plants and flowers and Freddy, given Phil's slower gait, for once had time to stop and stare without incurring the navigator's customary reprimand. 'When spring comes there'll be lots of yellow celandines here,' he said.

But Phil still kept his silence. As we left the dale by the steep lane, rising into Youlgreave village, I thought it time to raise the matter. But Freddy must have been telepathic, beating me to the draw. 'Stevens,' he said. 'Either you're sickening or it's some devious ruse to get us to stay out longer. What is it?'

Phil paused in his laboured climb, standing below the stone cottage which serves as a tea room during the spring and summer months, removed his anorak hood and took a deep breath. 'Well,' he said, exhaling. 'I might as well tell you. It's bad news. It's NASA. I had a letter this morning. It's a no go.'

'Oh dear,' said a sympathetic Freddy, concealing his delight. 'No free Mars bars then.'

'No,' grunted Phil. 'No nothing.'

'Hah well, probably all for the best,' said Freddy affably. 'There's no guarantee you'd have outlived radiation poisoning. In fact in your case, all things being equal, I reckon you wouldn't have. Not by a long chalk.' Freddy shot a quick grin at me.

Phil gave him a dismal look, 'Why?'

'What?' Freddy sounded surprised. 'You want to live for ever, well you wouldn't. You'd be fried chicken. You've got all those container lorries arriving at the surgery stocking up the 'Phil Stevens Wing' built specially to house all your pills and potions – what's all that about if not to cheat the Grim Reaper? You wanted to be packed in ice and brought out in 1,000 years time. It would have all been a total loss if you'd gone with NASA, death, disaster, kaput.' Freddy assumed a tender look, placing a hand on Phil's arm.

'Phil,' he said. 'We're behind you. As you go forth into your promised land of eternal youth that's where we'll always be. Behind you. Pushing you on. On and on. Us further and further behind.' Freddy's laugh rumbled upwards from his chest, then burst out explosively. Phil stared wearily at him, gave a quick, sickly grin and turned to stomp up the hill.

* * * * *

Freddy's joy that the 'DHSS Rocket', as he now called it, would be whisked off to the stars minus himself was to be short-lived.

We sat in our usual places in the Red Lion, one of the few tenanted pubs that have been allowed to fester in their original unfeminised – and thus less profitable – condition. The snug is dominated by the inglenook, surrounded by cream walls that, over time, have mellowed into a nicotine-stained sludge yellow. The landlord said he would commemorate the smoking ban by returning it to its former colour, but so far had done nothing about it. The huge ash pit, curiously only emptied each year on All Fools' Day by the landlord's long-suffering wife, had also contributed to the décor with a general grittiness that defied vacuum cleaners.

Phil loved its earthiness and sat in his Windsor chair in expansive and determined mood. 'Well, if I can't fly in space I'll fly in air,' he said, face ruddy in the firelight. Characteristically, he had made a rapid recovery from his daytime blues and after a couple of pints talked as though Freddy's diatribe at his aerial aspirations had never taken place.

'I used to sit in that control tower ordering those blips about on the radar screen, thinking why I aren't I up there?'

'A consummation devoutly to be wished, for all of us,' said Freddy, poker faced.

'The fact is,' Phil went on. 'Learning to fly has three parts, the actual flying, navigation and communications. I'll pass the r/t exam, no problem. I'm pretty good at navigation, army style – dead reckoning, all that stuff. The actual flying bit – rudder, stick, flaps – all that needs is time and practice. I'd guess I'd have a licence within a year – providing this global warming gives me enough dry days to practise in.' He raised his tankard and drained it in one swallow.

To my surprise Freddy didn't react as I would have expected. 'But you haven't had that medical yet,' he said lightly. 'How do you know you'll pass it? You're 67, not 27. Pilots have to have rapid reflexes, don't they?'

'No they don't,' said Phil. 'Flying is all about procedures and responses, not reflexes. You don't normally do anything on instinct flying an aircraft. It's think, check, act. You're not dodging around missing collisions like you are on the M1. It's much safer up there.' He leaned forward to place his empty glass on the table, giving Freddy and I the opportunity to exchange ironic smiles.

'Hmm,' murmured Freddy thoughtfully. He raised his head to stare above the fireplace at the large 1901 colour print of the Meynell Hunt. A crack in the glass that went right across the frame was delineated by a thin line of smoky dirt, some of which had filtered through to the painting itself, turning some of the red coats into a dark burgundy and the solitary grey horse into a black.

Freddy's eye glinted from the intense pleasure of a thought that he kept hugged to himself and wouldn't reveal until he and I were alone.

Later, the three of us walked through the village, a fall of light snow melting as soon as it touched the road surface. Phil said his usual goodnight as we approached the church and headed home. As soon as he was out of earshot, Freddy took a deep, self-satisfied breath and uttered guttural noises, either in pain or in delight, I knew not.

'What?' I said, puzzled.

Freddy was in his seventh heaven. 'I went on the internet before we came out,' he chuckled gleefully. 'I looked up the general aviation site of the CAA. I found medical requirements. It's there, in black and white. It says no pilot can take any supplements or medication that affect the nervous system. His heart, lungs and legs may be fine for racing up hills, but his nervous system? God, all the stuff he packs in every day? He's so full of pills he rattles. He won't get a pilot's licence. No chance.'

'But does he have to declare them?' I said.

'Oh yes! On the medical application form! He says Autogenics has cured his insomnia. Well, we know he still takes amiltriptyline and a load of other things that aren't allowed. Oh the glory, the glory. Deliverance!' Freddy raised his head to the black sky in blissful relief.

I was less euphoric, wanting to sound a note of caution, but held back in the face of his enthusiasm.

Freddy raised an arm in a gesture of victory.

'We'll see,' I said. 'Let's hope.'

We came to Freddy's tall Victorian semi on the hilltop. It reminded me of a Herman Munster abode. I could imagine the carol singers below being treated to a downpour of boiling oil from the battlements.

Freddy glanced up at the lit attic window. 'She'll be up there,' he said, 'embroidering and plotting my downfall.' He grinned at my dubious smile. 'Oh, Jean thinks Phil is always right. I'm never right. But she won't be able to help him this time. The law's the law. God be praised. 'Night Don.'

I watched him cross the gravelled drive, still chuckling to himself. He passed the battered old Land Rover to walk up the worn stone steps to the front door. Over it was a Victorian glass panel, featuring a yellow diamond surrounded by dark red roses.

MARCH

From late February the steep hill outside Freddy's house had been gritted almost daily. The British Isles was in the grip of a deep freeze with some alarmists paradoxically arguing that global warming was responsible. Apparently partial melting of the Arctic ice cap had stemmed the northerly flow of warm currents from the Caribbean. On this hike day, 1 March, it seemed they had disappeared altogether.

Freddy called Phil with a warning, his direst yet.

'Mark this,' he said gravely. 'It will be so cold that birds will freeze in the air and drop like stones. Did you know that tree trunks can shatter in this? And you want to take me out into the Arctic as you did on Taddington Moor when it froze my blood?'

'Yes, Freddy, but…'

'But me no buts Gruppenführer. You masochists may like cryogenic comas, but I don't. Anyway, I've got to take a book back to the library.'

Phil broke into laughter. His refusal to take offence at Freddy's complaints is a strong factor that helps keep the hike going. 'Freddy,' he said, 'I keep telling you. Think how you'll feel after…'

'Afterwards,' interrupted Freddy. 'The great afterwards. The trouble is life isn't lived in the afterwards. It's now.'

But Jean wouldn't budge an inch. 'Hiking can only do you good, Frederick.' And that was that. But he made sure he took some creature comforts with him on today's hike, five specially selected chocolates, from his secret cache.

'The route,' Phil announced, once in the car, 'is the northern and southern Hartington loops, in that order.'

Freddy chortled in disbelief. 'You're going to drive down that hill into Hartington in this freeze up? The Cresta Run's less dangerous. They don't go over the edge. They just slide on their backsides. We'll sail off at the first bend. Stuck on tree tops!'

In the event we survived, by virtue of the council's thoughtful deployment of gritting trucks. The long descent from the A515 was made in silence. Phil, to his credit, did not say 'I told you so.' Instead he gave me a smug grin, which left Freddy in the back seat, muttering to himself.

We parked in our usual place, the village square.

'Hah! Wonderful!' exclaimed Phil, getting out of the car and taking a deep breath. 'Champagne, Freddy! Get your lungs full of that.'

Freddy slowly crawled out of the warmth, his breath condensing in the sub-zero air, and looked about in dismay. 'Why do I suffer?' He coughed weakly. 'My chest won't stand this. Mind, you've got to die some way. I've told Jean which bank to go to for the house deeds.'

This brought a chuckle from me and a delighted cackle from Phil.

Clad in anorak, scarf, woolly hat and boots, we set off past the duck pond and then the famous Old Cheese Shop. Ten minutes later we began to climb the hillside, being careful not to slip on frozen earth. Halfway up a tinny sound was heard. Music? Yes, orchestral music, getting louder as we neared the summit and then identifiable as Barber's *Adagio*, but oddly in keeping with our wintry environment in its sadness and beauty.

Close to the hilltop a man was in the process of rebuilding part of a stone wall, his transistor radio on the ground. Was he the same waller we had met three years ago, close to Dovedale? His appearance suggested it was. He was smallish and balloon shaped, wearing a brown overall on top of several layers of padded clothing. On his head was a scratched, brown leather helmet with dangling ear flaps. His get-up reminded me, for some reason, of a mediaeval monk. Although the music he played was classical, as it had been on our first encounter, I stayed uncertain as we approached. He had his back to us, running an eye over the scattering of rocks on the ground. Behind him was the gap in the wall which he was busy filling in, around him the tools of his trade: measure, building lines, pickaxe, mattock and shovel. He had already laid the foundation stones and now faced the task of building two walls, both running alongside each other a few inches apart and gradually tapering towards the top. The gap between them would be filled with smaller stones as the work progressed.

He turned and saw us. 'Hiya!' he called out. I could see that two fingers were missing from his glove-covered left hand, conclusive proof of identification. We exchanged greetings, reminding him of our first encounter years ago, which both surprised and pleased him.

I expressed my amazement that he could handle stones in such cold weather.

He looked at me, his face the colour of red steak, but with twinkling eyes. 'I'm working, but brickies can't, can they? Their mortar freezes up in this. I only build dry walls!'

In spirit he was a descendant of the rural craftsmen of Shakespeare's day, especially in the interpretation of weather lore, using his own powers of observation. 'Tell yer what,' he went on. 'This freeze up's goin' to last a long time.'

We asked him how he knew that. Wasn't it nearly the end of winter?

He took his chance for a break and took out a thermos flask from an ex-army pack. 'Well, it's been cold ever since January. The first sign we 'ad was a warm November. Then we 'ad masses of holly berries, another sign. Then it was Bewick's swans comin' over, in front of them cold easterlies. So I reckon we've got this for some time.'

Freddy wondered aloud if we could hire him as our very own weather forecaster with a direct line to the navigator. The encounter broke up in laughter and us wishing him well.

As we left, Freddy said, 'He seems happy enough. Lucky man.'

He meant it, having looked forward to retiring from his glue factory since the age of 21.

* * * * *

The waller's forecast turned out to be correct. Winter stayed stubbornly defensive, pushing back westerly lows with easterly sorties of snow.

On the second hike day of the month Freddy rang Phil. 'This is Reich headquarters, Berlin. Attention all Gruppenführers. Buxton, Bakewell, Ashbourne and Matlock are cut off. Stand by your radios for further announcements.'

'Who says they're cut off?' Phil speared a piece of black pudding with his fork.

'My grandmother.'

Phil chewed on the black pudding that went so well with sausage. 'You haven't got a grandmother in Buxton. It's an aunt.'

'I didn't say she was in Buxton. I said…'

'Freddy,' Phil broke in. 'The roads are clear. I checked them on the internet.' He took a sip of Ruth's killer coffee. 'Anyway, we can turn back if it's bad. But we have to try, don't we?'

Freddy sounded world weary. 'Why? Why do we have to try? What in life makes that necessary?'

'Because it keeps you up to the mark.'

'What is this mark I have to keep up to? I don't like marks. I'd much rather sit by the fire and read my book. Where are we going?'

'It's a surprise.'

Freddy groaned heavily, 'Oh Lord deliver me from surprises.'

'You'll like it. Just hang in there and you'll be fine.' Phil drank a slurp of coffee and enjoyed the sudden bump of the wind against the conservatory roof. 'Oh, en route we'll stop at Ashbourne and watch the start of the Shrovetide football.'

'Oh lors. Not that riot. Not again.'

An hour later we stood on the edge of the 5,000-strong crowd in the Shaw Croft, waiting for the ball to be 'turned up', hands plunged into pockets and chins dug into chests against the cold.

Close by stood four men, who could have been part of the rampaging pack that had knocked out Phil in a previous game. They were without head coverings (likely to be torn off in 'the hug') and wore either rugby or soccer shirts over warmer clothing beneath. They would wait until time and exhaustion wore down fellow members of the 'Down'ards' team in the 10 hours of play that would follow. As substitutes, they would take their place in heaving scrums that might not move an inch in 30 minutes and then explode to another grinding standstill only 20 yards away.

Phil took off his beret for the National Anthem, a tinny rendition played through a speaker mounted on a car roof. He replaced it army style, left hand pressing it down over the forehead, at the same time the right hand tugging it close to the ear. 'Wonderful,' he said, surveying the crowd. 'This is great, one in the eye for the Health and Safety Executive. Hell's teeth, what's a spot of concussion when you have an event like this?'

Freddy gave him a dry look. 'You got a blow to the head that could have killed you and you say it's one in the eye for Health and Safety?'

'Freddy!' Phil was scornful. 'As kids we used to walk across unfenced sewer pipes over rivers. What do they do now? Watch a computer screen and eat crisps.' Phil nodded towards a group of men and women wearing yellow vests. 'See those, over there? They're marshals. For the first time in hundreds of years they've put in safety marshals! It's the first step. In five years they'll stop play going past the shops. Then they'll try to ban it.'

'Well,' said Freddy. 'Derby had this game. They stopped it 160 years ago, said it was savage and uncivilised. The likes of Caligula must have ruled here – and obviously still do. But…' – and Freddy pulled out a hand to make his point – 'I have no objection to anybody's mayhem so long as they leave me out of it. And while you're not navigating I'll be Gruppenführer.' He pointed to the mass of young men gathering in front of the podium from which the ball would be thrown. 'My orders are that you will not approach those heathens and you will not, under any circumstances, catch the ball should it inadvertently spring out to you. You are the hike driver and we want to arrive home at the end of the day.' He glanced at his watch. 'I give you 10 minutes and then we're away on the hike. Understood?'

Later that morning we climbed the carbuncular Ecton Hill, near Wetton village. Copper had been mined here, adding to the wealth of the Dukes of Devonshire, already rich through centuries of lead and coal mining.

Freddy laboured behind Phil, who was bent on a personal best, thrashing his way uphill, arms swinging madly, legs driving boots into soil for grip. Reaching the top he fell in exhaustion, but managed to press his stopwatch. After a few seconds he sat upright to grin at his weak compatriots struggling below. As soon as we joined him, sweating and panting, he snapped his stopwatch yet again. 'You'll be pleased to know, Freddy, you did that in 10 minutes 10 seconds. That's nine seconds off your record. Well done that man.'

'The letter to my solicitor,' puffed Freddy, 'is behind the Toby jug on the mantelpiece. This will initiate proceedings on behalf of my family for a minimum of £15 million.' He dropped into an adjacent hollow. 'And I believe it's coffee break. We're within 10 minutes of the hour.' He sat on a flat-topped rock, taking off his rucksack, breathing heavily.

Phil frowned down at Freddy. 'We stop when I say so,' he said.

'Appendix B,' wheezed Freddy.

'We've been through this. The navigator is the only one who can use Appendix B,' Phil replied.

Appendix B was a fictional rule which overrode all rules. Phil used it with abandon. We were not allowed to use it. Freddy, as always, was incensed.

'Why are you a fascist? Why should you dictate and not the two of us in the majority?'

'Because of danger. The navigator's job is keeping his team safe.'

'What danger?'

'Freddy, you were once in danger from hypothermia, remember? We were all in danger when we were lost on Kinder Scout.'

'And whose fault was that? Who forced us out in freezing rain? Who got us lost by falling for a Mrs Gruppenführer because she was decked out in sexy GPS and stuff? I vote we get a new navigator. I vote for Don.'

'Fine. Good. Excellent.' Phil spoke in the brisk, military fashion he adopts for such occasions. 'If Don wants to be rung up at eight o'clock every hike morning with your aunt's or grandmother's news from the front that's fine. If he needs to be warned about rain, frost, fog or snow when the forecast is for a sunny day I'm sure he'd like to deal with it. I do my best. Let him do his.'

I laughed at the routine posturing.

Freddy remained cool. 'I propose a new rule that no one should have the right to ignore all rules. Let it be called 36a. Don, you have the casting vote.'

Before I could answer Phil blew out a sigh of exasperation.

'This is mutiny,' he said. 'I'm not listening to it.' He disappeared back to the footpath. I queried Freddy with a grin and a raise of the eyebrows. The rule was that wherever the leader went we had to follow.

'Buckets of blood,' said Freddy, standing upright and packing away his thermos. 'I am an ordinary chap who asks for little, just the odd comfort.'

As we rejoined Phil, starting the descent on the northerly side of the hill, Freddy decided that a spot of serious Phil baiting was overdue. 'I've been thinking about dying, Stevens,' he said.

'You're dying?' Phil shot Freddy a look of interest.

'Not me. Dying in general.'

'Oh,' Phil said heavily and then pronounced, 'Fredeee!' in a warning tone. Phil doesn't 'do' dying in any way, shape or form.

But Freddy continued. 'Dead people do not bracket themselves as dead. Only the living see them as dead. So there are no dead people. They do not exist. I know it's hard for you Gruppenführers to understand, but can you imagine what life was like before you were born?'

'Hell's teeth, Freddy,' said Phil peevishly. 'I haven't got a clue what you're on about, and this is a hike not a funeral. Please?' Phil raised his stick. 'It's depressing.'

'Oh I thought you'd be happy knowing this death that you fear is nothing. It's only the fear of it that's scary. And insane navigators, who want to go on navigating for eternity, are the worst. And it's only fear that we may only be clever animals that makes people create all these gods. If we accepted there are no gods, we'd all be wondering why we're here and...'

'Freddy,' Phil cut in, 'can we talk about something less...'

'Of course!' chimed in Freddy. 'I forgot! You're not going to die, are you! You'll be neatly tucked away in your freezer. People would be able to pay to look at you, like the Elephant Man. We could all come and watch those flaky bits drop off.'

'What flaky bits?'

'The bits that drop off, ends, noses, chins and things. And you'll miss no end of World Cups. No football, no rugger, no cricket. You'd hate that.'

Phil wrinkled his face in distaste. 'You don't flake. All cryogenics does is put life on hold. You're still alive but suspended. It's already happening in nature. Some creatures do freeze up and go into suspended animation. Nothing bad happens. Ice doesn't destroy their cells. When they warm up they wake up.'

'And who warms you up? What if there's a nuclear disaster or the Avian Flu or whatever? And there's nobody around with a blow heater? Stevens stuck in the freezer for ever and ever.' Freddy laughed out loud at the image he'd created.

We came to a 'kissing gate', a wooden enclosure with the gate in the middle, a jokey and traditional construction that forced the swain or sweetheart to close it behind them, after which they could then turn and demand a kiss from their lover as the price for allowing them through.

After closing the gate Freddy stuck out his lips. 'Kiss me Gruppenführer.'

Phil sighed patiently, sending me into a fit of laughter.

We spent lunch sheltered from the north easterly on the leeward side of a grassy knoll overlooking the village of Hulme End. Being the week of Freddy's birthday, Jean had thoughtfully placed three mints in his lunch box with strict instructions that Freddy only ate one of them. He wrestled with his conscience, but it won. Nevertheless it was painful, doling out two of his favourite Old Originals.

'Thank you,' said Phil graciously, taking the mint. 'I take back everything I said. By the way, when's the dreaded duo arriving?' He referred to Freddy's aunt Cynthia and cousin Max.

'Don't remind me. Soon enough,' grunted Freddy. 'You know what she does, soon as she gets here? She's 84 and she wanders about all bent, horrible and wrinkly, pretending she's looking at new things we've done to the house and all the time her long nose is probing. Searching for my personal box of chocolates.'

'Good thing too,' said Phil. 'You'll get diabetes eating all that sugar.'

'And Max. All he does is boast about his bailiff's job. How wonderful it is chucking people and furniture into the street.'

I laughed at the mental picture of Freddy trapped with his monsters. It even brought a faint chuckle from Phil.

'So what fun will you have with them this time?' he asked airily. 'You can't tell them you've won the national lottery again.'

It had been, by any yardstick, Freddy's best wheeze ever. He had told them at breakfast that he'd had a dream in which all six numbers had been revealed and which he had written down immediately on waking. That night, with Jean taking a bath, he had sat in front of the television checking the result, after warning the guests that he would not be revealing – by even 'a flicker of an eyebrow' – if he had won or lost. He also said that, due to his Puritanical disposition, there would be no display of suddenly accrued wealth. He had then left the house clutching his lottery slip. Max had followed him and came back with the news that he had witnessed Freddy making a call from a public telephone box. Despite Jean's protest ('Oh of course he's not won it, it's only one of his silly jokes, you know Freddy!'), they had to wait 12 months – until their next visit – before making certain. Aunt Cynthia had made an instant beeline for the outhouse and was relieved to find that the 20-year-old Bendix washing machine was still there, something that Jean would certainly have replaced with even the most modest of wins.

Phil grinned. 'It's a wonder they ever come to see you. They'll stop soon.'
'I'm working on it,' said Freddy.

'So what cunning plot have you got in store for them this time?'
Freddy dallied with the cup of coffee at his lips before taking a slow sip, after which he let out a comfortable sigh. 'I'm going to be an intellectual,' he said.

'Oh crumbs,' grunted Phil in a self-critical tone suggesting he was an idiot to have raised the matter.

'Jean will be out when they arrive. She's got a charity meeting. I'll be wearing my deerstalker and long scarf. Intellectuals wear those. And I'll have a pipe, but I won't light it.'

'Oh,' Phil nodded, bit into his thin brown bread sandwich of lettuce and tomato and kept his peace. He would wait to hear the outcome of the visit, rather than have Freddy regaling him with his crazy plots ahead of the action. Nothing that Freddy did was a surprise to him any more.

The next day I met Phil in the electrical aisle of B&Q, both of us coincidentally searching for the same item, a doorbell extension. He lost no time in conveying his concern at Freddy's life games and 'weird goings-on'. They were so mystifying, he said, that he wondered – as if he'd never voiced it before – if I thought that Freddy was genuinely insane.

I put it to him. Hadn't he learned that the effect was precisely that intended? Wasn't the arousal of bewilderment at his own behaviour his essential goal? He wanted people to think he was bonkers, didn't he? Freddy had told us often enough, hadn't he? And if Freddy wanted to be thought of as crazy – shades of Yossarian in *Catch 22* – he couldn't be mad, could he? Crazy people don't want to be thought of as mad. They're too crazy to see how it can benefit them.

'Well, I've been thinking of something radical,' said Phil, popping his head around the corner of the aisle in case Freddy made a magical appearance. 'I'm thinking, what if we got somebody else to join the hike? A decent bloke, somebody who'll talk about the need for more prisons.' Phil grinned. 'Or football. And somebody who doesn't ring you up every hike morning and moan.'

Phil went on to say that he had nothing against Freddy, it was just that he sometimes got a bit too much. Another hiker would provide welcome relief, somebody to escape to when things got 'Freddy heavy'.

I suggested that he bring the matter up at our next meeting in the Red Lion as though I knew nothing at all about it. It was a diplomatic reply and the best I could do. Phil mulled over the idea, finally agreeing.

On the following Friday evening at the pub Phil bought the first round, an indication that the radical proposal was about to be formally put. Freddy was expecting his in-laws the next day and was in a gloomy mood. Phil sympathised and after a couple of pints tentatively asked the question, 'Don't you think, chaps, we're a bit claustrophobic on the hike?'

Freddy stared solemnly at Phil. 'Yes. You occupy the air I breathe.'

'No, I meant the three of us. Why don't we make it four?'

Freddy looked at him in deep suspicion.

'Then we don't have to talk three ways.' Phil spoke lightly. 'We can walk in twos so you couldn't complain I dominate you all the time.'

'Who? Who've you got in mind?' I asked Phil, playing the innocent.

'No, no. First, we each find somebody we want to put forward. Then we interview them, without them knowing – meet for a drink or something. Then we discuss them and choose democratically.'

'Fine,' said Freddy. 'We suss them out and then you choose your man under Appendix B.'

'No. We have a majority vote. Don's witness to it. Or we can put names in a hat, the shortlist.'

Freddy shrugged. 'Alright. We'll do that. But I don't want a Stevens Mark Two. I want somebody who's not a fascist dictator,' he warned.

Phil chuckled. 'Somebody idle like you.' He drew a deep quaff of ale and then, sprawling back in his armchair, smiled affably at Freddy and rolled the word 'intellectual' out of his mouth as 'intellectuwarl'. 'I thought intellectuals were born, not made.' He said it as though in itself it was a profound statement. 'How are you going to convince Aunt Cynthia of that? She thinks you're barmy doesn't she?'

'Yes, but not enough.'

'She's underestimating you Freddy!' Phil guffawed at his own wit.

I had never seen Phil so relaxed in a conversation with Freddy. He obviously felt safe in the pub and was near enough home to flee there if it became necessary.

'Just put me right,' he added. 'To make out you're an intellectual you must have brains in case they ask intellectual questions. How can you pretend you've got them if you haven't?' Phil grinned and nudged my elbow. 'Go on then. What do you do? You've got your deerstalker on and scarf. So what happens?'

Freddy shrugged. 'I shall have the pipe in my hand to point out things.'

'Things. What things?' Phil sounded less enthusiastic. A 'Freddy' chat was veering, as usual, towards the fringe of logic.

'I've got a stack of old Pelicans, all about music and philosophy,' said Freddy. 'When they arrive I'll be carrying them as I answer the door. I'll say they're for my thesis. They'll ask what thesis? I'll say it's called "The philosophical implications of Cornish jazz". Something for a PhD I'm doing at King's. I shall be playing Dave Brubeck. The Royal Festival Hall. 1954. Our vicar's daughter wrote the sleeve blurb for it. Max hates jazz.'

Phil had a glazed look. It did sound intellectual, he had to admit. Then he felt annoyed at having been made to think about it. 'Cornish jazz? Never heard of it,' he said irritably.

'Exactly. Who has? That's the whole point.'

Phil looked into his beer glass. 'Freddy.' He hesitated. 'Has anybody – like a doctor or, you know, a psychologist or somebody – talked to you about these things? I mean, if it was me, I'd get some advice.'

'I don't need advice. I have it all worked out.'

'Oh. But just, what if, what if what you're working out is too...'

'Weird? I hope so. That's the intention.'

Phil stared gloomily at Freddy, making a mental note that a fourth hiker was now definitely top of his agenda. 'So, go on then,' he said, feeling the first pinch of boredom. 'What happens next?'

'I'll show them a video of Alejandro Jodorowsky's film *El Topo*. It's a western full of dwarfs and monks.'

Phil's jaw dropped and looked incredulous. 'What the blazes is *El Topo*? And who's Ally thingy? You do my head in Freddy.'

'Great! Hah! That's precisely what will happen to Max and Cynthia!' Freddy beamed in delight.

'You are mad. Don? He is mad, isn't he?'

I grinned. 'Let him finish. What next then, Freddy?'

Freddy outlined his route to goal. The mystery and confusion would be topped up by him asking Aunt Cynthia if she'd read Robert Persig's *Zen and the Art of Motorcycle Maintenance*. He would then urge her to read it for her own peace of mind. The next ploy would be to say something very intellectual but entirely meaningless.

Freddy told us of something he had witnessed when he and Jean were staying at a hotel in the cool hills above Florence. A thin bearded man from Bath, who had looked fed up with the mundane conversation of his fellow guests, abruptly announced in a high piping voice that Italians were unsuited for democracy, mentioned Mussolini and had then inhibited any argument by referring everyone present to *Plato's Republic*. 'It was a master stroke,' said Freddy. 'Who reads *Plato's Republic*, apart from intellectuals? It makes them impregnable. So I thought I'd use it. I'll start at breakfast, because they'll get here late tomorrow night. I'll deliberately burn a slice of toast, then hold it up to peer at it in an intellectual way, while humming.'

'Oh Lord,' murmured Phil, his eyelids shutting. 'Send for men in white coats.'

Freddy continued, 'When they're staring at me I shall say, "The toast's in mourning for the loss of its doughy soul."'

Phil stared at Freddy. 'Oh yes.'

'And then I shall say, "have either of you read *Plato's Republic*?"'

Phil paused and then said, in a flat voice, 'What the hell's going on?' He turned to me. 'Do you get this Don?'

I shrugged with a neutral raise of the eyebrows, always the one balancing on the wire while the other two threaten to push each other off. Phil nodded at me and gave a tired smile. 'So that's an intellectual.'

'It's simple,' said Freddy. 'Intellectuals say crazy things, but because people know they're intellectual it forces them to think, well, they must have a point else why say it? That's when the intellectual gets right on top. Teflon coated.'

'Oh,' said Phil. 'I see.' The glazed look returned. Then he shook himself and spoke kindly, in sympathy. 'You know Freddy, I didn't need to get you on that rocket to Mars. You're already there.'

Then he cracked up.

* * * * *

The doorbell rang on Sunday evening. I opened the door to a light fall of snow. Freddy, with Montague on the lead, stared at me under the lit porch, his face pale and stretched.

'Was it that bad?' I said.

'Worse.'

I went to fetch my fleece and hat. As we walked through the village a preoccupied Freddy quickly dismissed his 'vampires' as a topic, saying it had gone well. Aunt Cynthia and Max had not been so much bewildered as repelled and had left him alone. They had since gone home.

No, something entirely unexpected had happened, far worse than anything Aunt Cynthia could produce. 'Phil turned up,' Freddy went on abjectly. 'He brought the *Derby Evening Telegraph*. Had Jean read about what her charity was up to? Yes, she said she knew about it. It was about them wanting people to take part in a sponsored hike. Guess where?'

I thought about it. 'Does it involve camping?'

Freddy gave me a glum faced nod of the head. 'Yes.'

'A two-day hike?'

Freddy shook his head.

'Not Kinder Scout?'

'No. Peru.' Freddy repeated it, 'Perooo', in a sepulchral tone.

I laughed. 'Come on, you're kidding.'

'No. It's Peru. And Phil showed it to Jean. And Sargent, cancer care for children, is the only charity that Jean supports.'

I let it sink in. 'But could it be Phil scaring you with Peru and then cancelling it for a day round Kinder Scout? You're so relieved you jump at the lesser evil? He's done it before.'

'No. He wouldn't have showed it Jean if that's what he was up to.' He groaned. 'God, that camping at Kinder Scout, that was painful enough. But this! It's as bad as his Mars trip. I might as well be out in space, up those Andes with no oxygen! Ye gods,' he went on. 'It's billed as a challenge lasting *10 days*. Ten days of sheer unadulterated torture at the hands of the most dangerous man in the world.'

I would have laughed had I not also been struck by the thought that I would also be expected to join in. 'Freddy,' I said. 'Hold on. You can't be expected to pay your way for a fortnight in Peru. What about your holiday with Jean?'

'No,' said Freddy. 'All it costs is £300 because you raise the rest by sponsorship.' He stopped under a lamp near the entrance to the cricket field. In the white lace of falling snow, his eyes drooped, giving him the look of a sad spaniel. 'I'm trapped. If Phil hadn't chosen me, Jean would have. She gets Sargent's circulars before any press release. She was waiting for the right moment to ask me to do it, anyway. So I've got both of them at me, plus that dark angel up there, Phil's handler.' Freddy stared upwards, blinking at tiny snowflakes. 'You remember that blizzard two years ago at Middleton Top? It'll be ten times as bad. He'll go like Jack Nicholson in *The Shining*, mad with snow. He'll take over from the hike leaders. He'll have us climbing those ice towers in a hurricane, slipping up those glaciers, frozen to the bone. This time it's not happenstance. It's not coincidence. It's enemy action.'

Freddy plucked a comfort bar of nougat from his pocket and chewed on it as he watched Montague sniffing around the bus shelter. 'If I don't make it you can have my deerstalker.'

Freddy scowled upwards. 'And you, Stevens, can get pickled in ice.'

* * * * *

Freddy spent the next day collecting his thoughts. His only hope of escape, he decided, was by the force of undeniable logic. He drew up a list of reasons for being excused the Peruvian plot, as he now termed it. Listed, in no particular order, were his age, claustrophobia caused by proximity of mountains, fear of heights, lack of motivation, his natural laziness and a mental illness that forced him to stop hiking and examine wild flowers. The only other disorder he thought he could get away with was air sickness. He presented the list to Jean, which soon had her laughing.

'Air sickness? You've never had that.'

'I was sick on that flight back from Greece.'

'Freddy, that wasn't air sickness. That was an overdose of Greek chocolate.' She dug an ice cream out of the freezer. 'Listen. This is my charity, my only opportunity to shine. Think what I can say – my husband's gone to Peru to find the lost city of the Incas to raise funds for those children.' She handed him the ice cream with a winning smile.

Freddy argued, but it was to no avail. Jean was insistent and saw other benefits accruing. 'Freddy, just think how it will restore you with the neighbours!'

Freddy told me later that he had to close his eyes at this point lest his anguish betray him. Jean added more salt to the wound, saying it would not only impress Aunt Cynthia and Max but also those other relatives who were seen only at weddings or funerals, all possessing excellent memories. All of them could recall 'the wedding' when Freddy had turned up as groom in a weird get-up, a carry over from the 1950s, Teddy Boy fashion. The relatives were solid, upper working-class people, Methodists mostly. Freddy, with his winkle-picker shoes – changing to brothel creepers for the honeymoon – duck's arse haircut and long, wide-shouldered jacket, had raised more than one eyebrow.

'That Freddy', as they called him, had caused many to shake a head. How could Jean marry so far beneath her? And she was always making excuses for him, wasn't she?

Thus Jean was highly motivated. Canada was inappropriate. Peru was perfect. In the face of Freddy's continuing protest she pointed out that he had hiked a total of 5,000 miles in the Peak District. 'It's just hiking, that's all it is. It doesn't matter if it's in Peru or Matlock, does it? And what better way to get fit than the weekly hikes with Phil?' She looked up at Freddy's face, and saw his stoicism vying with despair.

'Now it won't be all that bad,' she said, adjusting his tie and running fingers to straighten out his crumpled shirt. 'Now listen. You know how you've become a bit of a laughing stock with all your eccentricities. Well this will put it straight, won't it.' She patted him on the shoulders. 'And always remember if ever the going gets tough in Peru don't think about it. Ignore it. Just think how you'll feel afterwards.'

*****

Freddy and I walked Montague on a damp, drizzly night. The situation had already got out of hand, he moaned. Jean had already informed the next door dentist's wife of his intended, great charitable adventure. Freddy said he was fearful it might lead the dentist to think that the Land Rover was all part of his training, to equip him with the kind of hardened bum one needed for bouncing around in the Andes. He would be respected, not puzzled over, an unmitigated disaster. Going to the other end of the spectrum in order to collect hero status would set him back years in his search for the meaning. He remained philosophical as to his fate. 'Remember to tell Jean to sue for no less than £16 million for all the pain I've been put through. And tell Phil he can't have his cigarette cards back, not the cricket ones.'

We were passing the post office when a man in a track suit came running towards us. It was Phil, a heavy looking haversack on his back. 'Full of bricks,' he called out. 'Can't stop!'

'Oh Lord,' said Freddy miserably as he watched Phil trundling homewards. 'The only madman in the village and he's selected me for special treatment.' He watched Phil disappear round the church and then screwed up his face. 'Why aren't I somebody who is listened to? Why do I have to do everything everybody else wants? Somebody please tell me.'

* * * * *

The next day Freddy woke up to the recollection that he had been excused National Service because of dermatitis brought on by a temporary job in a factory, putting screw threads on bolts. He was known as a 'semi-skilled screwer', long before we copied America in giving the term an entirely different meaning. But when Jean's relatives interrogated him as to why he was not serving Queen and country he said he suffered from the 'Camella de Lange syndrome'. He had found this in a book of rare illnesses, a disorder that compelled the victim to bite their own lip. Freddy had banked on his persecutors not having the wit to do any research and said it was a disease which made him subject to temporary brain stoppages when questioned on delicate matters, such as National Service. He had not been able to prevent himself romanticising the illness – it was well before he dreamed up onedownmanship as an art – and had told them it had been 'passed down the centuries by Simon de Lange, a French baron who had arrived with William the Conqueror'. Only those of aristocratic stock usually succumbed, he said.

The history of his syndrome was so detailed – as with all his wheezes – that outright disbelief was not the predominant reaction in Jean's camp of relatives, more a general scepticism.

None, at that time, had dared declare him insane, if just for Jean's sake.

As Freddy sat down to breakfast he wondered if he could tell Jean that he'd failed his army medical on account of flat feet, hoping she had forgotten his dermatitis. But he quickly junked the idea as a non-starter.

How had he managed to hike all these years if that was the case? Peru would not be defeated that way.

'Say something suddenly. Four and two.' Jean looked up from her *Times 2* crossword at Freddy, who groaned suddenly and touched his leg. 'I'm getting a pain down here. Must be my old injury.'

'What old injury? Frederick?' She pointed her pen at him. 'Don't try it on with me. It won't wash.'

'Yes, but I remember I had this well before hiking. It's worse when I'm at heights. I think it's called density pressure, which you get at great altitude, like…'

He tailed off at Jean's look. 'Alright then.' He picked up a piece of toast. 'I'll just have to walk through the pain. I'm used to it.'

'No, Freddy,' butted in Jean firmly. 'But no. You are not getting out of it. You can't. You'd be letting everybody down. And think what Cynthia and Max would say.'

After breakfast Freddy stumped up two flights of narrow stairs and entered his attic room. He switched on the computer and searched for 'Foreign Office warnings to travellers'. Ten minutes later, clutching a print-out, he went downstairs back to the kitchen table.

He showed her the list of dangers. She was sending him, he declared, into a country where street crime, acts of terrorism, general violence, road accidents and bites from vampire bats were commonplace. Foreigners were frequent targets for attack, and although the Shining Path terrorists were less active it was clear that Peru was not a country to wander around in without some form of military protection. In some areas, Freddy said, hiking groups had been victims of a spate of attacks by armed bandits. He would hope that Jean accepted that these grave risks should not be borne by himself but by the likes of Phil who revelled in that sort of caper.

Jean patiently explained that a well-known charity such as Sargent would never send volunteers into such a dangerous situation. She then turned to the urgent matter of the coal bunker. 'It's Neolithic, Freddy. Get rid of it.'

After breakfast Freddy went outside to gaze at the ugly, squat brute of a bunker. The thought of bashing such a monstrosity with a lump hammer made him flinch. He turned to the task, instead, of completing his painting of the shed. The reason he had not finished it, he had told Jean, was on account of his 'allergy to paint smell.' He wondered if a similar debilitating condition could be blamed on the bunker.

Why not? Obviously the percussion effect of striking concrete with a hammer would lead eventually to repetitive strain injury. In the short term it would cause muscular trauma in his right arm which would prevent him from carrying Jean's shopping out of Tescos and into the car. Yes, that was a pretty good wheeze, he thought. It might even become true.

Hike day. 8.01am. Phil put down his grapefruit bowl to answer the phone. Freddy began the offensive with a declaration. 'While I couldn't get to sleep on account of paint fumes, I spent hours on the internet. I have evidence that Peru is the most dangerous place in the world, and if you knew what was happening there you wouldn't want to risk your life seeing how precious you hold it.'

'Okay,' said Phil. 'You've been on the advice for travellers site at the Foreign Office. They don't say you mustn't go there…'

'Kindly hear me out. A team led by Dr Emile Gonzales has studied the hormone levels of 210 people living at above four thousand feet in the mountainous area of Peru.'

'Who's Dr Emile Gonzales?' Phil wiped his mouth with a paper napkin.

'A doctor. Let me read to you.'

'It sounds like one of your wheezes, Freddy.'

'It can be nothing further from the truth. This is serious.'

'Okay, tell me,' said Phil, resigned.

'Ready? Right. Here goes. "For comparison they looked at a control group of a 170 people of similar age and ethnic origin who lived at just 150 metres above sea level, in the Peruvian capital Lima. They found that the hormone dehydroepiandrosterone of this group…"'

Phil butted in, 'Say that again. Dehydro…?'

'It's a hormone. The Lima people have 60 per cent less of it than the mountain people.' Freddy paused, then said firmly, 'This hormone is called DHEA for short and I remember that Dr Strangebugger, your personal health guru, prescribed it for you.'

'DHEA! Why didn't you say so!' Phil sparked into attention. 'Yes, I still take it. Go on.'

'I emailed Dr Pedro and he emailed back that anyone who takes DHEA as a supplement should on no account go into mountainous country.'

Phil interrupted him. 'You said he was Dr Emile Gonzales, not Pedro.'

'Did I? That's because I'm tired. The point is do you understand the danger? I've no wish to die on a mountain in Peru, which I will do, roped to you.'

Phil heard the mail dropping on to the parquet floor in the hallway. 'Got to go. We'll talk about it on the hike.'

An hour later Phil picked me up and said nothing. But as soon as Freddy was in the car he spoke. 'No need to worry Freddy. It's off,' he said tersely.

'What's off?'

'Peru.'

'Off? You mean...?'

'Off. I had a letter after we spoke. Just like the space trip. A kindly note explaining that elderly people might encounter problems of insurance. They don't say we can't go. It's a gentle hint.' Phil snorted. 'I am 55 in reality. I am not old. I have worked damned hard to keep young.'

Freddy closed his eyes and sank his head back to touch the head rest, his mouth open. 'Oh Lord, thank you,' he gasped.

For the rest of the journey Freddy tried to create a cocoon around himself, to enjoy his reprieve from certain death. He dreamed about Sunday tea, sticky ginger cake, a walk in the woods, reading his book by a coal fire and watching his favourite antiques programme on television. Occasionally he was rudely dragged back into the present by Phil's sporadic outbursts.

'You see, dwarfs, cripples and gays have got everything going for them. But what about us? The big majority?' Phil railed at the windscreen. 'All forgotten. Written off.'

Freddy was so drowsy that he could only reply in a murmur. 'I keep telling you to relax and enjoy what's left of life. It's all you've got.'

'You don't get it, do you!' exclaimed Phil in a loud voice, annoying Freddy by bringing him to the alert. 'Anything we do to improve our lot gets stymied by these silly ageist sods! They go on about racism, but do nothing to protect us!'

He reminded Freddy that his 'great philosophers, Kant and Wittgenstein,' whom Freddy had raved about as having possible answers to the meaning, had both stated that what mattered about fact and reality was the human perception of it. 'That's what you said Freddy. And that's why I'm upset about time. My perception of one hour is 40 minutes. It's an absolute scandal.'

'Gruppenführer, look.' Freddy continued the argument as we left the car park and walked near the village of Sheldon, three miles to the west of Bakewell. 'You perceive fact and reality in your way, because you're insane and other people aren't. You should contact your satanic handler, tell her to quit. You're changing your email address and she won't be given the new one.'

'You see?' Phil appealed to me. 'This is what I have to put up with. Have either of you come up with a fourth hiker yet?'

At coffee break we sat on a stone wall at the side of the Magpie mine, its surface machinery still standing, owing to the efforts of the local historical society. Freddy became interested in two figures walking towards us along the footpath. 'I do not believe this,' he suddenly hissed. 'Look who it is!'

The male was unmistakeable, still wearing his bright orange anorak and green bobble hat. And still chattering like a machine gun. It was Clifford, our tormentor, the human limpet who had condemned us on two occasions to death by talking. But this time there was no need for a quick getaway. He had a female with him, slack-jawed like himself and showing buck teeth as she gabbled. She wore blue ski pants and a yellow storm jacket. Neither looked at the other as they chattered and passed by without giving us a glance, each soliloquy unintelligible, lost in the rise and fall of their contrapuntal chat. And they had not given us, or the mine, a glance. As they strode out of sight we began to laugh. Freddy was kept so amused by the incident that he ceased jibing at Phil.

But his euphoria was to be short lived. On the drive home, after a quiet five minutes, Phil spoke. 'You know,' he said. 'Now Peru's off the agenda I shall have to concentrate on other things where these ageists have no dominion.' He glanced at Freddy with a smile.

Freddy looked across at him and emitted a false groan. 'Oh yes? Flying aeroplanes? Well I won't be doing that.'

'You don't have to,' said Phil. 'I'm the pilot. You'll be passenger.'

'Canada or bust is it?' Freddy gave me a mischievous grin. 'Oh really. In fact I bet you none of us will be doing either.' He folded his arms, hugging his smugness.

Later that evening, as we walked Montague, Freddy was adamant. 'Oh yes, no doubt. He would have flown us to Canada. Thank God he'll fail that medical. Else we'd be in for it. Give him a piece of rope and he'll take a mile.'

Again, I voiced caution. 'We never know with Phil. I wouldn't be surprised if he finds some way round it.'

'If he does then there's only one thing for it. The next time he takes us up on those gritstone edges, that's the time. Just one push, that's all it needs. Off the cliff. There'd be no forensic evidence. He just fell, m'lud. Just sort of fainted on the edge. Oh glory!'

* * * * *

On the last hike of the month we trudged up the hillside towards Alstonefield. The naked dummy was still in the upstairs window, now wearing a Jane Austen type of hat. A woman drove up to park outside the cottage, got out to open the boot and took out a cardboard box.

'Morning.'

We exchanged greetings. Freddy, the most eager of us, was the first to get into conversation with her. We discovered that the cottage was not lived in, but was actually a clothes museum which exhibited a large array of outfits and accessories dating from 1790 to the 1970s.

The lady, by a curious coincidence, knew my wife, Liz. I was at home, penning a sequel to this book, when I took a call. A female voice declared she was 'Notty Hornblower', and could she speak to Liz please, in connection with an NSPCC function.

At first I thought it was Freddy, either simulating a voice or embroiling a woman as mad as himself in one of his many wheezes. Fortunately I decided that discretion was best and summoned Liz. Afterwards she told me that Notty ran a 'costume museum', with an Alstonefield address. And she was, if not famous, well known as a costume and accessory expert, appearing on TV programmes such as *The Antiques Roadshow* and *Heart of the Country*. No doubt the lack of an advertising sign outside the museum was due to Peak Park planning laws. Anyone might be forgiven for not knowing about it, due to restrictions on advertising signs. The owner, Mrs Hornblower, conscious of our muddy boots, invited us into the yard to look through ground floor windows at her collection. But Phil, glancing at his watch, shook his head in apology. 'We have a timetable, I'm sorry. Very nice of you to invite us.' Freddy grumbled as we resumed our upward climb.

'Gruppenführer, you have no soul. You must have an iron cross instead of a heart. You'd have enjoyed that. Didn't you see the military uniforms?' Phil stopped walking. 'Military?'

'Yes, I just caught a glimpse of one, in red, with medals on the chest. You weren't looking.'

'Oh. Well, we'll try to look in next time.'

Freddy gave a whoop. 'You see Don! Anything he wants to do, we do! Anything I don't want to do, we do! Right. The George is five minutes away. We shall partake of a pint in exchange for you looking at military uniforms. Fair?'

'Yes, Freddy,' said Phil, for once seeming to give way to justice. 'I was actually going to allow it, anyway.'

'I don't believe you. You are a dissembling...'

'No,' Phil cut in. 'I owe you for supporting me in the Dash. You deserve some reward.'

Freddy grumbled, generally pleased, but put out by Phil's patronising air. 'I know what you're thinking, Freddy,' said Phil. 'But you're wrong.' He smiled benignly. 'I've got another reason as well. I'm inviting you to celebrate a very special occasion.'

'Oh God,' said Freddy. 'What occasion?'

'No. Inside the pub. These things require a formal toast.'

'Lors,' groaned Freddy. 'And there I was thinking I was getting a drink without any payback.' He took a deep breath and remembered something. 'By the way, it's your turn.'

Inside the snug Phil passed the Boddingtons from the small bar to where we sat by the fire. As Phil sat down Freddy said he hadn't seen him pay for the drinks.

'No,' Phil said. 'I didn't have to. Last time, if you remember, Richard offered us a drink on the house, but we turned it down. They let us have it now.'

'Just a minute,' said Freddy. 'You can't have a free turn and I'm expected to pay next time?'

'Alright Freddy,' said Phil putting up a hand in a placatory mood. 'I'll pay next time.'

'Right then,' said Freddy, his outraged sense of fair play mollified. 'Well come on. Give us the worst.'

Phil raised his glass, 'Well, here's to it fellers.'

'To what?' I asked.

'The treat I told you about. The big one. Can't you guess?' Phil grinned at me. 'What had I *got* to do?'

Freddy put his hands to his face. 'Do? No idea. Tell us the bad news. Come on.'

'You know I failed to fly in space. Well, I've made up for it.'

Freddy lowered his hands and stared at Phil. 'Made up for what?'

'Okay. What did I have to pass?' Phil grinned at Freddy's stare. 'I've passed that medical, you'll be pleased to know. So here's to the future.' He raised his glass. 'You're both going to love flying. That's a promise.'

Freddy looked at me, and then back at Phil. 'You've…you…couldn't have,' he stumbled. 'You take all those pills. They're not allowed.'

'True. They're not. But I stopped taking them two months ago. The Autogenics does the whole job now. I'm cured.' Phil chuckled as he raised his glass to his mouth.

Freddy stood up. 'You…' There was so much he wanted to say but in the end said nothing at all, so he sat down abruptly and stared blankly into the fire.

APRIL

'Gruppenführer.'

It was the first day of April, a bright cold day with a westerly wind, and Freddy was in combative mood. Adding to his annoyance were Phil's tactics of walking faster whenever he was challenged. And Freddy had challenged him, all the way in the car and now all the way up the worn steep footpath through Froggatt wood. 'Stevens,' he panted. 'I want to know – whooh – how you conned your way through that medical. And – whooh – your intentions now that I ban you from playing any part in my downfall which is – whooh – all the way down from 2,000 feet in an aeroplane. Do you hear me?'

But Phil maintained his dogged and brisk pace. Freddy tried to keep within conversational distance. It was difficult. 'Just to repeat – whooh – you are the worst ever Gruppenführer and – whooh – the whole village is preparing for your blitzkrieg and will – whooh – defend itself on the green and in the street and on the pavement – whooh – we shall never surrender. If you keep walking – whooh – like this I'm quitting. Do you hear me?' Freddy popped a Werther's Original toffee into his mouth.

'I've passed the medical. I'm fit to fly!' called back Phil. 'And there are strict rules. I'm not allowed to fly over villages at below 1,500 feet or at a height from which I can glide clear if the engine fails! I've told you that a dozen times!'

On learning that Phil had passed his medical, Freddy's initial disbelief had led him to spin a web of disinformation in the hope that general unrest within the local populace would drive Phil back to earth.

First he spread the news in the Hawk and Buckle and the Red Lion that Phil had left his senses behind on the ground by taking to the air. Freddy also dropped the odd remark in the post office and church vestry, the latter by virtue of becoming the sole tenor after the retirement of Tommy Telfer at the age of 98.

It was Jean who had put Freddy's name forward. 'He has a fair voice and it will do his lungs good,' she said. 'And did you hear about Phil Stevens taking up flying at *his* age?'

There was general concern burbling around the take-away and surgery. Freddy circulated everywhere, planting his seeds and nurturing them with added tales of Phil's increasingly strange behaviour, such as the time six months ago when Phil had persuaded Freddy to go on a day trip to see the War Cabinet Rooms under Downing Street and then to tour Hyde Park. Instead of catching a tube back to St Pancras railway station, Phil had insisted on walking, 'as you'd expect from a madman'.

It was a hot day, Freddy said, and Phil was sensitive to traffic fumes. To his horror Oxford Street was full of diesel buses and taxis, and so he would dive into a store and breathe in a lungful of air, then dash out into the street to walk 50 yards without taking a breath and then dive into another store for another intake of oxygen – and so on.

At one point in his manic state he ran into a security man who was seven feet tall, bounced off him and was nearly arrested for assault.

Phil's cause was not helped by some of the villagers' antagonism towards the airfield, owing to summer days in the garden blighted by the drone of aircraft.

'It's only visitors who make noise,' Phil protested. 'Every pilot at the airfield is instructed not to fly over villages, and they don't because the circuit for landing doesn't go over them.'

His explanation only served to convince the complainants that, at 67, he had to be insane.

'Mind you,' said one large and loud regular in the Red Lion. 'Remember when he was an air traffic controller at East Midlands? I avoided going on holiday when he was on duty.' He raised his voice over the laughter, 'Now the bugger's a pilot I'm scared stiff!'

Freddy joined in the laughter and helped stir the pot even more.

'He'll use it to prove some theory of rejuvenation. He'll dream up personal bests like how long he can dive without hitting the church steeple. And Jean's got me doing lots of jobs in the garden this summer. I can see him, zooming down on me, one of those white kamikazi headbands round his forehead and that crazy grin. He'll buy one of those redundant RAF Bulldog aircraft because he can keep the roundel and "Group Captain Wizard Prang's" name on its side. He'll create his own flying circus. Baron von Stevens, putative Reichsmarschall.'

All agreed the phoney war had begun and would continue until Phil went solo. Then it would be enemy action – and defence.

Phil took it all in his stride – literally – and walked faster than ever. The last hike had been particularly punishing, a 13-miler. He enjoyed making waves or, as he put it, 'airwaves'. Openly – now that the secret of his monetary windfall was out – he told us that he intended to spend some of the money on a 'nip and tuck' job. Freddy was aghast. 'You're going to have plastic surgery? I do not believe it. That's for women. You! Gruppenführer macho mein leader?'

'Why not?' asked Phil in all innocence. 'I'm fit inside and it helps to look fit outside. It's good psychology. Look young, feel young.' Phil grinned. 'You're always on about the "human spirit" Freddy, you could do with a face lift. You look like a mournful spaniel. A nip and tuck would put a smile on your face. You might even turn into a keen hiker.'

Phil returned to his normal operations, punishing himself on his devil's machina. He would row fast for 3,000 metres, then push up a series of 25 kilos before collapsing in a heap, stopwatch in hand.

On this first day of April Freddy was still demanding to know what the treat might be. He said that it was certain to involve flying with hiking as the end result.

And, as an aircraft was to be used, it was not rocket science to work out that Phil would make the destination a long way off, which brought in north Wales and the Cairngorm mountains as likely choices, with Canada as a long-standing aim should any of those be successful.

Freddy was still demanding answers as we broke out of Froggatt wood on to a giant stage, a gritstone clifftop poised 700 feet over the River Derwent. Phil had his back towards us, standing on the edge of the cliff looking out into distant mists towards the villages of Eyam and Stoney Middleton. Freddy stopped on the footpath and spoke to the back of Phil's head. 'I need to know to get my affairs in order. So tell me.'

Phil made no reply, still gazing out into the distance.

'There's that film of Hitler gawping at the Eiffel Tower. You're just like him,' said Freddy, trying again. 'A self-made man who worships his creator.' He paused, hoping his wit would strike home. It didn't. 'Don't tell me you're admiring the view?'

'No, I'm just trying to work out the distance to the horizon,' Phil said.

'Oh that's good. You frightened me. Nature can't have you as a worshipper. What would Wordsworth have said?'

Phil turned to face us, the silvery hairs sprouting from beneath the beret glinting in the sunlight. 'Freddy, there's nothing to stop you celebrating it,' he said. 'If that's what you want. What about one of your poems? Bet you haven't got one for April,' he grinned.

'Yes I have,' pouted Freddy and began:
'Whan that April with his showres soote
The droughte of March hath perced to the roote,
And bathed every veine in swich licour,
Of which vertu engendred is the flowr...'
Freddy broke off, trying to recall the next line.

'That's French,' Phil said.

'No it isn't. It's Chaucer. To be more exact it's Old English. 'I used to know all of it,' he complained. 'Every line,' he sighed.

'You have to do memory exercises like I do Freddy,' Phil said, setting off with his head erect and focussing on the horizon in complete disregard of nature's beauty around him. He had never lost his military bearing on the hike, whereas Freddy over the years had become more round-shouldered. It had the knock-on effect of making his long arms seem longer and his gait that of a carthorse, heavy, deliberate and slow.

Phil had dismissed him as 'shambolic' and delivered frequent admonishments, as today, 'Freddy, if you don't straighten up and sharpen up you'll spend the rest of your life in a neck brace.'

'Splendid,' retorted Freddy. 'Absolutely splendid. A delight. That's exactly what I want to be, an invalid. Glory, no hiking.'

Nevertheless, Freddy made an attempt to keep up with Phil, drew level, then said, 'Oh,' and stopped walking. His eyes went upwards and after another, weaker, 'Oh,' he crumbled gently to the ground. Phil and I were quickly by his side, memories of two years past when Freddy had collapsed from heatstroke.

'He's got a pulse,' said Phil, breathing hard. 'Let's roll him over, get his head lower. That's it.'

'That's so much nicer,' murmured Freddy. 'My idea of exercise is a good brisk lie down. It's so much nicer than walking.' He winked at Phil. 'April Fool.'

Phil stood up, adjusted his rucksack and set off muttering and shaking his head.

For the next half hour he punished Freddy with a light infantry pace.

Freddy shouted at his back. 'You see, the Hun can never take a joke. That's your problem Gruppenführer, you're like Himmler your boss, no sense of humour!'

Later, Phil's annoyance having abated, we walked along the cliff edge above Baslow village. To our left lay a wilderness of heather, home of grouse. The sharp westerly coming from our right glanced at the cliff wall and then shot rapidly upwards so that anyone standing on the cliff edge would feel the force of its updraft. Phil, true to nature, walked as near to the edge as he could, drawing a groan from Freddy.

However, the footpath took Phil inland, towards a massive weather-eroded sculpture standing in solitary splendour. This was the Eagle Stone – and, yes, from a certain angle it does look like an eagle.

Young men of Baslow, as a rite of passage, once had to climb this rock formation before they could marry. 'They've stopped that lark today,' said Phil, always keen to have a go at Health and Safety. 'It's a wonder they've not surrounded it with barbed wire.'

Phil's meditation on the decadence of English society in the 21st century continued as we reached the Wellington monument, a stone obelisk-with-cross erected in 1866 in honour of the Duke of Wellington. 'Wonder what he'd have thought of the compensation society,' murmured Phil.

But neither Freddy nor I paid much attention as we gazed in a southerly direction towards the great park of Chatsworth House, home of the Dukes of Devonshire. 'Baslow,' said Freddy his gaze falling towards that village. 'They used to take the waters there for joint and muscle pain. That's precisely what I suffer from on account of hiking, and I shall be raising my claim to £5 million with a charitable donation for the relief of victims of other mad Gruppenführers.'

Freddy likes Baslow village, he told us, everything about it conforming to his idea of the perfect English village with its thriving school, also used as a community base for activities by local societies. Baslow also retains some events, dropped by other places, such as the annual carnival and procession with bands. It also has a well dressing, combined with a church fête with tea in the vicarage garden and a barn dance in the evening.

'That's my England,' Freddy murmured wistfully. 'Soft, warm and friendly. Not yours, Gruppenführer, all torchlit processions and swastikas, blood and iron.'

Phil, for once, humoured Freddy by raising his stride into a goose step. I laughed, but Freddy continued in his reverie. 'The true Englishman likes to fish,' he said. 'That's my idea of exercise, sitting by the Wye with a rod. I'd bring a large flask of tea, my personal box of chocolates, a Mars Bar and two cans of best Pedigree. Oh yes, and I'd smoke a pipe, Dutch tobacco like Graham Goodall's, smelling of toffee.'

Freddy's imagination catapulted him away from the hike to his car parked under an oak tree by the church, any village church. 'The only hiking I'd do is the short walk from there to the river bank. I'd settle down like Ratty or Mole and write poetry like Wordsworth, catch a trout and cook it over an open camp fire – but no camping overnight,' he added hastily. 'Nothing horrific. A nice warm bedroom in the local pub after an hour or two in front of the log fire with a good malt whisky. Doesn't your scarred soul, Gruppenführer, stir itself just a little at these fine thoughts?'

Phil nodded, then consulted his pedometer and watch. 'We're bang on schedule. Our ETA for lunch is 13 zero five hours.'

'Oh God,' said Freddy. 'Where is this man's soul?'

But Phil was away, legs extended, arms pumping and shoulders back.

'Oh Lord,' said Freddy and called out, 'Gruppenführer, I have stopped walking. I shall stay stopped until you slow down. Do you hear me?'

'You're lucky you're not running,' shouted Phil. 'Another fake collapse like that one and you will be.'

Lunch was spent near Bubwell, home of the ancient Bassett family, one of whom had fought with King Richard on the Crusades. The field in which we sat was partly surrounded by a copse. I noticed that Phil was staring towards it, having paused in his salad pecking. I followed his eye line.

There, to my amazement, was a corps de ballet that had just entered the grass arena from the copse, a company of cavorting, dancing and pirouetting – hares. Against the green of the grass and the dark background of the wood, a bright shaft of sunlight singled out a threesome waltzing around in a carousel and two boxers standing upright, scrabbling their forelegs at each other's faces, but landing no blows.

There was even an audience of four hares watching – and were they applauding? And was the boxing and dancing a rite of spring? Were the females preserving their virtue at the aggressive males? I pointed at the two pugilists. 'Look at the male. He's so much bigger. Why does he have to do that? He's strong enough. Why can't he just take her?'

The answer came from an unexpected source. 'That's not a male, that's a female,' Phil said. 'The females are nearly always bigger. She's fighting off the male. If the male's strong and brave enough she'll give in. They have three or four litters a year. During the day they're like the SAS, they lie in depressions in the ground, out of sight.'

'How do you know all that?' Freddy frowned at Phil. 'You know nothing about the countryside. You're making it up.'

'No,' said Phil. 'They eat herbs in summer and grass in winter. They're ignoring us. That's another reason why we say they're bonkers because they're so obsessed with what they're doing they sense no danger.'

'Stevens. Since when were you an authority on hares?'

'Can't remember,' said Phil, taking a swig of coffee and nibbling at a piece of apple. 'I just know it. I've always known it. Oh and another thing. If they don't like you near them they'll scream and grind their teeth.'

Freddy's laser beam penetrated Phil's skull but could find no flaw and so he continued to smile at his leader, eyebrows pulled together, in an expression of curiosity mixed with surprise. Phil, for his own part, smiled back and adjusted his red beret in such a way as to suggest that he had not been found wanting.

That evening Freddy called on me with Montague. When Freddy first acquired the dog, Phil used to join us for the evening walk but gave up when Montague kept sniffing his crotch. Phil couldn't understand why he didn't fancy either of his two companions, but it was Freddy's joke about gay dogs and gay men that finally sent him on his way. Freddy alluded to this before telling me that Phil's obsession with his macho image gave the clue as to why he possessed so great a knowledge of hares. 'Boxing hares would delight him,' Freddy said. 'Phil's memory banks are reserved for anything on the planet that competes or shows aggression.' He sighed a little. 'A pity that flowers don't all bash each other. He'd have been a great botanist and my hiking life would be so much nicer.'

* * * *

The next hike a week later also had an animal as the centre of attention and most welcome, as Freddy's patience was finally rewarded.

The route took us from Mill Dale into Dovedale, then across the wooden bridge and up a steep, rocky path to the hill top where, nearly three years ago, we had been strafed by a fast jet fighter.

Just after this we had been entertained by a transistor radio playing Vivaldi's *Four Seasons*, the Winter Movement. This, in turn, had heralded a stone waller, a trade that went back to the time of Shakespeare.

Shortly after that we had approached Stanhope hamlet, as today. And, in a repeat showing, we rounded a bend in the road – and there she was, the lady of Freddy's dreams. He spotted her, as before, sitting on a wall.

'She's there! Jenny! Ha hah!' Freddy was jubilant. 'She's alive!'

The bitch border collie watched the three of us as if asking herself the question – were we legitimate hikers and, as such, ready to be led? She stirred herself but was not yet ready to jump down from the wall, as on the previous occasion. We drew nearer. I could see her eyes alive with expectation. And then came decision. She jumped down to take over from Phil as hike leader.

It was at that moment that we saw the plastic covered notice on her back held in place by a harness made of red leather. The notice itself had the same wording but was bolder and blacker, drawn by a marker pen. 'PLEASE SAVE MY LIFE. SAY "GO HOME JENNY".'

Freddy wanted to stroke the dog. 'Jenny, come here, girl,' he commanded. She ignored him, but paused, waited for him to catch up with her and only then was happy to be stroked and fondled. But only for a few seconds. Then she was away in front, business-like.

'Watch her,' said Freddy. 'Watch her jump on the wall.'

But Jenny did not jump on the wall, nor the other one. Instead she trotted about 20 paces at a time, after which she would stop and turn her head to ensure we were in tow before setting off again.

And so we continued our strange procession, a dog showing canine authority over humans that tickled Freddy's fancy no end.

'Wonderful,' he enthused. 'Absolutely wonderful. What a dog. She has just got to be a reincarnated hiker. Lab Sum would say so.' He referred to the time we visited the Tara Buddhist Centre in Etwall, culminating in an episode of sheer embarrassment that kept us clear of monks and their followers for a long time.

'They don't believe a dog is human. A dog is a dog,' said Phil, scornfully.

Half a mile later Jenny was still acting as pacemaker, and Freddy's eulogy on canine intelligence and friendliness had begun to run short of adjectives and adverbs. Then he had a thought. 'I know what she wants,' he said suddenly. 'A drink at the George. That's what she's after.'

'If you're thinking of using that dog to get a lunch time drink forget it,' said Phil, always alert to Freddy's wheezes. 'Drinks are out today. We've a long way to go.'

He remained resolute in the face of Freddy's protests. 'You may as well send her back now because we are not taking her to the George.'

'You're the worst ever Gruppenführer in the whole world,' Freddy said grumpily. 'You're jealous because she's a better navigator than you are.'

We reached Hope and started the climb up towards Alstonefield.

'Time to send her back,' ordered Phil.

'Not yet,' argued Freddy. 'She'll go home when she gets to the village.'

'You're a dangerous romantic Freddy. She might get run over.'

'This dog, never, she's far too clever for that,' Freddy said. But he spoke without conviction, accepting that parting was inevitable. He walked quickly to catch up with Jenny and stopped her with a raised finger. 'Jenny.'

Jenny stared back at Freddy.

'Jenny, go home.'

Her tongue, pink and fresh, lolled over her lower front teeth all of a quiver, her breathing sharp and urgent.

'Jenny, go home.' Freddy thrust out his arm, pointing back towards Stanshope.

She lowered her head, ignoring the command, and carried on with the hike. 'Jenny!' Freddy's voice was sharper and louder. Jenny stopped and turned to look at him, eyes full of pleading.

Freddy kept his arm raised and spoke patiently, but firmly. 'Good dog. Jenny, go home.'

For a moment she stood motionless then, with Freddy's arm still pointed homewards, turned round and plodded back, stopping to stare up at Freddy in one last appeal. Finding him implacable, she walked on. After a few yards she broke into a trot and then into a run.

We watched her sprint until she was out of sight over the hill. 'She ought to get a medal,' said Freddy. 'If you were stranded as I was, with hypothermia, she'd fetch help, no doubt about it. What a dog.'

I did believe that there was a slight break in Freddy's voice. But then I remembered that Montague was his second dog. The first had been Butch, an English springer spaniel, a loveable and affectionate creature that had Freddy once declaring that animals had souls.

His passion for them did not extend to foxes. Unlike Phil, who was outspokenly pro-hunting, he came from the same generation which had spent hours as children playing in the countryside. During World War Two he had been evacuated to a small village in Herefordshire where the 'pig man's visit' had been a regular occurrence. Slaughtering animals, although a nasty business, had been part of his life that could not be disavowed. It was essential to maintain rural tradition lest we lose touch with the reality of living, he said. I was not quite sure what he meant, but it sounded sensible.

*****

Phil wondered what it would be like to live in a world without women. It had been the basis of a TV reality show. It was appropriate that he put the question in the Red Lion, still a male preserve, not much changed from the days of spit and sawdust. We were, as usual, sitting around the inglenook fire. 'You see,' he said. 'Think of all the time saved. And you can always learn to do a bit of ironing and get ready meals from Tesco.'

'I rarely agree with you, but this time I do,' said Freddy.

'Good man.' Phil tossed his empty crisp bag into the fire. 'Why?'

'On account of Jean going into my shed.'

'You've got that too?' Phil looked interested. 'That's amazing. Ruth's started doing that as well. It's all this equality stuff. They don't need to be there, but it's like a dog marking its territory. Instinct. Does she poke around?'

'Yes, checks what I've got. I keep my personal box of chocolates there. And everything I need in case of emergency.'

'What emergency?'

'If her relatives arrive unexpectedly. I retreat there. I've got books, a lamp and a heater. I hide most of it.'

Freddy's tone changed from matter of fact to one of suspicion. 'Why don't you want women?' He sat back in his Windsor chair, giving Phil a wry smile. 'I know. Without women we'd have cold baths every morning. Then a day spent hiking – every day. A lifetime of unending pain. Give me women every time. Because they're civilised.'

Phil shook his head. 'They undermine you, all the time. How many times does Jean make you wear something you don't want to wear, like a tie? And when you get there everybody's got a sweater or an open-necked shirt. Freddy, correct me if I'm wrong, but Jean stopped you getting a Trabant, didn't she? And Ruth has made me take my exerciser out of the garage so I have to keep it covered up outside. It's all aggro with women. Every aspect of life.'

'Hmm.' Freddy looked thoughtfully at Phil. 'You mean like dropping egg down your new jumper and she never lets up on it.'

'There you are,' said Phil triumphantly. 'You know exactly what I mean.'

'And throwing away the sweater you've been wearing on the hike for six years. Your favourite sweater.' Freddy beamed at Phil.

'Precisely.'

'And likely to stop a lunatic dragging you up flying?' Freddy's smile remained fixed. There was a pause.

'Hah. Now there's a thing.' Phil looked uncertain.

'Stevens,' Freddy said laconically. 'Shall I make your day? She wouldn't.'

'Wouldn't what?'

'Stop you dragging me up in the air.'

'Really?' Phil sat up in his chair. 'You mean…'

'If you went to her – as you do – and wheedled round her – as you do – she would support you, yes. She likes flying you see.'

'Freddy, that is the best news I've heard in…'

'No it's not,' interrupted Freddy. 'And if you think you can take me up in a plane forget it. Because I will have a doctor's certificate if needs be. I will have back trouble, really chronic. And going above 1,000 feet makes my teeth ache. I also have panic attacks. And claustrophobia. I can't bear the noise of an aircraft engine. I get air sick. It also makes me deaf.'

'Are you telling me you don't like flying?'

* * * * *

Freddy looked at the coal bunker. After the long and generally damp winter it had changed from being a bare, concrete piece of ugliness into a bright green structure, festooned and dripping with moss and spreading out from its base to invade adjacent territory. Pots, a pile of bricks and a garden roller, which was never used, were all smothered by the stuff.

Freddy went indoors and told Jean to come outside and look at the bunker. She complained that she was busy, but that was her standard reply to anything that Freddy suggested she looked at. Eventually she went outside and looked at the bunker.

'Well, what about it?'

'Don't you think it looks fascinating?'

'No. Why?'

Freddy tried to articulate his feelings about it. He even called upon the name of Damien Hirst to back his cause.

Jean saw no art exhibit, just a coal bunker covered in moss. 'Frederick, I want that gone by May. It's the ugliest thing and it depresses me.'

'Why don't you let me take a photo of it and send it to a magazine?'

'You can take a photograph of it. Yes. But get rid of it.'

Jean went back indoors and Freddy, after a pause, went into the shed.

He located his personal box of chocolates, selected a hard Brazilian and sat down on his chair. He ate it then picked out another chocolate, without making any selection this time. Then he had another.

* * * * *

It was the morning of the last hike day of the month. Phil sat at breakfast bathed in gentle sunlight, diffused by the roof blinds of the conservatory. There was, as yet, no complaining phone call from Freddy. Phil was content to read an article about 'happiness' in *The Times* supplement. He learnt that there was evidence to show that people who bestowed gratuities or gave assistance to needy people shot up the joy scales. According to a psychologist at the University of California, the best way of all was to 'turbo charge' your happiness by making a 'gratitude visit'. One should write a testimonial, the researcher said, and read it out to the recipient. Phil turned down his mouth at that idea. It wasn't the British way at all, he thought, munching his cornmeal crepes laced with dark, Greek honey. He was about to turn to the sports pages when an idea struck him. He went outside to his shed, where he kept a lot of his outdoor stuff, and rooted through a pile of hiking papers. He found what he was looking for, a book titled *Peak Hikes*, and took it back to the conservatory.

He searched for a hike that he had not done before – usually because it was either too 'tame' or too short. He found one which made him feel happy. He was happier still when 8am passed and Freddy had not made his call.

As soon as Phil had climbed into my car he made an announcement. 'I think today should belong to Freddy. I think it's time he had a hike all to himself.'

'Oh yes.' Freddy's suspicions were quickly aroused. He turned round to stare at Phil in the rear seats. 'I don't like the sound of that.'

'You will. I promise.'

'Stevens, you don't give away anything unless it furthers your demented pursuit of wearing out your body and mine in the process. I…'

'Freddy, just listen,' Phil interrupted him. 'It makes me happy to know you're a botanist and so today you can loiter to your heart's content.'

'Where?'

'It's a river hike.'

'And what's the payback in terms of the pain scale?'

'None.'

'I don't believe you.'

'Freddy, you will be able to stop as often as you want because it's only a four to five-miler. That's all. If you don't believe me, read it.'

Phil handed Freddy the hike book. 'Page 44.'

Freddy looked at the book's cover and then found the page. 'A Short Walk to Chee Dale and Back'.

'That's it,' pointed out Phil. 'See, it only says four to five miles?'

'Okay, but what's the payback? Am I to be lashed by whips up Kinder Scout on all fours, or taken to the Arctic to be forced to hike in sub-zero temperatures?'

'Neither. You'll see. I'm just happy to know you're happy.'

Freddy grunted in disbelief. 'This is going to be awful. I know it.'

The hike began at the entrance to Deep Dale and Topley Pike, two miles east of Buxton on the side of the A6 road and directly beside the River

Wye. We followed the rough track alongside the river, soon passing under a railway bridge. The air was fresh and cool, a perfect day for a hike.

Phil had to restrain himself from marching ahead and allowed Freddy, who remained at critical alert, to set the pace.

Freddy obliged, but warned Phil that he was on the look out for 'any funny business' either today or in the future. He then turned to his task. We had not walked 10 yards before he stopped to scrutinise the deciduous woodland that reached upwards on our right. He then turned to survey the river.

He spotted a dipper standing on a stone in the bubbling water. 'See that?' he said. 'What could be more beautiful than that? The wagtail is like it but a bit smaller. Let's watch it dive.'

Freddy stared at the bird. We all stared. It was brown with a white neck and it stared at the water and bobbed up and down. This display was all it did, for two whole minutes.

Phil let out a small sigh and followed it with an uncomfortable sounding cough. 'Wait for it,' whispered Freddy. 'Any minute now.' But the dipper was content to stand on the stone, and Freddy was happy to stand by the riverside.

Another minute went by. Phil glanced at his wrist watch, a Torgoen flight chronograph, which cost £230. It could compute speed and distances. Phil had proudly produced this acquisition on the previous hike. It was a mark of his growing frustration that he looked at the watch again inside the next 20 seconds.

'It will dive. Don't worry.' Freddy maintained his pleasant interest in the bird.

Phil, who was losing happiness by the second, took a short breath.

Freddy concentrated on the dipper. His contentment was such that he looked positively happy.

Phil coughed loudly.

The dipper dived into the water in its search for insects and larvae under the stones on the river bed. And then it surfaced and returned to the stone, back to its routine of bobbing and waiting.

'Yes,' said Phil, taking a step. 'Very interesting. Not seen one do that before. Er… shall we…?' He waited for Freddy to take over the lead.

Freddy turned to him. 'Wasn't that good?'

Phil agreed it was good. 'Now, if we can…?'

The hike, such as it was, continued with Freddy spouting a few lines from Wordsworth as he pointed out the flora, a rich and diverse display all along the riverside. He showed us a mallard and then suddenly hushed us, standing still, ear cocked, picking out the sound of the wood warbler from the chattering background of the tit family.

Phil's heroic display of interest in Freddy's discourse on nature was waning sharply as Freddy spouted more lines from Wordsworth.

After a coffee break he trudged behind Freddy, with a pained expression, staring at the ground a few yards ahead.

Freddy next showed us a treecreeper. It was creeping down the branch of a tree, creeping slowly. Then came the examination of the flora, with herb Robert and bluebells pointed out as examples. Freddy was thorough in his examination of the plants, crouching down beside them to make a closer and more detailed examination.

Phil remained stoic in his silence. Beads of perspiration stood out on his forehead.

We returned by Monsal Dale.

The hike, declared Phil, had taken four hours to complete at an average of one mile an hour. He was anxious to elicit from Freddy some acknowledgment of his achievement. 'Note no running up hills Freddy? No dashing on?'

Freddy agreed that was so, which encouraged Phil to plough further. 'We could hardly call it a hike, though. I hope you enjoyed that.'

Freddy agreed that he had enjoyed it. There was a pause before Phil spoke again, 'So I'll make a note in my hike book when I get home. One treat for Freddy. And one due to...er...me, I suppose?'

Freddy made no reply, smiling to himself.

* * * * *

Phil's magnanimity brought him no brownie points as Freddy kept to his programme of disinformation. He cultivated the acquaintance of a garage owner, a regular at the Hawk and Buckle and a member of the local flying club, owner of a Piper Tripacer aircraft. Freddy pretended to be amused by his stories – the type who told tales about pilots who landed without flaps or forgot to lower landing gear, poor souls who were nature's fall guys.

Freddy cleverly dropped Phil's name as a vague acquaintance during one session to see what reaction it might elicit.

'Oh Phil? Phil Stevens? Oh crikey, old Phil. What a character. Absolutely crackers. I could tell you a story.'

'Do. What happened?'

The story was told. Phil had gone up with an instructor, climbing over open countryside to 4,000 feet, to learn about spin avoidance. The nose had been pointed upwards with throttle power at idle. At the last possible moment before stalling, the instructor had kicked the rudder bar to send the aircraft hurtling downwards into a spin. It was Phil's task to prevent that happening.

'Yes. And?' Freddy could hardly wait.

'Well, he did that but then volunteered to do the actual spins, dive bombing vertically at the ground. Which you don't have to do. But he wanted to do them. The G-force is terrific. All the blood in your body packs into your feet and then it rushes back again. At his age!'

'Oh, yes, he is quite old. So?'

'Well, when he got back to the airfield he had to spend two hours sitting down and had to drink three mugs of tea before he could drive home. He was so dizzy. He's really weird. Do you know he reckons that he's only 55 and keeps a diary? Every day he writes down "I am only 55." Isn't that weird?'

'It is.' Freddy nodded sympathetically. 'Strange chap. Sounds really weird.'

Later, in the Red Lion, I came in to find Freddy handing a pint of Boddingtons to Phil. I caught the conversation. 'I heard about your spin avoidance,' said Freddy. 'Or rather lack of it.'

'Who told you that?'

'Doesn't matter. What does matter is you trying to get me up in the air risking my neck.'

'Do you know, Freddy, there's worse things than air crashes. Last week I paid £35 for a test of mercury in my body.'

'Dr Strangebugger.' Freddy nodded.

'Do you know that mercury is the second most lethal metal on earth next to plutonium? And I have a bucketful in my mouth?'

'So have I. So have millions.'

'I want it out but I can't because they say I'll get more mercury poisoning from the drilling.'

'But what's that got to do with flying?'

'Nothing. But it's worrying.'

'You know,' Freddy said. 'If you find living that bad you should find other ways of spending your time.'

Phil grinned and pointed a finger. 'Funny, Freddy. Very funny. Give you that. Look, I did those spins with an instructor. I would never do them on my own or with another pilot.'

'But you would with me. Because you have been sent to do things like that, to me. And you are 67 years old. And I don't believe you. You'll go diving under bridges or looping the loop with me hanging on by my front teeth. I know you.'

'Not true. Simply not true.' Phil tried to placate Freddy, explaining that pilots were trained in keeping safe. 'But you must admit you owe me something for Chee Dale. That was a nature ramble. Not a hike. I did it for you Freddy, not me.'

'You see,' said Freddy, gesturing with his hand at Phil. 'What did I tell you Don? I am expected to give payback. Well no I'm not.'

'Freddy, all I'm saying is that one good turn deserves another.'

'It does not! I have had years of torture on the hike. I've had to run up hills and down them. I've lacerated my feet, hurt my knees. I've been frozen to death and had sunstroke. I've been lost up Kinder Scout in a fog that could have killed me. All these things I have done, I've done for you. There is no payback owing. None whatsoever.'

Freddy quaffed his beer in stoic and dignified fashion.

Another week passed, during which Phil made no mention of flying. It was a case of letting sleeping dogs lie. Phil would wait until his first, real opportunity.

MAY

An unexpected frost, during the night of 30 April, soured the large pink blooms on the magnolia tree by the garden gate. The intense cold also silenced the swallows in the old barn across the lane, at least until the sun was up. The white-as-linen blackthorn flower remained pristine and unaffected, but the hawthorn buds of creamy white, spread over miles of countryside, now looked jaded.

Freddy woke up on May Day thinking about the fourth hiker and decided to relegate him. Instead he would be called the Third Man, after Carol Reed's film of that title, a neat misnomer as the movie's main character was also a shadowy figure. A suitable hiker, someone who had a compatible temperament, the time and the inclination, was proving difficult to recruit. Freddy, however, remained nonchalant. 'No need to bust a gut,' he said. 'If we don't like Phil's hiker – as we most likely won't – then we just vote him down, simple as that.'

Freddy's complacency and my lack of urgency were, before the month was out, to prove fatal mistakes.

* * * * *

The prospect of a frosty and sunny hike got Phil's juices flowing as he ate breakfast in his conservatory. Breakfast was a Ruth special, bought at Bakewell market, consisting of sausage, an egg from a springwater-fed hen and bacon which had been dry-cured using sea salt and raw cane sugar. This was followed by a muffin soaked in honey. Ruth had also bought a supply of water buffalo meat from a herd near Chesterfield, one of a handful in the UK. The water buffalo has low cholesterol compared with beef, and twice the calcium and protein. Succulent slices of this rare meat would be on Phil's plate for that night's meal.

Phil's mobile trilled at 8.01am. It was Freddy, his nemesis, of course. Before Freddy could speak, Phil nipped in. 'Freddy, you can't be serious! It's going to be a beautiful day. You are not cancelling…'

'Gruppenführer,' Freddy interrupted. 'I'm not. I just remind you that it's International Workers Day, which I always celebrate on account of my 40 years in the sulphur mines. It happens that my grandson is celebrating it in a different way, and I would like that to be our treat for the day. It's a surprise.'

'Surprise by how much it shortens the hike. Go on, what is it?'

'It won't shorten the hike at all. If we can get to Monyash by 10 o'clock we could stay for...'

'Freddy,' Phil intervened, painfully patient and stressing each word. 'The hike today goes nowhere near Monyash.'

'Well, you can change it to the Lathkill hike. That starts from Monyash.'

Phil sighed. 'Freddy, your relatives, who make up much of the population of the Peak District, only ring to warn of impenetrable snow, severe gales and thick fog, the purpose to slow down, shorten or cancel our hike. What difference is it with this one?'

'I told you, it's a treat,' said Freddy.

Phil paused. Then, uncharacteristically and unexpectedly, gave way. 'Okay, but you do realise we're getting to know Lathkill too well? I warn you, we spend no more than 20 minutes in Monyash.'

'Gruppenführer, you are a Scout and a gentleman.'

Phil resumed his breakfast with a smile. He had not given way on anything. In fact he had benefitted. He had decided that the lost 20 minutes would be made up by extending the hike. A further 10 minutes would be added on as a penalty. Freddy was getting a bit too big for his boots: it was time to drive home the lesson that backsliding would not be tolerated. Pleased with the way the day had started, Phil poured out a steaming mug of Ruth's killer coffee.

We drove into the village of Monyash at 10.25am, making for the old market cross, which still stands on the village green, its base supposedly made from old village stocks. A maypole stood in the middle of the green, children surrounding it, the boys wearing short trousers, white shirts and red ties, and the girls, pretty dresses. An audience had gathered to watch the dance, made up of schoolteachers, villagers and tourists.

The maypole was made of wood, about 10 feet tall and about five inches in diameter. Coloured ribbons, attached around the crown, were each held by children, all standing to attention, dutifully waiting for the dance to begin. Half the children faced the other half, trying hard not to be distracted by the others' smiles. A piano accordion, played by one of the teachers, let out a loud chord and the dance began to the tune of

Barwick Green, the children hopping and skipping around each other in interweaving patterns, the tape winding around the pole in a colourful downward spiral. When there was no more tape to be added, the dance came to an end, to enthusiastic applause.

The maypole may have been a phallic symbol, a 'stinking idol' to Oliver Cromwell, but to Freddy and me it was a nostalgic reminder of old England.

Phil had his mind on other matters. 'So where's your grandson, Freddy?' he said. Freddy scanned the children. 'He's not here. He might be practising his piano,' said Freddy, seriously. 'He has to practise three hours a day. He's only nine, but he can play Chopin's *Polonaise* like Stephanie Chen. The teachers say he's a musical genius.'

Phil gave Freddy a hesitant look, uncertain how to react. (On my return home I checked the internet to find that the 17-year-old Chen had shared first prize in a piano competition in Texas.) Occasionally, as today, Freddy will toss in some name or fact that in itself is undeniable, thus helping to create in his victim the doubt and bewilderment he finds so amusing. Sometimes the story is wholly true, as Phil has found out to his cost. He could justifiably regard a new Freddy wheeze with scepticism but never outright disbelief.

'Well,' Phil glanced at his watch. 'I make it 20 minutes off the hike so we'll extend it by half an hour.' Phil gave Freddy a skewed grin and led off for Lathkill Dale.

The entrance to the dale is by a gate from the roadside. After a plod across two wide grass fields, the dale funnels down to being only 20 feet in width, covered in rocks and boulders. Care has to be taken here, lest a knee collide agonisingly with a sharp edge.

As we left the jumble of rocks behind, Phil broke his silence. Evidently thinking of the children's dance, he brought up – yet again – his problem with that remorseless enemy of his, time. 'I've been thinking,' he said. 'And I'm convinced that kids live in the present. They don't know what tomorrow is. Every moment they're involved. But they're not like us, looking for a target for each activity. They don't seek a result of anything they do. They just do it. Why can't we still do that? Time would go so much slower.'

Neither Freddy nor I said anything, merely grunting a little in acceptance. For once Phil had made an interesting proposition, with only a modicum of his usual crankiness. But he swung back to his common obsession. 'Did you read about the big asteroid? It's going to just miss us at 15,000 miles, but then – get this – it might be drawn into our gravity a couple of years later! It could wipe us out. How about that for a bum deal?'

'Gruppenführer.' Freddy spoke with a lightness of tone when dealing with Phil's oddities. 'When is this going to happen?'

'2029.'

'And how old will you be then?'

'Biologically, 59.' Before Freddy could reply Phil was quick to add. 'And I will be here. That's definite. All I object to are things landing without permission from air traffic control.' Then he grinned and joined us in laughter. Once again it was a flash of the old Phil, before the onset of grumpiness corrupted his innate good humour. There was hope yet.

About a quarter of a mile further on we came across a group of adults ranging from early 20s to mid-40s. They wore work clothing, mainly jeans and open-necked shirts, but some were in the kind of pale blue overalls that looked institutional. Using lengths of wood they were busy reinforcing grassy steps on the hillside that led down to the narrow wooden bridge crossing the river, the site where we had taken over care of the injured kestrel.

Having nodded and said the odd 'hello' to those who caught our eye, we caught bits of their conversation... 'screws'... 'remand'... 'category A in Gartree,' indicating that they might be criminals on community work. Whatever, they seemed placid and at ease with each other, women as well as men. I noted a middle-aged man wearing a dark green anorak, supervising the work. Was he a prison officer or someone from English Nature or the National Trust?

We walked carefully, picking our way along the winding, stone-strewn footpath. Phil, thinking of the work party we'd left behind, spoke strongly. 'That's where we went wrong. We should never have had an industrial revolution but stayed agricultural. Tradition, continuity, that's what we should have kept. They tied people together. Now look at us. Falling apart.'

Freddy and I pointed out, yet again, that there had been terrible times in rural communities, with famine and poverty rife on the land. But we had to agree with the general thesis. All three of us, as children, had lived through years of war and post-war austerity. With no consumer society and everyone linked by family and country to a common goal, there was bags of discipline, little crime and the kitchen door was nearly always unlocked.

* * * * *

Freddy's interest in birdwatching had been strengthened on his birthday by Jean presenting him with a colourful bird book, slim and lightweight enough to be slipped into his anorak pocket. This, she hoped, would get him 'out from under her feet' one or two days a week, in addition to hike day.

And it had worked. On a fine day Freddy would relinquish the Peak for a solitary stroll along the rivers Derwent and Trent, hunting for whitethroats hopping about with their scratchy song over the hedges or listening to the cascading song of the willow warbler. The chiffchaff was his favourite, darting between the oaks, melodious in song.

On the next hike in May Freddy stopped for a whole minute to watch a blackcap flit through trees, an unusual sight as they are shy of being seen. For Phil it was a stop too far. He jabbed his hiking stick to emphasise his displeasure. 'We came hiking,' he asserted. 'To keep fit and to live longer. What good is it sloping around, stopping to watch birds?'

He appealed to our logic, as well as drawing attention to rule 17b, which neither Freddy nor I had heard of: 'All hikers shall maintain the walk between coffee and lunch breaks. Any unauthorised backsliding will result in additional mileage ordered by the navigator at his sole discretion.' Then he issued a yellow card warning. 'I gave you a complete hike of your own last month, Freddy. That was more than generous. There is to be no more stopping for bird or flower. Any more and we shall have to consider your position!' And with that he set off, quickly.

'Oh wonderful!' shouted Freddy. 'Can I go home now?'

Later, north of Hartington, we climbed a hillside, sweating with the effort. Phil turned to find Freddy pausing for breath. 'Come on Freddy!' 'I could see the gleam in Freddy's eye amid a lot of blinking. This, together with a knitting of the eyebrows, I recognised as likely precursors to a Phil baiting session.

'I've had a breakthrough.' Freddy joined us, puffing to a standstill and placing hands on knees.

'What breakthrough?' asked Phil.

'Quantum physics.'

'Quantum…' echoed Phil with a heavy sigh. 'What are you on about?'

'Quantum physics. I know how you got here.'

'I know how I got here,' said Phil. 'By hiking, not backsliding.' He continued his hill climb, tutting disparagingly as he went.

Freddy struggled to keep up. 'I'm talking about your mission to plague me. I now know there wasn't any. You arrived here by accident.'

Phil turned and gave him an Oliver Hardy look, all frustration and tired impatience. 'What are you talking about?'

'Matter. We now know there's no law of cause and effect. It's chaos. That's how you dropped on me from your alien world. It was a total accident. My bad luck.'

'Really. I must have taken the wrong turn,' said Phil ironically and carried on with his climb.

'Look at Japan Electric,' called out Freddy. 'They've built a car only half a millimetre long. So how small were you when you slipped from your universe into mine? You know about parallel…'

'Parallel universes,' cut in Phil, shouting back. 'We know! You've told us before! It's getting a bit of a bore, you know. Seriously. Can we hike now?' He set off walking quickly, shaking his head.

'You never minded when we talked about my drains and the problems with the car,' Freddy called after Phil. 'What's more boring than that?'

Phil paused before speaking. 'They're not boring because they're man's things,' he said slowly. 'Drains are things you can get into. And I mean *you* should get into. Give me some peace.' He chuckled in black humour.

'I thought you'd want to know how you arrived,' complained Freddy. 'Your universe was probably no more than a millimetre from my big toe. You, in your dark satanic world, full of black arts, slips into mine…'

'Freddy,' pleaded Phil, cutting in. 'You're right. Amazing. Now can we talk about something else, interesting though your topic is? Please?'

'No. I'm coming to the important bit,' said Freddy. 'It's vital.'

'Oh cripes. Send for the men in white coats.' Phil gave a desperate chuckle.

Freddy persisted. 'Don't you realise that's why you get uptight, racing around like a lunatic? It's because you're not in tune with our universe. You're an alien.'

Phil snapped. 'Good grief! Give it a rest can't you?'

'Oh lors.' Freddy stopped to stare at the side of Phil's head. 'Oh dear.'

'What?' Phil screwed up his face at Freddy. 'What are you looking at?'

'Oh dear.' Freddy looked sombre. 'I'm wrong. You were sent after all.'

'Freddy! Hell's bells!' Phil brandished his stick. 'Say what you've got to say and have done! Please? You're driving me bonkers!'

'Hmmm.' Freddy peered at Phil's head, took in a deep breath and exhaled before speaking. 'Yes. That's it then. Maybe I shouldn't tell you. You'll be shocked. Because the truth is out. Anybody can tell what you are.'

Phil sighed heavily and lowered his head, trying to calm himself down. 'Okay. What am I?'

'An android.'

Phil paused. 'Right!' he barked out. 'I'm an android. Can we hike now?'

'But you're leaking.'

'What?'

'There's white lubricant leaking from your ears. And there's a tear in the back of your head. And I think... yes. Your ears have turned yellow.'

Phil turned and stumbled on, muttering incoherently, a hiking King Lear driven mad by chicanery, lies and deceit.

Freddy turned to me with a big grin, raising his arms in victory.

Later we followed the rim of a steep-banked hollow, where we had once saved a sheep from a predatory fox. Now began the weather god's shenanigans, in the exact spot where, two years ago, he had magically turned winter into summer in the shake of a dice. Incredibly, it happened again. A wind sprang up, driving horizontal hail, stinging our faces. It was over in less than a minute and was followed immediately by hot sunshine, melting the white carpet. No sooner had we uncoiled ourselves in the heat when the wind spun round on itself in a mini tornado, threatening to hurl us off the hilltop while straightening out Phil's silvery locks. Then, as quickly as he had entered, the weather god skipped off stage and quit the theatre.

An hour later we approached a farmhouse. The date inscribed in the stone lintel over the green door was 1790. We had been here before. But the sagging gate to the cattle yard was no longer sagging. And all of the derelict outbuildings inside and beyond the cattle yard had vanished. New steel-framed buildings had been erected in their place. And the rubbish that had littered the yard had disappeared. A freshly painted sign proclaimed 'Betty's Cottage Ice Cream. All dairy products, butter, cream, eggs, cheese.' My heart leapt. Freddy exclaimed. Phil merely said, 'Hell's bells.'

This was the farm where Jim Oldroyd and his son, Benjamin, had lived, a place where the poverty of the hill farmer had never been better exemplified. But – and this was the cause of our amazement – Jim had told us that he had failed to get a bank loan to finance an ice cream business at the farm, the only way he could see out of his financial mess. Had he, at the last, managed to secure the loan and get into business? Or, by sheer coincidence, had it fallen to someone else to start it? Our question was answered immediately.

A Land Rover Discovery rounded the corner and stopped, facing us. A short, tubby man in his 30s got out. He wore a blue shopkeeper's apron and had a cheerful face. 'Morning,' he said affably. We returned the greeting. He opened the metal gate, returned to his Land Rover and drove into the yard. I just managed to read part of an advert stuck in the rear window: 'Betty's Ice Cream. Hillcrest Farm' before the vehicle disappeared around the rear of the buildings.

We walked on, digesting the news. 'Jim was a tenant farmer,' I said. 'He didn't own the place so he couldn't use it as collateral for the loan. This chap either didn't need it, or he owns the place.'

'Mind, Jim got his revenge, didn't he?' Freddy grinned. 'On the bank. A ton of it!'

Unknown to his father, Benjamin had driven a tractor into town towing a muck spreader. He'd backed up against the offending bank's large doors and let rip with the pumping unit. When the bowser was empty he got down from the tractor to view his handiwork. He was soon joined by a growing crowd, all of them transfixed. At one point the bank door had opened and the bank manager's head had appeared. As he cautiously looked out, a drop of slurry from the Grecian-style pediment had plopped on his bald head. This spectacular event had made the national dailies and all TV news programmes. It became the sole talking point in pubs, cafés, clubs and coffee shops. Jokes abounded. An art teacher, remembering that a Turner Prize entrant had displayed a number of elephant droppings, had seriously wondered whether the attack had anything to do with 'performance art'. The reply came: 'Yes, but it was the usual load of shit.'

Phil, who had said little since we left the farm, returned to a familiar theme. 'Three years? Three years?' He stared, almost threateningly, at me. 'You sure it was three years ago when we were last here?' Freddy and I assured him of that fact. Phil exhaled sharply. 'You see. It proves it. I am losing a third of my life.' His face set in grim realisation.

'Phil,' said Freddy, relenting after his earlier attack and showing sympathy. 'It's the same for everybody as they grow older.'

'Well, how come I'm the only one who complains about it?'

'Look,' said Freddy. 'At the age of five the next year represents 20 per cent of existence to date. That's a lot. At 67, the same length of time – between annual renewal of your bus pass – represents less than two per cent of your existence. You whip through it. That's the reason. We've talked about it no end of times. In fact it's boring.' Freddy burst into a chortle.

Phil grunted, humourless. He couldn't argue with arithmetic, but it gave no satisfaction. 'So why isn't everybody complaining about it?'

'Because they're not like you, crackers.'

'Rhubarb,' scoffed Phil. 'I know what's going on. I study time. It's because I'm not crackers I've been able to analyse it.'

We walked on, Freddy looking melancholic. 'Rhubarb,' he said heavily. 'That's what I've got to do when I get home, make rhubarb jam. I have to do it every year when Jean goes to her sister's.'

'What's this, some religious ritual?' Phil was perplexed.

'No. She doesn't like the smell of it cooking. She only likes to eat it when it's jam.' A smile broke out on Phil's lips. He glanced favourably at Freddy. 'Rhubarb? Do you get enough to make rhubarb pie? With custard? Does Jean like that?' he asked mildly, anxious not to appear too eager.

'No, just rhubarb jam.'

'If ever you want to get rid of any, let me know. I love rhubarb. It's got a real kick in it.'

'Hah! That's it!' Freddy seized the moment, pointing at Phil. 'That's the reason you're insane. Oxalic acid. Rhubarb's full of it. Didn't you know? Nothing will eat the leaf, not even rabbits. And it's in the root, not as much as in the leaf, but it makes people obsessive and mad and want to go walking. They go mile after mile. They can't stop. It makes them believe they're immortal.'

'Rhubarb rhubarb,' chanted Phil, giving me a grin. 'Rhubarb.'

'Well you ask Dr Strangebugger when you next see him,' said Freddy. 'He'll tell you. Less of the oxalic acid and we might have a sane navigator.'

We sat for lunch by a stone wall, close to the ruin of the 11th-century Pilsbury Castle. In the Middle Ages the castle recorded the first appearance of the Derbyshire oatcake. It became the area's staple food and is still eaten to this day.

Phil's mobile chirped. 'Sorry about this fellers,' he said and stared at the caller's name. 'It's Graham Goodall. Hello?' he said. 'Oh…crumbs…really.' Phil listened intently. 'All of them? Unbelievable. Yes, we can. See you soon.' Phil switched off the phone and put it in a waterproof pocket of his anorak. 'Graham's had a court order against him. Half the nation's press are there.'

Freddy and Phil melded in unity as the concerns with time, the universe and drains were put on hold as we raced towards Middleton, only to be slowed down on the final mile of country lane by a tractor. Phil cursed and fumed, but we had to wait. It was only for a minute or two. The tractor soon swung off into a field.

The scene that we found, as we came into Middleton village square, pulled us up short. It was like something out of *MASH*, the combat zone hospital film and TV series. A roaring helicopter was positioned over Graham's secluded garden. A photographer leant down from it, snapping the 50 Trabants parked in neat rows. The rotor wash bent the surrounding bushes and trees and swept the line, full of Graham's washing, horizontal. Photographers scurried around the front yard, clicking at the few Trabants that stood there. A crowd of villagers had gathered in the square, holding on to their hats and wondering at all the commotion. BBC, ITV and Sky news crews were in action.

One of the locals being interviewed for BBC News was Major General Peter Cavendish, the chairman of the parish council. As we parked the car Graham came from the house dressed in the helmet and light blue uniform of the German Democratic Republic's *Volkspolizei*. He instinctively ducked his head at the noise overhead and climbed into the grey border patrol vehicle that had been instrumental in saving

Freddy's life three years ago. He was immediately surrounded by press photographers. 'Look this way Mr Goodall!', or 'Pretend to be driving, can you?' they yelled.

We climbed slowly out of the car, watching in awe. 'I created all this,' said Freddy, open-mouthed. 'I told him to put them in the garden.'

'What do you make of Mr Goodall's car collection?' shouted the BBC news reporter at the General.

'I think it's a pity,' growled the General. Encouraged to speak up against the helicopter racket and taking half a step backwards as the microphone was shoved into his face, he then stood his ground and raised his voice. 'We can't enter for the best-kept village competition can we, not with that lot of rubbish around.'

'But most of the cars are in the garden out of sight. Why is it a problem?'

'Fine, but look at the yard. They're in there as well. It's a mess. He's had a planning authority order to get rid of them.' The General was being reasonable. 'He hasn't done that so the authority has had to go to court. What else can they do?'

'What if he doesn't get rid of them?'

'Hah, well. The law has to be observed. If it isn't…' The General shrugged.

A short fat man wearing khaki shorts, exposing knobbly knees, held down his panama hat against the turbulent air and stuck his reddened face before the camera lens. 'Goodall is an egocentric maniac!' he bellowed. 'He should be arrested!'

Graham sat in his patrol car answering reporters' questions. 'Folk are so narrow-minded,' he boomed, nearer to the helicopter than the General. 'I can't believe they call these beautiful, ecological and economical cars an eyesore! I think some of the villagers must be anti-German!'

'And what about those rabbits!' cried out a small stout lady, clutching her head.

'It wasn't that bad!' called out a thin-faced elderly man with a stick.

'Oh yes it was! The place was knee deep in them!'

The Sky reporter summed up to camera. 'Well there we have the Trabant, the most awful car, a symbol of divided Europe and now responsible for a war breaking out in this…' – he glanced up at the helicopter – 'normally quiet village. Graham Goodall does have his supporters, but can he win the war?'

It was an hour later. We sat outside, at the rear of the house. Most of the media's vehicles had departed. The few that remained dotted around the square had reporters inside quietly tapping laptops, equipped with the means for instant transfer of news. Within hours newspapers, radio and television would splash the story. It would, not surprisingly, reach Germany. Graham Goodall was destined to become a curiosity beloved by the media.

Graham came out of the house bearing a tray heavy with mugs of coffee. For no apparent reason the *Volkspolizei* patrolman had been replaced by a Texan cowboy. He wore calf-length boots, a white shirt with tassles over the two breast pockets, Levi jeans, a belt with a decorative metal clasp and a bootlace tie.

Freddy looked puzzled, but not by Graham's attire. 'What I don't get is that you've hidden most of the cars in the garden. It took a helicopter to actually see them. So what's everybody so worked up about?'

Graham dismissed it, with a gesture. 'It would have happened anyway Freddy. They were determined to get rid of the Trabbies. But why did the planners tell me it was all okay and I could keep them?'

'What?' Phil glanced sharply at Graham. 'When did they say that?'

'You've forgotten.' Graham sat down to ream out the burnt remnants of Holland House tobacco from his pipe. 'It was three years ago. You were here.'

'That's right,' I said. 'The planning officer, that day, about three years ago. He said Graham could keep them, provided the yard was tidied up.'

'I remember,' said Phil. 'Yes, he did. God, three years,' he sighed.

'Yes,' went on Freddy. 'We forgot because of all that trouble with the taxman and those Germans calling at the same time. The planning chap said the yard had been an overflow place for parking cars from a garage in Youlgreave.'

'And because of that there was no need to get permission for a change of use.' Graham stuffed tobacco into the empty pipe, pressing it down with his forefinger. 'So what happened in the meantime?'

'What you want is a good lawyer,' said Phil.

'Or us to act as witnesses.' It was Freddy who spoke.

Phil and I murmured our approval. We agreed it was an angle worth exploring.

As we drove away from the house, Graham waving a last farewell, a photographer popped out of a Range Rover to snap his change of identity from border policeman to Texan cowboy.

The drive home was spent absorbing the dramatic events at Middleton. It was Freddy who spoke. 'They shouldn't be persecuting Graham,' he said. 'They should be praising him. He's taken 50 cars off the roads. If everybody collected 50 cars we'd bring down carbon emissions tremendously. It's like the Rolls-Royce that Donald owned at Milldale. He never drove it, except to fill it up with petrol. We should do what they've done. That's the way to save the planet.'

* * * * *

In the week leading up to the next hike, Phil decided that Freddy's lengthy baiting session earlier in the month, taken together with all the other teasing, flippancies and taunts of recent hikes, had gone too far. It was, literally, beyond a joke. It was essential, he felt, to secure that fourth hiker, urgently. Finding the right person was proving difficult. Men who had the fitness, time, drive and personality required were thin on the ground. The ideal person would be a man who could 'talk the talk' (sport, discipline, the need to put more people in prison) and, literally, 'walk the walk' alongside him, someone whose very presence would deter Freddy from launching any more of his lengthy, tedious and irksome attacks.

Phil's ideal choice had backed out due to a knee injury. He was an ex-policeman, six feet two inches tall and would have made an ideal security guard. How to find a replacement? He was surprised that Freddy hadn't already tried to nip in with one of his lazy cronies, in an attempt to ruin the hike. Phil had the gut feeling now that to be anything less than swift in the matter could bring disaster. He went to his study and picked up the hike log book from the safe to record these thoughts. He found a pen and froze as his eye caught a photograph of himself standing by a Cessna 152 aircraft. A man stood next to him, in friendly fashion. Phil peered at the photograph closely. Then he picked up the phone.

In the history of the hike the stratagems and secretive planning of the two opponents, Phil and Freddy, would be written down as part of the 'phoney war', the prelude to 'Der Tag', the day that would be etched in Freddy's memory for ever. ('Der Tag' had been the code name for the first day of the intended Nazi invasion of England in May 1940.) Its mention would always bring to mind those things that happened when we finally met our 'Third Man'.

* * * * *

Morning broke on the third hike of the month and began as any other hike day, with Freddy putting through a nuisance call to Phil at 8am for no other reason than to moan about a cold front moving in, only to be reassured that it would not arrive until the late afternoon.

It was my turn to drive, and I picked up Freddy as usual. On arriving at Phil's house I pipped the horn, while noting a Range Rover parked outside, a vehicle I'd not seen around the village before. The personalised number plate included the letters 'G T', set apart from the remaining digit and letter by more than the legal limit.

The front door opened. Phil stepped outside, carrying his gear as usual. He stopped, turned round and allowed another man out of the house, before turning to lock the door.

They walked towards my parked car, the stranger carrying not only an anorak and rucksack, but also a walking pole. Fixed to his brown belt was a GPS, compass and multi-function clasped knife. Around his neck hung a neatly-folded Ordnance Survey map, sealed in a see-through waterproof wallet. He was in his 60s but had a lean, hard body, evidently used to exercise.

'Oh no,' whispered Freddy, aghast, taking him in. 'Gruppenführer clone.'

Phil leaned into the car. 'Fellers, this is George. He was at a loose end so I invited him along. Just for the day. Hope you don't mind.' Phil gave a false chuckle and addressed me to escape Freddy's black stare. 'Yes, we didn't know it was on until half an hour ago. I just rang him up on the off-chance. He's a pilot, like me.' He waved a hand at me. 'George, this is Don.'

'Hi.' I stuck my hand out. It was gripped in the jaws of a car crusher.

'Hello Don.' George's voice was light and assured, and he smiled while continuing to break the bones in my hand. Through the mist of pain I registered a slightly tanned face with an aquiline nose and pale blue eyes. His blond hair, now greying heavily, and pale skin gave him what I thought was a Scandinavian look.

Later, Freddy told me that he saw George as a dead ringer for Reinhard Heydrich, the 'Butcher of Prague', one of the most-feared Nazis in the Third Reich. There was certainly a hint of a cool, detached mind – Heydrich was regarded as a rare intellectual of the thuggish regime – behind the ubiquitous smile.

'George, this is Freddy,' said Phil, anxious to finish the introductions.

'Hi.' George smiled again as he extended the maw of his right hand, soon drawing a wince of pain from Freddy. 'Hope I'm not going to tread on your toes, you chaps?' he continued. 'Or stick my pole into you. Bit of a novice at hiking, I'm afraid.' Only now did he let go of Freddy's hand. A novice? What was the guy doing with a hiking pole, GPS, map, compass and clasp knife if he were a novice? Freddy nursed his injured hand and turned to grimace at me. I feared he was about to get out of the car and storm home. But he stayed put, his face set in a fixed, dark frown.

With all hiking gear safely locked in the boot, the two men climbed into the back of the car. I had a good view of George in the rear-view mirror.

'You a commercial pilot, George?' I half turned my head.

'No, private.'

'That's how we met – at the airfield,' said Phil. 'He's building his own aircraft from a kit.'

'*What aircraft? A Stuka dive bomber?*' That's what Freddy would have loved to have said, he told me later. Instead he said nothing, his mind ticking away, thinking, thinking, his hand throbbing, throbbing…

At one point on the run towards Ashbourne, Freddy and I exchanged knowing smiles. There was no doubt that we had been 'jumped', that Freddy's fears had been justified. George, we discovered, lived in Duffield, north of Derby. He was divorced, without children and had spent his working life as a wine importer. He had kept fit all his life – he was a regular squash player – and any outdoor activity appealed to him. He owned a cabin cruiser moored nearby on the Trent and Mersey Canal. In winter he went skiing.

I noticed that he listened attentively and was diplomatic enough to remain deferential and show interest if anyone broke into his conversation. Phil was fulsome in praise of his man. 'You see, George is the best example I know of a man who can live without a woman around. That right George? There's nothing to stop him doing what he wants. He can hike at the drop of a hat or go to the pub if he feels like it.'

'He could even go hiking in Canada,' Freddy added, with a dry look at Phil.

'That's right!' Phil seized eagerly on the suggestion, at first missing the irony. 'Yes, Canada. There's a thought.' But then he fell silent, annoyed with himself for being so easily led on.

'Canada,' said George. 'Great place. I did a bit of ski-jumping there once. But that's another story,' he added modestly. I looked in the rear-view mirror. George still bore his pleasant smile as he looked out of the window.

On the A515, rounding a bend near the turn off for Thorpe village and Dovedale, I braked sharply, causing a screech of tyres.

'Wow!' exclaimed Freddy. 'How did *they* get out?' Cows were everywhere, on both sides of the road and on the grass verge. It was impossible to see how they'd escaped, there being no sign of damage to fencing or hedgerow. There was a closed metal gate on our left-hand side.

'Let's get them in there,' said Phil. 'I'll try and open it.'

'Yes, do that.' George was quickly out of the car. 'Freddy, if you go back round the bend and stop the traffic, I'll stop it this side.'

Freddy did as he was told, at as fast a jog as he could manage. Lives were at risk, not least his own. Phil and I tackled the gate. But it was held to the wooden post by orange-coloured binding string. And the knots were impossible to untie by hand. 'Anybody got a knife?' I shouted.

George ran forward. 'Don, take my place.' I jogged away, ducking and diving between the cows. Fortunately a heavy truck, with a hiss of brakes, came to a standstill on my side of the herd, forming a substantial road block. I turned my attention to keeping the cattle in some semblance of order.

George had his clasp knife open at the sharpest blade to cut through the string. Within seconds the gate was open. Freddy reappeared. 'I've stopped the traffic that side,' he called out.

The immediate danger over, we concentrated on getting the herd through the gate, with Freddy and I acting as drovers on the Ashbourne side and George and Phil on the other. With much rough shouting and prodding with hiking sticks, we managed to pass one cow through the gate, then another. The rest were glad just to follow.

'Like sheep,' Freddy said, to some amusement.

With the last one through, George picked up the sagging gate and humped it back into a closed position. Then, with impressive dexterity, he produced a length of twine from the knee pocket of his commando-style trousers and cut off a length with which he refastened the gate to the post. It took less than a minute.

We were impressed. 'Well done,' I said.

Phil concurred. 'Yes, good job. Lucky you came along. We don't carry string or anything. Maybe we should.'

'I always carry some,' said George. 'And the knife. You never know when they might be needed. Anyway, it's good to be tested occasionally.'

'Absolutely,' said Phil. 'That's what it's all about.'

We returned to the car and resumed the journey north.

Freddy looked thoughtful. 'George,' he said. 'Were you in the Forces, like Phil?'

'Yes,' he said. 'Royal Marine commando.'

'Ah yes,' said Freddy. 'That explains the knife and stuff.'

'Well,' said George. 'That post and string was easy. One of the tests in the Marines was to duck under water to free a rope that had wrapped around a boat prop. Dive, cut, lungs bursting, surface, breathe, dive, cut – takes about 20 minutes. You're left with bits of rope. Then you have to splice them together back into the original length.'

'You see,' said Phil, with a proprietary smile. 'This is the kind of man you'd want on a hike. Wouldn't you agree, Freddy?'

'Of course,' said Freddy, with a wry look at Phil. 'It'll come in handy when our boat fouls up in the Dove.'

There was a pause. Phil gave a mechanical chuckle. 'I ought to warn you George, Freddy's our joker in the pack. Keeps us happy.' Freddy met Phil's eyes and gave him a tired smile.

The hike started from Calver, heading west into Coombs Dale, a haven for plants and wild flowers. Ash woodland guards its entrance, effectively deadening noise from the outside world. As we walked in silence among hawthorn, hazel and blackthorn, Freddy's attention was taken by the abundance of wild flowers. He drew our attention to forget-me-not and celandine. Then – great news – he found that elusive flower, the delicate green moschatel. Further up the dale, Freddy found the rare limestone fern, protected from the hungry sheep by the rocky screes.

I could see Phil holding back his impatience. Was it an attempt by Freddy to provoke him into an outburst and so embarrass his guest? Well, he wouldn't give him the pleasure. Not on this hike, anyway. It would not do to show his putative 'unter-Gruppenführer' any weaknesses or conflict associated with his leadership.

A thunderclap, reverberating down the dale, broke my thoughts. 'It's not thunder,' said George. 'That's a quarry explosion.'

'They're mining fluorspar.' Freddy joined us, pointing south-westward. 'Or say they are. In fact it's illegal. They were only given permission to remove as much limestone as it takes to get to the fluorspar, but they're taking loads. They've had a legal stop notice from the planning board. So what did the company do? They put in an appeal – which takes ages – so they're taking as much as they can before they're shut down.'

'Graham's had the same stop notice,' I said. 'I bet he has to give in before the mining people do. And who's the real threat to the environment? Them or Graham?' My question was met by murmurs of appreciation from Phil and Freddy.

Later, we climbed out of the dale in a southerly direction, heading towards Hassop and Bakewell. George pointed out the danger of walking near any of the numerous nettle patches. 'They'll sting you for the last time,' he warned. 'They hide old mine shafts.'

I looked at Freddy, which prompted him to chance his arm. 'You seen to know a lot about the area for a non-hiker, George,' he said.

George smiled modestly. 'I've got a photographic memory. I mugged up on this hike before we came out. I can remember the whole route.'

'So why do you need an Ordnance Survey map?' Freddy wasn't going to let go too easily. In for a penny, in for a pound.

'Ah, no,' said George. 'Nobody should go hiking without a map. You never know what might happen.'

'So, Gruppenführer,' said Freddy in cod German, pointing accusingly at Phil. 'You haf been endangering our lifes! No map!'

Coffee break was spent on the ridge above the western end of

Coombs Dale. To the far north lay the great, brooding mass of Kinder Scout. As we descended southwards we could hear the constant roar and grind of machinery. Soon gigantic trucks, bigger than armoured tanks, came into view trundling along the wide, brown steps cut into the sides of the vast quarry, sending up clouds of dust. It was total devastation, a gigantic bite wrenched from the landscape, not a sight for the faint-hearted or those who love the beauty of nature, and especially the Peak District. Yet how do you manage a national park when it is one of the few places where fluorspar is found and is in such demand?

George seemed cheerfully unaffected by it all. He had Phil engaged in a shouting conversation to overcome the noise of the machinery. So far the two of them had walked together – Phil's tactic of keeping Freddy at a distance was paying off. I caught snatches of football chat about a proposed revision of the offside rule. Freddy, meanwhile, kept the pair under scrutiny, his lips pursed in deep thought.

The conversation between Phil and George had petered out by the time we started the long climb up the northern side of Longstone Edge. Early on it became apparent that both men were climbing quickly, George in the lead, his elbows tucked in and arms moving like pistons, his footsteps measured and equal. Pound for pound he was using less energy than Phil, whose technique was to attack with an extravagance of arm movement, his feet digging into the ground in varying lengths of stride, one moment short, the next moment long and sometimes side-to-side, thus losing distance covered.

'Interesting,' said Freddy, viewing all this. 'Very interesting.' We lost sight of the pair as they neared the ridge, but with George clearly in the lead.

On reaching the top we found Phil and George sitting on rocks, rucksacks open and sipping coffee. Phil stared at the ground in front of him. George, looking relaxed, tinkered with his sat nav.

'So who won?' Freddy asked.

'George,' said Phil readily. 'But I did a personal best. Chopped two seconds off. Not bad eh?'

'Excellent,' said Freddy lightly and nodded at the instrument on George's knee. 'Find much use for that?'

'Yes,' George replied. 'You never know. A sudden hill fog and you're lost. You'd need one of these. Imagine if you were lost up Kinder Scout in a thick fog. You can die up there. You know that?'

Freddy hesitated. 'Phil? What would you do if you were lost on Kinder Scout? Use a sat nav?' Freddy ended the question with a teasing raise of the eyebrows.

Phil scowled at Freddy. George looked at the three of us with a blank face. 'Sorry, have I missed something?'

'Yes,' said Freddy, trying to look earnest. 'It's a bit of a coincidence, that's all. That's exactly where we were – on Kinder, in fog – when we got lost with that GPS thing.' He nodded at the sat nav. 'Tell George, Gruppenführer, how you got lost with that GPS. On Kinder.' He referred to the bizarre hike of two years ago when our navigator had fallen in love with an Amazonian female festooned in hi-tech gear.

The Amazon had been leading a small group of PR women across Kinder Scout on a test of initiative. Freddy had spotted one of her charges, a young and vulnerable woman, in tears. Knowing too well how miserable she felt, he'd had a word with her privately. After that she had completely turned the tables, to the chagrin of the Amazon and the sorrow of Phil, who had become disenchanted with his 'superwoman'. George listened to the story. 'The wrong coordinates must have been put in before you started,' he said. As he spoke, I decided that his eyes were a pale, ice blue, the smile superior. Freddy was right. He was Reinhard Heydrich.

Everything exploded – a massive detonation, from the direction of the quarry. I felt the ground tremble beneath me. It served as general notice for the end of the coffee break.

We continued the hike, first watched by a kestrel, in turn watched by a buzzard high in the cloudless sky, circling slowly in majestic surveillance of all things animate. The hike ended on a quiet note, without any mention of George joining us next time.

* * * * *

Freddy, seriously peeved, kicked at a loose stone, sending it skittering into the hedgerow, startling a pheasant into a flurry of noisy flight. 'The way Phil dumped George on us would be like the queen asking guests at a palace garden party if they supported the monarchy. And look at that bruise on my hand!' Freddy showed me the mark between his finger and thumb.

I showed him my own bruise. 'He made his mark on both of us,' I said. We were on our usual evening walk with Montague.

Freddy mimicked George. 'Hope I don't tread on your toes.' Then he fell back into his own voice. 'No, just my hand, no problem, be my guest,' he said airily.

'I don't think it will last,' I said. 'I can't see Phil putting up with a sadist who's going to beat him uphill all the time. And the guy's a know-all. He'd take over the hike if he could. I think Phil will kick him out.'

'I'm not so sure.' Freddy paused to pluck a green stalk out of the undergrowth lining the lane. 'Phil didn't mind being beaten up the hill. It improved his personal best. Phil doesn't hike for hiking's sake. He does it to stay young. I think he chose George to keep him up to the mark, simple as that. You know what I really think? I reckon George won't come on the next hike. He'll come on the one after that. Then he'll miss two more and pop up on the next. They'll keep doing this until we get used to him. He becomes a fixture. Fait accompli.' Freddy chewed on the sweet end of the stalk.

'Okay,' I said. 'In that case what we should be doing is finding our own man and putting him up for election before George gets bedded in.'

There was no immediate response from Freddy. He caught me looking at him with a curious smile. 'What?'

'I know your expressions,' I said drily. 'You've got somebody, haven't you? Come on, admit it.'

'No, I haven't.'

'But you've got somebody in mind.'

'No. I know what I'd *like* to do.'

'Oh yes? To Phil or George, or both?'

'I don't know. Look.' Freddy tried to slice through his indecision. 'Let's wait till we know George is definitely turning up. Then it could become interesting.' He refused to say any more on the subject. Irritated, I persisted.

'Come on, Freddy!'

'No, I can't tell you. It all depends.'

'On what?' I was determined to get it out of him. 'Don't tease me like you do Phil. Who is it? I'm not going to tell anybody.'

'But you might tell Liz and she might tell Ruth. And she'll tell Phil.'

'I promise not to tell Liz. Scout's honour.'

'Hmm.' Freddy debated with himself. 'No.' He made short, shaking gestures with his hands. 'I've got to set up something. It's a bit delicate. It depends on reactions, even yours. If I told you, your reaction wouldn't be the same as if you didn't know.'

I clicked my teeth. 'This is a big wheeze.'

'Oh yes.'

'The biggest ever?'

'Could be.' A big smile spread over Freddy's face.

As we neared the old barn near my house, the crimson sky in the west was turning dark blood red in the twilight. Swallows squeaked on their last arcing flight after insects. I caught the black flash of a bat circling around the barn. The tang of wood smoke drifted downwards from our chimney pot. In the silence I could hear the clink of a hammer on anvil coming from the distant forge.

A young, saffron-robed monk with shaven head approached. We bade him good evening. He returned our greeting with a gentle smile. After he'd gone I began to laugh as a memory surfaced. 'Do you remember that night when we went there to…'

'Don't remind me,' Freddy broke in. 'I know exactly what you're going to say.'

The three of us had attended a meditation evening at the local Buddhist centre. Beforehand we had eaten a strong curry. The genteel silence had been broken by a melodious gurgle from Phil's midriff, followed by a high-pitched squeaking. Freddy had then joined the refrain as second piccolo. In that utter quiet the sounds were as disruptive as they were embarrassing. It was all too much. Freddy had farted.

We laughed at the memory as we said goodnight, Freddy lugging Montague out of the hedgerow as he scrabbled after a rabbit. As I let myself into the cottage, I could hear Freddy lightly singing The Beatles' 'All you need is love, ta ta da da der,' the song punctuated by the first of the night hoots of the barn owl.

JUNE

'Unfortunately,' wheezed a voice, speaking through tissue paper. 'I shall not be available today, on account of my hay fever.'

'What have you got in your mouth Freddy?' Phil switched the phone to 'loud and hands-off,' placed it on the conservatory table and popped a 500mg tablet of glucosamine sulphate into his mouth.

'Stevens, are you aware that I attended the allergy clinic in Derby? And the news was not good?'

'When was that, 60 years ago?' Phil knocked back a selenium tablet.

'Did you know we have the greatest variety of allergy-producing grasses in the whole of Europe, except for the area around Montpelier in France, and that Derby and Montpelier clinics are twinned for allergy research?'

Freddy was interrupted by Jean. Coolly, she took the phone from him. 'Phil? Freddy is hiking. He's just being silly. Take no notice. I've packed his lunch and flask.' She handed the phone back to Freddy, smiled sweetly and returned to the kitchen.

'Oh lors. I've been press ganged. Did you hear that?'

'Yes, I did,' said Phil, downing a dose of calcium. 'And do as she says. Stop being silly. See you, usual time. Don's driving.'

'Is George going?'

'Yes. See you.' Phil ended the call quickly and reached for his omega-3 capsule.

Freddy slowly replaced the phone in its cradle and sighed softly. His optimism that George would give today's hike a miss had been misplaced. It wouldn't have been so great a blow if we had been any nearer to finding a compatible hiker. He was further frustrated by the recent heatwave. Having no wish to succumb again to sunstroke, he had reluctantly stopped himself from going out to photograph the wild flowers of summer. In particular he'd wanted to capture a floral vignette seen the previous spring near Ilam, featuring campion and bluebells among spreads of wild garlic. The simple beauty of it all had enthralled him. He'd also intended to visit Lathkill Dale, hoping to find 'water aven' and the rarer 'lords and ladies' under the shaded limestone cliffs. Then there was the extremely rare and protected Jacob's ladder, near Monyash.

Adding salt to his wound was the weather forecast for today's hike. It gave 'normal temperature with a cool breeze,' ideal for flower hunting. It was yet another example of Sod's Law, which seemed to gravitate in his direction, especially when something really enjoyable was in the offing. Unfairness blighted his life, he thought. He didn't ask for much, really, when he came to think of it. Automatically he headed for the shed to choose three soft-centred, personal chocolates.

And then he realised he hadn't eaten any breakfast.

As soon as I arrived at Freddy's house he gave me the gloomy news about George.

'So the big wheeze is on,' I said.

'If I can get one going.' Freddy's spaniel eyes drooped. 'Him coming today, I don't need a wheeze. I need an assassin.'

The Range Rover stood outside Phil's house as we arrived. This time George appeared with kit additional to the GPS, compass and knife. A pedometer was attached to his belt and a compass watch to his wrist. A bright silver whistle dangled over the map slung round his neck.

'Going somewhere dangerous?' Freddy nodded at the equipment.

'Hah!' George smiled. 'But if you'd been on expeditions like I have…' He left the rest weighing heavily with a smile.

'Gruppenführer? You see?' said Freddy, shaking his head. 'What have I been telling you? All those years we've hiked without a whistle. Who knows who we could have called up? Mountain rescue on Kinder Scout? Jenny the dog? A truck to tow us out of that snow drift at Middleton Top? I don't know how we survived without one.'

Phil chuckled politely, first in a low monotone and then louder, to demonstrate his imperviousness as leader and camaraderie as a chum. If George was impressed by Phil's show of munificent leadership he gave no sign, his smile remaining as fixed and as enigmatic as ever.

We parked the car in the short cul-de-sac outside the primary school in Calver, north east of Bakewell. The hike began with a short road walk, approaching the River Derwent. At this point Freddy, for some reason, overtook both Phil and George, making sure he would be the first to enter the narrow riverside footpath. I had never seen him out in front, while Phil was navigator. There had to be a reason and I guessed rightly.

Some distance along the footpath Freddy suddenly came to a halt, bringing us to a stop behind him. He sniffed the air deeply, then murmured rapturously, 'Hmmm. Smell that.' The lightest of zephyrs wafted the scent of wild honeysuckle into our path.

Phil and George momentarily indulged him, nostrils extended, Phil politely murmuring 'great' and George 'super'.

Freddy resumed his walk, but shortly afterwards stopped once more. This time his purpose was to examine cock's foot, mallow and bird's-foot trefoil in every detail and from every angle.

Phil and George's patience wore thin and both refused to spend time staring at a dog rose. 'Get on Freddy,' urged Phil. 'We're behind time already.'

'But this is important,' huffed Freddy. 'The dog rose has a change of colour. It's like a chameleon.'

'Hmm, like you, Freddy,' said Phil mildly, conscious of George. 'A rear guard who suddenly pops up in front.' He forced a chuckle.

'Get fell in you 'orrible little man!' beamed George at Freddy. 'Don't you know, platoon leader at the front, men behind? Make way!' He gave a short and dry laugh.

Freddy gave me one of his po-faced looks, betrayed only by a slight twinkle of the eye, but stayed in front for the remainder of the footpath.

Later, as we began a steep climb towards woodland, Phil stopped and frowned down at Freddy, who was wandering slothfully in the rear. 'Come on Freddy!' he called, in as encouraging a tone as he could summon. 'He holds things up both ends.'

'Yes. Quite a lad,' George said, smiling. He cupped his hands to his mouth and shouted. 'If you don't buck up, Freddy, we'll put you on jankers!'

'He won't know what jankers was,' Phil grimaced.

'Oh? Didn't he do National Service? He wasn't a conchie, was he?'

'Of that type,' muttered Phil. 'You know them. They'd get out of anything.'

'I know them. I can imagine.' George nodded, smug with the idea.

Freddy drew nearer. 'Jankers, what's that?' he asked, puffing.

'Confined to barracks. Punishment parades.' George looked at Freddy with a paternalistic air. 'You don't know how lucky you were.' As we set off again, he went on. 'By the way, Phil tells me you're a searcher for the meaning of life. I was after that once.' Pride lifted George's chin a notch. 'A Philosophy module. Open University.'

'Did you find it?'

'Hardly. We looked at things like "What was God doing before he created life?"'

'What *was* God doing before he created life?'

'Ha. Good one.' Phil pointed a finger, giving credit. 'Good one, Freddy. First rule, always bounce the question back.'

'Yes.' Freddy nodded solemnly. 'I'll try to remember that.'

'My advice is not to bother. Enjoy the hike while you can. Right Phil?'

'Absolutely. I'm always telling Freddy that.' Phil caught Freddy's weary 'thank you for nothing' smile.

At coffee break, as we sat on a slope near Baslow, George came out with a joke. 'Freddy. What comes between conception and death?'

Freddy frowned. 'Life?'

'No, the hokey cokey.'

'Hokey cokey?' said Phil in bewilderment.

'Yes, that's what it's all about.' George put his head to one side, drilling out a staccato chuckle, looking to the three of us for an amused reaction. None came, but George continued unfazed. 'And never worry about the world ending today. It's already tomorrow in Australia.'

His mechanical chuckle was broken by Phil suddenly standing up and pointing. 'Look at that! Look, over there! Can you see it? That big black animal?'

We jumped up to stand beside him, peering down the line of his pointed finger. Some 300 yards away, sloping through the bracken, was a large and dark cat-like creature. To whispered 'Good griefs' and 'Hell's bells', we stared until the animal had disappeared into the trees.

'Amazing,' said Freddy. 'There was a TV programme last night. About black panthers.' He said it had dealt with exotic creatures that had escaped into the English countryside. He was about to launch into a summary of its findings when George broke in.

'Freddy, these tales have been going for 40 years. Since the mid-1970s lots of big cats have been seen.'

'They said that on the programme,' said Freddy.

'Yes,' said George airily. 'But if you look at it from a scientific point of view it's obvious these species have freely interbred. They reckon offspring of these cats are about six feet long and a dark brown colour.'

'Yes,' said Freddy. 'That's what the programme said.'

'But there's not been one attack on a human until a woman found a big cat asleep on the top of her wardrobe. That was in... er...' George searched for the name.

'Hayfield,' said Freddy. 'That was in the pro...'

'That's right. Hayfield,' broke in George. 'When she woke up there it was, right on top of her wardrobe. Fast asleep, would you believe it?'

'I would,' said Freddy flatly. 'It was in the progr...'

'Yes,' George cut in. 'Isn't it all amazing?'

'Where did you read about it, George?' Freddy said casually.

'It was in *The New Scientist*.'

Phil looked at him. 'I take *New Scientist*,' he said. 'Can't remember reading about it in there.' For the rest of the hike Phil wore a preoccupied look.

* * * * *

On arrival home Freddy and I sat in the car outside his house, watching a thatcher work on a cottage roof, one of a cluster at the heart of the original village. He was using a 'legget', a wooden tool, with which he dressed the ends of the water reeds hanging over the eaves.

At last Freddy spoke. 'Did you notice George said "*The*" *New Scientist*? It isn't. It's "*New Scientist*".'

'Oh.'

'I think he's a poser. I think Phil's started to rumble him. But how does he get rid of him? I can't see him saying, "Sorry mate, we don't want you any more." And can you see him admitting he dropped a clanger? I can't.'

'No,' I said.

'It's going to need a big wheeze. A very big wheeze. One of my best.'

* * * * *

On the eve of the second hike of the month, towering cumulonimbus clouds erupted in thunder and lightning, followed by hours of rain. Freddy rang Phil to say that he wasn't going on account of the mud created by the storm, the kind that sucked his boots down so much that his feet rose inside them and made his big toe hurt.

'Okay Freddy,' said Phil. 'No problem. As soon as your big toe hurts we'll carry you out of the mud.'

'I suppose George is going?'

'Yes. See you.' Phil put the phone down quickly, then told Ruth of Freddy's latest complaint. She screeched with laughter.

The following morning we joined Freddy in his Land Rover, destination Longnor, a village south of Buxton. As soon as we moved away, Freddy restated his dislike of mud. What was the point of heaving one's body through clinging mud, he said, with boots getting heavier all the time? It wasn't logical. And 'glutinous hikes' always reminded him of his workplace, the glue factory. The idea was to hike, not wallow, wasn't it?

'It's a challenge, Freddy,' said George brightly. 'Good for the old leg muscles.'

'Not mine,' said Freddy. 'Mine weaken in mud. It's a condition called legorophilia.'

I burst out laughing.

Then came an unexpected observation: 'Phil,' said George carefully. 'Freddy may be right, you know? It will be very sticky. What about doing the Tissington Trail to Parwich instead?'

Phil answered steadily. 'No, because half the year we're in mud. We never give in to mud, otherwise we'd have to hike for six months on hard trails.'

George looked out of the window and pointed towards the horizon. 'See that black stuff, right in the distance?' He had changed his tone to one of concern, speaking slowly. 'It should be with us about 12.30. Now then, according to your records, Phil, the Tissington hike's got that bus shelter in Parwich. We can have lunch there, in the dry.' He had borrowed Phil's hike log book, which recorded weather, lunch stops, times, temperatures and speed of walking. Initially, Phil had been reluctant to allow the log book out of his care, but George had faithfully promised to return it the following day.

In response to George's suggested change of plan, Phil said nothing for a moment, and then spoke in as light a tone as he could manage. 'No, I think we'll keep to the plan, if you don't mind.'

For a moment George was silent, still preoccupied with the distant cloud formation. 'Hmm, that's rain alright. Remember the army motto, Phil? March wet. Eat and sleep dry? I think you should reconsider.'

I could see Phil's mouth working as he tried to frame a suitable reply. 'No,' he said with finality. 'We'll stick to the Longnor hike.' The forced lightness of his tone indicated the tension he felt.

'I checked your notes, though, Phil.' George sounded like a doctor with a difficult patient. 'There's that bog halfway round. You say to give it a miss if it's that muddy. After all this rain, perhaps... what do you think?'

Silence from Phil.

'Well,' said Phil eventually, his voice dropping in pitch and volume. 'I think we'll be fine. Don't worry, we'll be okay.' The words slipped out between tightening teeth.

Another hiatus.

Hikers share with the crews of midget submarines the need to be 100 per cent compatible. Time spent hiking is always full of conversation. Hikers, thrown together for hours on end, chatter like magpies. In weeks, certainly months, they nearly always reveal their true personality and character. Through an aside, an unwitting remark, a reaction to a particular situation, in confessions about politics, views on society and personal philosophy, the totality of character and personality are revealed. There are few situations where such insight into fellow man can be gained in such a short space of time. In the 'pre-Georgian age' – Freddy's term – despite the battles between him and Freddy, we knew each other well enough to accept our faults and failings. And there was always something to laugh about – but not with George.

The tension continued to ratchet upwards.

It was now that George made a fundamental mistake. 'Come on, Gruppenführer,' he urged with a smile. 'You know a good officer entertains ideas from his subordinates.'

After a pause Phil answered quietly. 'Ah well. I was never an officer. Just a sergeant.'

'Exactly,' replied 2nd Lieutenant George, preening himself yet again in the hope it was funny. 'As your superior officer, sergeant, it's the Parwich hike. Company will parade at 0800 hours, dress – denims and working boots.'

It fell on stony ground. No one found it funny – except George.

My mind swam around trying to find some quip – anything – to break the embarrassing silence.

It was Freddy who came to the rescue. 'Of course, Gruppenführer, you know rule 33d, don't you? After a new member has joined the group they're allowed to choose the second hike. Yes?'

'No, I don't know that rule.'

'Yes, you do.' Phil was being completely thick. He'd been offered a lifebelt and had ignored it. 'You made the rule,' Freddy continued. 'You can allow George his request.'

'33d.' Phil thought about it. For some reason his brain wasn't working. He had a momentary panic attack. 'What?' he said, to cover it up.

'Gruppenführer. You made the rule so you could bend a little. It was your idea, remember?'

'Was it? Oh yes! Of course!' Phil had tumbled to it, at last. 'Yes! I did, didn't I. Yes, I'd forgotten. That's right. I can allow the Parwich hike. Permission granted.' He felt so much better.

George turned his head to look out of the window, looking well pleased.

I sagged and sighed silently, in relief.

Freddy changed the subject. 'See that fox?' he said. 'There look, running into the wood. That's what hiking's all about. Nature, not all this blood, sweat and pain.' He shot a mischievous smile at George. 'We don't go in for masochism, do we?'

George glanced at Phil in hesitation. Freddy had tipped him neatly off balance. 'Well, it's both, isn't it?' he said lamely. 'Health and nature.'

Did I detect a flicker of uncertainty in the cold blue eyes? Ridiculously, an image popped into my head, that of the villainous penguin in *The Wrong Trousers*, one of Nick Park's Wallace and Gromit animations.

We began the hike from the car park at Tissington and were immediately forced to step aside to allow a pack of cyclists to pass. All of them, men and women, were dressed in cycling gear and wore rucksacks. I caught the pleasant lilt of the Dutch accent. Travel between Holland and the Peak District is quick and convenient, with regular flights from Amsterdam to East Midlands airport. Half an hour's drive from there takes the flatlander into the Peak to revel in our hills and dales.

One cyclist, a man with long hair and a beard, trying to catch up with the main group, clipped the straps dangling from Phil's rucksack.

After an expletive, Phil applied the only literary quote he knew, that from Dickens. He had employed it in so many situations that Freddy was ready for it. 'Cyclists,' Phil said, 'should all' – and here Freddy joined in – 'have a stake of holly through their hearts and be boiled in their own pudding.'

At the conclusion of the duet Phil stared at Freddy, giving an emphatic Oliver Hardy slow blink of the eyes, while expanding his chest in a deep intake of breath. Freddy reacted with a sheepish smile, tickling the top of his Stan Laurel head. This short bonding with Phil served to encourage him to be bolder. 'So, George,' he said. 'With you knowing such a lot I'm surprised you don't have an idea what God was doing before he created the universe.'

George raised his chin in thought. 'I think he probably created hell to be filled by people like you who ask impossible questions.'

For its cleverness it drew polite laughs from all three of us.

I made it my business to walk just behind – and to the side of – George, so I could give him closer scrutiny. The man *is* clever, I thought. Strange and clever. And I knew there existed men who feel compelled not to dominate an individual, but a group (religious, political, whatever). George seemed to be this type of control freak. Incipient megalomania?

Ten minutes later Freddy gave Phil further moral support. 'Coffee break, Gruppenführer? Have we your permission?'

'Yes, we're within the 10 minute rule.' Phil gave a quick glance at Freddy. Was it in appreciation?

'That rain's getting nearer. Do you really think it wise?' said George.

'I thought you marines were tough,' I said teasingly.

'Hah, no.' George sounded serious. 'I'm thinking about Freddy. I read about his hypothermia in Phil's notes. A bad do. We have to look after him, you know.'

'Hmm. Patronising clever devil,' I thought. Ingratiate himself with Freddy and undermine Phil at the same time.

'Don't worry about me,' said Freddy in cheerful martyrdom. 'Dying is what us poor bloody infantry do well.'

Phil said nothing. Tight-faced, he increased his pace. We came to an old bridge, part of the old railway. It had side walls, ideal for sheltering from the wind. 'Coffee break,' declared Phil, in a louder and firmer voice than usual.

After sitting down with his back to the wall, Freddy took a small book from his rucksack, opened it and began to read. Phil glanced at it. 'Bird book?'

'No, poetry.'

'Wordsworth?'

'No. Stuff I learnt at school. See if I can remember it.' Freddy put back his head and closed his eyes in concentration: 'Oh to be in England, Now that April's there, And whoever wakes in England, Sees, some morning unaware, That the lowest boughs and the brushwood sheaf, Round the elm-tree bole are in tiny leaf, While the chaffinch sings on the orchard bough...'

'Freddy,' said George, causing Freddy to stop in mid-flow. 'Awfully sorry, but if there's one thing I can't stand it's having sentimental poetry read to me. I don't know why, but it makes my flesh creep. Probably something to do with my school days. Can't remember what it was, though.' He gave one of his machine-gun like chuckles.

Freddy stared ahead, while Phil kept his eyes lowered.

On the way home Freddy insisted that we stop at the Bentley Brook Inn, situated just outside Ashbourne. He said he had just enrolled as a member of 'The Friends of the Peak District' association and had read, in one of its leaflets, about a brewery based at the inn. Its award-winning beer was called 'Leatherbritches Ale'. Beer connoisseurs travelled from far and wide to sample the brew. Freddy argued that since we loved real ale, it would be a good way of 'supporting Peakland commerce'.

'Hah,' said George in a cautionary tone. 'I don't think your Gruppenführer will be enamoured.' He grinned at Phil. 'What rule is it?'

'It's allowed when the hike's finished,' Phil said tautly. 'Permission granted.'

George pursed his lips. 'I quite like real ale myself. So I'm happy. What about you, Don?'

'Fine by me,' I said.

On arrival at the inn we declared our interest. The Head Brewer was called and was only too willing to take us to the old washhouse at the back, which now serves as the brewery. Long before the days of scientific analysis, he told us, the tax man would arrive to check the strength of the brew. This was done by pouring some of the beer on to a barrel top. The tax man, who wore leather britches, sat on it for a while, then got off and felt the seat of his trousers. The duty paid depended on how sticky the beer felt. (When Freddy had first told us this story he had been met with 'Gerrout of it!' from Phil and a cynical 'Oh yes?' from me.) Now vindicated, Freddy downed his half pint with great pleasure.

That evening, Freddy and I met for a late and extended Montague walk, wandering further away from the village than usual. He said little to begin with, savouring the peace of the quiet country lanes and enjoying the lyrical music of song thrush and blackbird in the high hedgerows.

Through the leaves and branches filtered yellow beams of dying sunlight, illuminating myriads of tiny, dancing insects. Neither of us spoke until we walked into the shadow of a wood.

Here, Freddy let Montague loose. He scampered off into the trees. 'Right,' said Freddy, surprising me with his businesslike air. 'It's on.'

'The big wheeze?' I looked at him in hope.

'Operation Heydrich.'

I guffawed. 'Oh lovely! Operation Heydrich. Terrific. When does it kick off?'

'Not yet. Certain things have to happen first. I'll fill you in as soon as I know.'

I said I could hardly wait. We turned back, homeward bound.

As we walked at the side of the church we spotted Phil jogging back to his house opposite, rucksack on his back, no doubt full of bricks.

'Good grief,' I said, amid a long groan from Freddy. 'He's hiked 10 miles already and now...' I broke off, shaking my head in a mix of pity and amusement. We carried on walking.

Between the church and the pub was a group of barn conversions, large and expensive houses around what had once been a farmyard. One outbuilding bordering the road had been singled out by the local planning authority for the use of a 'local craftsman'. It was now the village forge.

We had been fortunate in having attracted a young blacksmith, who spent most of his time making ornamental gates and fences. Shoeing horses seemed to be a thing of the past. I would often stop to watch him strike a piece of iron just out of the furnace, which he would then beat and twist into a finished piece, its colour changing quickly from white-hot to red. Then came the sharp hiss of steam as it was plunged into water, coming out black. The furnace was dead or damped now, and the inside of the smithy dark.

Beyond the smithy was an entrance to a large paddock. We leant on the five-barred gate and stared across a rich swathe of meadow foxtail grass, topped by silvery, silky looking spikes. Further on a chestnut mare stood against a white blaze of hedgerow blossom, its foal beside it. In that deepening twilight, when colours are strangely more vivid than in daytime, Freddy smiled gently. 'Did you like chemistry at school?'

'Not much. Too much smell of gas and acid. Why?'

'I loved it. That led to my downfall, the glue factory. But you remember the first thing you learnt in the lab, acid neutralises alkali. Am I right?'

'Yes,' I nodded. 'But I think it's two parts of acid to one part of alkali needed.'

Freddy clicked his fingers to summon up the mare and foal. 'Well, that makes it even more interesting.'

* * * * *

The opening gambit of Freddy's 'big wheeze' had much to do with food. He is fond of culinary jokes, sometimes using them in 'Phil baiting'. His latest was: 'This Cornish pasty you bought, Phil, tastes awful. They could make a fortune selling it in health food shops.' Recently, he put the question: 'What would be our last meal on earth, forgetting healthy food as a bit irrelevant at that point in life?'

Phil and Freddy had – curiously – opted for the same thing, venison and a rich salad, with syllabub to follow. I had plumped for Greek lamb and parsnips cooked with apricots, followed by a rich custard-based pudding. We wouldn't waste time choosing the wine. It would be the house red and plenty of it.

Food returned to our agenda at the next Friday evening session in the pub, to which George had not been invited – Freddy and I would have been amazed if he had. Freddy produced a booklet that he'd picked up in the local market. All the foods within it were traditional and all from Derbyshire. 'Lumpytums' (oatballs in milk), Buxton pudding and posset were listed, along with the more famous offerings: Bakewell pudding, Ashbourne gingerbread and Hartington cheese. The booklet claimed that the success of these businesses had boosted the local economy.

'So did I,' said Freddy. 'With Leatherbritches.'

Freddy, Phil and I counted ourselves lucky in having wives who enjoy cooking, since we are pretty well useless at the art. Who did domestic science at school? We didn't. They did. It was a proper arrangement and neither our wives, nor the three of us, could fathom out why society, with its laughable 'political correctness', would want things otherwise. At the previous year's Christmas pub celebration we had a competition in which the wives had to dream up jokes about their husband's cooking. Ruth said of Phil, 'When he cooks he uses the smoke alarm as a timer.' Not to be outdone, Liz said of me, 'If he had a black belt for karate and one for cooking, he'd kill me either way.' Jean was even less kind. 'If I left Freddy for a week by the time I got back the kitchen would look like Sir Alexander Fleming's laboratory.'

She won our prize for the evening, a book on nouvelle cuisine inside which Freddy had written: 'For people who like to pay a hundred pounds for a meal and still feel hungry.'

Inspired by what he read in the booklet – I found out later – his first move of Operation Heydrich was to stage a barbecue in his garden, to which Phil and I were invited, along with our wives.

George was not invited.

* * * * *

As a starter for the barbecue it was Freddy's job to drag the gas barbecue from the back of the shed, where it had spent a moss-creating winter. He hauled it to the patio, where the paving slabs radiated warmth, calling for open-toed sandals. A huge coloured parasol shaded most of the table. Earlier, Jean had instructed Freddy on his duties. 'We don't want black pavement edges all over the steaks,' she had warned. 'Clean the grille and keep turning them over, that's the secret.' This peeved Freddy, because if there is one aspect of cooking that he excels in, it is turning over steaks. Jean made the 'rub' from one of her mother's recipe books, using a mortar and pestle, crushing peppercorns and mustard seeds with a sauce concocted from ketchup, Worcestershire sauce and red wine vinegar. She added one or two 'tasties' of her own including Dijon mustard, brown sugar, diced onion and bay leaf. There was no garlic on account of Freddy's allergy to the stuff.

When Liz and I arrived the aroma of sizzling Porterhouse steaks filled the house, and it intensified when we stepped out on to the patio. Freddy, wearing an apron, stood at the barbecue in a cloud of smoke.

Shortly after that Phil turned up with Ruth. She erupted onto the patio, letting off a high-pitched squeal at the sight of Freddy's apron, which had, in large red lettering, the printed declaration, 'No snails. Only fast food.'

While Ruth was venting her vociferous delight Phil marched up to Freddy, surreptitiously whipping from his pocket a small phial containing sunflower seeds and another containing omega-6 oil.

'What's this?' asked Freddy.

'Ssh,' warned Phil. 'Just whack 'em in the grub. We're talking immortality.' He winked and grinned, as if to prove he wasn't always mad.

Jean began talking about her trip round Blackpool Tower in a Tiger Moth. 'My father was a sergeant pilot in the Lancasters,' she said. 'He was one of the few who survived the war. My cousin flies. It's in the family. We have a distant connection with Amy Johnson on my father's side. Do you know she put on lipstick and painted her fingernails before flying thousands of miles with only an atlas for navigation?'

I gave Freddy a wry look, but he hadn't overheard. Was her devious purpose to groom Freddy for an eventual flight in Phil's aircraft? It would not be surprising. The two kindred spirits had joined forces against him on more than one occasion.

Freddy was still turning over steaks when a man in his 60s came out of the house, escorted by Jean. He was over six feet tall and heavily built. His balding head, as he walked, preceded a flowing cloud of frizzy white hair. He wore white trousers, and a short-sleeved yellow shirt. His spectacle lenses were the 'bottle glass' type. As a consequence, he peered pleasantly at the person to whom he was introduced, giving an air of bumbling geniality.

'Toby's our local historian. He used to run the reference library. He's a member of my poetry group.' Freddy handed Toby a glass of stout.

Ah yes, Freddy's poetry group. I knew the basic details; it met in an oak-panelled back room of the Red Lion once a month. Members were expected to write poetry as well as offer readings from poets they had come to like. According to Phil it was a meeting of 'weirdos', the type who wander about wearing peculiar clothing. One woman wore a sari crossed by a Scottish clan scarf and had a knitting needle through her hair.

Toby found himself cornered by Ruth, the complete extrovert when it comes to meeting someone. Her beady brown eyes fixed on him as she extracted his birthplace, school, work experience, likes and dislikes. Freddy reckons that Ruth would have been a stalwart of the Gestapo, complementing Phil's Gruppenführer role in the regular army.

During his interrogation Toby kept his head tilted backwards and his mouth open, his eyes looming large behind thick glass. Before answering a question he would drawl out a murmured 'Ye-e-es', followed by an 'er, um,' accompanied by a spreading out of his large hands, which were then clasped over his rounded stomach. He spoke slowly, stressing and elongating the sound of certain words, occasionally using archaic and superfluous expressions like 'All that transpired, I would say, of yesteryear.' I could imagine him in the old, dusty reference library, long gone with the advent of the internet, a catalogue of local history within his head, lover of ancient facts and customs, always delighted when someone wanted to know about the Bonnie Prince Charlie room in Derby or the whereabouts of the old Markeaton Brook that used to run openly through the town centre. Ruth discovered that one of his pleasures was to appear as Father Christmas at the Children's Hospital each year.

The meal began in a mild panic as people scurried around the table and to and from the kitchen, sorting out salad and baked potatoes, then distributing warm plates and deciding who should sit where, while dishing out and receiving sausages and beefburgers. On sitting down there ensued the general sort out of tomato sauce, butter, oil, vinegar and wine, after which conversation was limited to mundane exchanges of 'Pass the butter please,' and 'Extra baked potato anyone?'

Ten minutes into the meal Freddy tapped a spoon on his plate, bringing the table to alert. 'I've brought us together because Toby would like to join us on the hike. Any objections?' Freddy beamed around the table.

I had my mouth open, but Phil's was wider. There was a long pause as he struggled to regain his mental balance. 'Er… um…' he stammered. 'Of course. Welcome Toby.' He shot a quick and sharp interrogative glance at me. I looked quickly away.

Toby peered at me. 'Don?'

'Oh, no objections,' I said. 'Glad you're aboard, Toby.' I hid my amusement at the sight of Phil undergoing trauma. But what could he say? Toby had been recruited exactly as had George. Sauce for the goose? It wasn't difficult to see the point of the wheeze.

Later, I managed to buttonhole Freddy in privacy. 'Is Toby in on it, or is he just a pawn?'

Freddy tut-tutted. 'I wouldn't use Toby like that.' His smile turned into a grin. 'Don't worry. Watch this space.'

The next day I went back to give Freddy a hand in demolishing the coal bunker. Seeing my arrival, he waved his hammer forlornly at the cause of his frustration. 'I bet chain gangs don't have bigger rocks to crack. What crime have I committed that I should get this?'

The bunker had been reduced to a series of lumps of concrete, linked together by rusting iron rods. 'I mean, look at it,' he said plaintively. 'These things would have stopped a panzer tank.'

I produced a hacksaw from the boot of my car. Within the hour we had separated the pieces and secreted them under the large shed, before Jean returned from shopping. Freddy's cover story was that we'd taken the debris to the council dump.

He rewarded me with a gift of two of his 'personal chocolates', but only after making me promise not to tell Liz.

* * * * *

My high hopes for the first 'Toby' hike were dashed on its eve, when Freddy told me that Toby was indisposed.

When Phil heard the reason – 'a touch of gout' – he was incredulous. 'Gout? Whoever heard of a hiker with gout? What's going on here?' His suspicions intensified when Freddy then asked if the following day's hike could be extended.

Phil paused before speaking. 'Extended? Who's that on the phone? Who's this voice impersonator?' he demanded. 'For security purposes please give me Freddy's address including postcode.'

Freddy replied quickly. '43, Repton Road, New York.'

'And birthday?'

'Thirteenth of January, 1838.'

'Maiden name of wife?'

'Einstein.'

'Okay Freddy,' sighed Phil. 'What wheeze is this?'

'No wheeze. Scout's honour. Tomorrow is the longest day in terms of daylight, but I have the means of time-stretching – what you're always on about. If the hike could end about six we could then have some fish and chips, and then set about extending your life span. It's a treat. In fact there are two treats.'

'Freddy, you must be crazy if you think I'm falling for this.'

'For this to take place,' said Freddy, 'the hike has to be the Roaches.' Phil frowned. 'The Roaches. That's hills and climbing up rocks. You hate all that stuff. This is a wheeze! Come on, admit it.'

'You navigate, you lead the hike,' persisted Freddy. 'It can be as long as a 13-miler. You can drive us there. It's all under your control.'

'The Roaches.' Phil thought about it. The Roaches, in the south-western part of the Peak District, went up to 1,750 feet. There was a mountain rescue centre close to where we would start the hike, near Upper Hulme. Phil's taste for tough hiking set his juices flowing. Perhaps Freddy's 'time-stretcher' might only prove a minor irritation, some silliness with which he could cope. After all, it was the hiking that mattered. 'Freddy,' he said. 'I'll risk it. But I drive to make sure we get there. And I navigate the hike, ok? And I want your promise you'll complete the route.'

'Gruppenführer. I promise. To the death.'

The following morning George and Phil picked up Freddy and then me. During the journey Phil did his best to elicit more information. 'Where do we go after the hike ends? Is this wheeze anything to do with clocks? Do we have to go and see anybody?'

Freddy only answered the last question. 'No, there's nobody. It's a surprise treat. That is all I'm permitted to say.'

'Okay Freddy,' Phil said. 'But I hope we're not chasing wallabies.' He referred to animals that had escaped from a local zoo.

'No wallabies, promise.'

'Wallabies,' said George. 'That was also in the programme.' And then his face froze as he realised his mistake.

Freddy gave him a sharp, hard and lingering look. George hurriedly composed his features to look innocent, but it was too late. He looked flustered, the first time I'd seen a crack in his aloof expression.

We arrived at a lay-by on the road out of Upper Hulme, adjacent to the line of gritstone edges, lying north to south. The second most northern ridge of the Roaches has a spine of protruding sculpted rock fins, giving it the look of a gigantic dinosaur lying dormant under the clear blue sky.

After the ritualistic putting on of hiking gear Phil pulled back his sleeve. 'Right gentlemen, synchronise watches. It will be 10.20 on my count, five, four, three, two, one…10.20. We're off.'

Phil led the climb through the heather towards the two edges, the Lower and Upper tiers, with a set of rock steps connecting them. Built into the rocks of the Lower Tier was a stone-built house, known as Rockhall Cottage, a tiny, primitive building reminding me of the troglodyte hillside dwellings in the Dordogne valley in France.

A few yards from the front door the footpath turned left. At this point the door opened to reveal a middle-aged man with a beard and a black patch over his right eye.

'There's no climbing,' he shouted fiercely. 'Haven't you read my notice? At all times respect privacy of Rockhall Cottage and comply with the by-laws?'

Phil confessed we hadn't read his notice and reassured him that we would not climb his rocks, at which he softened.

'I'm the king of Rockhall,' the man announced proudly. 'There's no climbing within 110 feet of the back of the house. You're welcome to pass by. I make no charge.' And with that he bowed in a dignified manner and retreated inside his lair. Later, I did some research and discovered that the self-styled 'king' was Doug Moller, who had written a book called *The Wars of the Roaches* chronicling his battles with 'yobbos', the Peak Planning Authority and the police. Amid the text were extracts of letters from Moller to Margaret Thatcher and the Queen, each with the heading 'War Correspondence'. One of his chief complaints was that yobbish hikers would climb above the palace to pee down his chimney. Freddy would have liked to have stayed and chatted with the intriguing 'king'.

'No, Freddy, no.' Phil sharply reminded him of his promise to allow the hike to continue unhindered by wheezes. Freddy, in fairness, made no protest, but having run slap bang into a member of the eccentrics 'A' list – far above Graham – he made a mental note to return for a solo audience with King Doug. Here was a man whose non-brainwashed mind might help create the social vibrations that could lead to discovery of the meaning of life.

We walked a fair distance from Rockhall Cottage to ensure that no further royal displeasure was incurred. As soon as it was judged permissible, George climbed towards the ridge quickly and easily, Phil just behind. Freddy, far below, groaned as he laboured upwards.

Phil looked down at him. 'You chose it! I'm not to blame this time.'

For once, Freddy had no ready answer.

To the west of the main edge of the Roaches is a line of small subsidiary edges known as the Five Clouds. On one of these faces a rock climber leant out into space as he prepared his next move. It caused Freddy to catch his breath. 'Hell's teeth,' he grimaced, looking away. 'Why do they *do* that? It makes my legs go watery.'

We waited on the edge for Freddy to arrive, George peering down at him. 'You'd never make a marine Freddy!' he shouted. 'Take that man's name, sergeant!'

Freddy shouted back. 'If God had intended me to be a marine he'd have given me flippers.'

George gave one of his rat-a-tat chuckles and brandished his stick around with a proprietary air. 'This is some of the best gritstone climbing in the country,' he announced. 'They've got some classic climbs. Great names as well, the Sloth, the Swan, the Valkyrie and the Wombat.' It came out like information from Google. Throughout the rest of the hike he made references to rock climbing in so much detail that I was certain he had swotted it all up, seeking to impress us with his skill and knowledge.

At the conclusion of the hike, we exchanged boots for shoes and drove into Leek, Phil still highly sceptical about the evening programme. We sat, eating chips, on a wall near to the working corn mill named after James Brindley, the engineer who had built the Bridgewater Canal.

'When I was a kid,' I said, 'I bought my chips in the *Daily Sketch*. We took our own paper along to the chip shop.'

Phil said his was probably served up in the *Daily Mail*. Freddy couldn't remember his newspaper, but said that chips in those days were more delicious than the healthier, less fatty, ones of today. 'Sod's Law again,' he said mournfully. 'What we like best usually kills us.'

George waited a moment, for effect. 'I took along *The Times*,' he said. 'My old man was the town mayor.'

We could find no comment to follow. Nor did we wish to.

Phil became impatient, looking at his watch. 'Hell's teeth, Freddy. It's now half past six! When do we get these treats!'

Freddy indicated the mill. 'This is the first.' He screwed up his empty chip bag, dropping it in a convenient litter bin.

'How much?' Phil was not impressed.

'Oh no! It's buckshee. I'm paying. My treat, remember?'

'Oh. Oh, right then.' Phil gave Freddy a grudging apology.

'Most kind, Freddy,' said George. 'Fascinating things, mills. My grandfather owned one in East Anglia. I spent ages in it. I can tell you a thing or two about corn mills.'

We stepped inside the mill. The noise of the working parts was so great that it stifled conversation. I could feel the mass energy flowing from the outside water wheel, powered by falling water from the adjacent River Churnet.

'This is natural power,' Freddy shouted. 'None of your carbon emissions here!' Which of us would deny him? Even Phil had forgotten his peevishness, lost in the belly of the rumbling monster. We moved slowly through the three levels of the mill, the meal, stone and garner floors, hypnotised by the slow, rhythmic creak, rumble and grind of the cumbrous gears and beams.

All four of us had lived in the age of great engineering. It was regrettable that younger generations would never experience the power of water as we had experienced it, nor the massive energy of steam. How could I ever forget the thrill of the 'namers', steam locomotives roaring under the bridge at Tamworth, or grunting on to the platform at Derby? At these shrines we worshipped, armed with notebooks, writing down *The Royal Enniskillen Fusiliers*, *The Duchess of Sutherland*, *The Master Cutler*, all shrieking their whistles, thundering into history.

'How was that then?' Freddy asked as we left the mill.

We thanked him for an exciting experience. But tiredness had set in and there was a feeling that the next treat would have to be pretty special to keep up our flagging spirits.

'So what do we do now?' asked Phil.

'We wait.' Freddy sat on the stone wall.

'Wait? What for?'

'Well you can't rush time if you want to make time.'

Phil threw up his hands. 'This is a wheeze. I knew it!'

'No it isn't. Something happens at a certain time and I can't rush it. Just believe me, you'll be gobsmacked. I promise.'

George regarded Freddy as a myopic judge might, eyes narrowed at the accused standing in the dock. 'Young man,' he said. 'This has got to be good.'

Freddy ignored him. 'Now all we have to do is wait.'

'For how long?' demanded Phil.

'An hour and a half.'

'An hour and a half!' the three of us cried in unison.

'Well you wouldn't have come if I'd told you about it.' Freddy was all innocence, appealing to me for support.

'Wheeze! I can smell it,' declared Phil, abruptly. 'Why do I always fall for it! I must be insane. I'm going home.'

'No.' Freddy was insistent. 'I love to go home after the hike. Would I risk keeping you out all this time if it wasn't worth it at the end?'

'Freddy,' said Phil, sitting down on a low wall. 'Have you considered the possibility that we might not like it? We're tired and want to go home. You might like it because you're strange. But what's interesting for you may not be interesting for us. Have you thought of that?'

George surveyed Freddy, chuckling lightly, repeating himself. 'Laddy. This has got to be good you know. Or else.'

Freddy spoke with sincerity. 'Gruppenführer, I am going to add time to your existence on earth. That is what you seek and I am giving it to you. Can you turn that down?'

'Yes. Because it's baloney.'

George was still chuckling, still surveying Freddy, the miscreant. 'You'll be on a fizzer my lad, if this goes pear-shaped. You'll be outside company office at 0815 hours, best boots, belt and gaiters. The charge will be wasting officers' time.'

'No.' Freddy stood firm. 'You won't waste time. You'll be making it.'

Clearly, Freddy had something in store for us that could not be a mere wheeze. He was risking far too much for that kind of thing. And I, as his friend, had to support him. 'I'm okay, Freddy. Hope it'll be good.' I gave him an encouraging smile.

Another pause. 'Freddy.' Phil stood up sharply, demonstrating his leadership qualities of decision and resolve. 'This is what we do. We're going to hike for 45 minutes and then back for the same time.'

Freddy was aghast. 'We've hiked 13 miles already!'

'You should have thought of that. This is to pass the time and it can also be regarded as a punishment if it does turn out to be a wheeze. It'll also build stamina and use up those fish and chips, stop you from getting fat. Come on.'

* * * * *

It was 9.15pm. We arrived, wearily, back in Leek after the extended hike, having walked a total of 17 miles that day. Even I was getting fractious, in no mood for a second 'treat'.

Freddy led us to the parish church of St Edward the Confessor. We trudged behind him to end up in the old churchyard, facing west.

'Oh, my God. It's a Dracula job.' Phil looked at the headstones around him. 'Some idiot dressed up is going to leap out at us. No, I know what it is. It's a ghost walk! Freddy?' he said threateningly. 'We've been out all day and now half the night. I'm in no mood for it.' He hesitated. 'It isn't anything to do with dates on these headstones is it? If it is, you're in trouble.'

'Grave trouble,' said George and laughed at his own humour.

The sun was setting in a sky lit by brilliant red, crimson and yellow streaks. 'You see that hill over there,' Freddy said, pointing. 'Now watch the sun, everybody. It's going down behind it.'

Grudgingly, donning sunglasses, Phil obeyed the instruction. The red orb settled behind the hillside and, soon after, dropped out of sight.

We waited. 'Well?' said Phil, interrupting the silence. 'Now what?'

'Just wait and see,' said Freddy.

I suddenly realised. 'Hey, it's the longest day!'

'Oh no!' roared Phil. 'Freddy! The summer solstice doesn't stretch time!'

'I know,' said Freddy. 'But this does. Just keep watching. Any time now...are you ready?'

We stared into the darkening sky. And then, mysteriously, the edge of a red, thin hoop emerged to sit for a time on the ridge of the hilltop. Then more was revealed. It was the sun, back from the dead, rising in the evening sky. A few whispers of amazement were all that we uttered. It was George who finally spoke – and then only to himself. 'It must be an illusion.'

Freddy enjoyed our confusion. 'Keep watching.'

Over the next quarter of an hour the sun, unbelievably, moved towards the far horizon. 'You see, Gruppenführer,' said Freddy. 'The time between the first sunset and the next is buckshee. All this is extra time.'

'That is stupid. That is not happening,' said Phil.

'Freddy, how did you wangle that?' exclaimed George.

Freddy looked delighted.

'I don't believe that, either,' I said. 'Is there some back projector out there?'

We forgot our tiredness as we walked out of the churchyard back to the car, bombarding Freddy with questions, while he made hand signals for us all to calm down and listen to his explanation.

We quietened sufficiently for Freddy to tell the story. In 1686 an astronomer, Robert Plot, saw the phenomenon and thought he could use it to measure the Earth's angle of tilt. Currently it tilts at an angle from the vertical. But, because the Earth has a slight wobble, the angle varied over thousands of years. He worked out that the shifting axis on the longest day of the year resulted in the exact position of the sun slipping slowly towards the distant horizon. Plot suggested that he measured this slippage at Leek over a number of years. This would measure the change in the Earth's tilt.

'Did he do it?' I asked.

'No. He forgot one important detail, the English weather,' said Freddy. 'He needed regular annual sunsets. Chances nil. He'd be lucky to find two in successive years. I checked last night's weather forecast to make sure we'd see the sun go down.'

'What causes the phenomenon?' asked George. 'What actually happens?'

'Don't ask me,' said Freddy. 'I don't think anybody knows.'

Phil was magnanimous in his praise. 'Well, for once Freddy, that was pretty impressive. It would have done for the Christmas treat.'

Freddy positively preened himself, thrilled by his demonstration of an occult sunset. He had run a risk of it all failing. What if cloud had suddenly obscured the setting sun?

As soon as I had made sure that Phil and George were out of earshot, I asked Freddy if today's treats had anything to do with his wheeze. He looked at me in his usual po-faced innocence.

'So what is it? Come on, tell me.'

Freddy enjoyed teasing me. 'Well, Phil's life was stretched a bit. And he liked it. And I paid for him going into the mill. And I bought his fish and chips.' He raised his eyebrows at me. 'So?'

'That was to make him owe you one, wasn't it? Put him in your debt?'

'Well,' Freddy grinned. 'He's got to put up with a lot next week.'

'Next week? What happens next week? You mean on the hike?'

'Toby. He'll be on the hike, won't he?'

It gradually dawned on me. 'Hold on. You deliberately kept Toby out today. He didn't have gout, did he?'

Freddy started to chuckle.

'So you could get round Phil. Today's the start of Operation Heydrich?'

Freddy broke into a big grin. His spaniel eyes had a merry look.

'God, Freddy. Unbelievable. That is a wheeze and a half!' I shook my head and then, infected by Freddy's laughter, joined him. We were laughing so much that Phil and George, arriving at the car, turned round to look at us.

JULY

Warm, dry winds from North Africa followed weeks without rain, bringing dire threats from the water companies. Fortunately the Peak population was spared as the great dams to the west of Sheffield were above the minimum for the time of year – but only just.

The only unwelcome intrusion was the overnight sprinkling of sand dragged down from the upper air by a local thunderstorm, causing Freddy's neighbour, the dentist, to whip his cherished BMW into Derby for a car wash.

On the hiking front the two adversaries, Freddy and Phil, reviewed their individual situations. Phil was fully aware that the 'treats' of June were designed to soften him up for the advent of Toby. But he remained uncertain, and therefore suspicious, of Freddy's motive. Freddy, in contrast, was happily expectant that the hike would soon be free of George's unsettling attitude and behaviour.

As we set off on a Montague walk Freddy opened up on Operation Heydrich. Having kept it under wraps for a fortnight he asked me to guess its aim and outcome.

'Toby on the hike?' I said. 'Chaos. Phil insists we drop him?'

'And in return?'

'You insist he drops George.'

Freddy grinned. 'Do you think it will work?'

'More likely than not,' I said. 'Presuming Toby is in on it.' I gave Freddy a searching smile.

'Watch this space.' Freddy's lugubrious eyes twinkled a little. As we reached the footpath by the cricket pavilion he slipped Montague off the lead to watch him dash to and fro along the hedgerow, yapping at birds.

'There's a problem, isn't there?' I grimaced. 'Even if Phil wants to get shot of George he won't agree if it looks like he's been manipulated.'

'I've thought of that,' said Freddy. 'I reckon he'll want Toby hiking to show how useless he is. We'd have to agree then, no argument.'

'And you say fine. We'll drop Toby if you drop George.'

'He should jump at it.'

I nodded. 'Phil gets rid of George without losing face. We're all happy.'

'Hope so,' said Freddy. 'All it needs now is Toby on form and it should be an interesting hike.'

'Aargh!' I reacted to Montague, who stood wagging his tail, offering up a long-dead pigeon in his mouth.

* * * * *

Pre-hike day arrived. Freddy stared at the jobs list pinned to the kitchen notice board. Jean had left instructions to cut the lawn, get a haircut and prevent the Victorian bell-pull, when pulled, from dragging out a connecting rod as long as his arm.

By mid-afternoon, however, Phil had not made contact.

'Looks like "Plan A" is on,' Freddy said in a phone call.

Freddy waited a couple of hours on the slight off-chance that Phil might ring. As anticipated, he didn't.

At 7pm, with still no contact from Phil, Freddy rang Toby. 'It's on. Der Tag.'

A warm breeze sprang up, rustling the leaves in the beech trees by the church. Freddy, Toby and I waited opposite, outside the half-timbered house. The front door opened and out stepped George, followed by Phil.

'Good grief,' muttered Phil. 'Look at that. Hell's teeth.'

George grimaced and regarded Toby, open-mouthed. 'That scarecrow there?' he murmured incredulously. 'I don't believe it.'

Phil and George kept their eyes fixed on Toby as they approached, taking in the stained grey trousers halfway up the chest, the striped blue and white oil-stained shirt, a pair of ex-army boots already on and tied with clumps of thick white tape. Toby looked like a bloke less ready for hiking than mucking out a cowshed. Striking a bizarre note was the white cloud of hair struck by the sun, giving him the shining halo of a saint.

In contrast George – in pale blue shorts, short-sleeved shirt, fastidiously attired with hiking accoutrements – and Phil, in his militaristic 'Rommel' gear, looked the part.

I had a sinking feeling. Not only did they look the part, they also looked an item. What if George dropped his takeover bid for the hike? What if Phil began to like him? In that case Operation Heydrich would fail.

I didn't tell Freddy that I feared for the hike, that today would provide the crucible in which it was to survive or be doomed.

Phil frowned and looked down at the pavement as he made the introduction. 'George, this is Toby.'

'Hallo.' George gripped Toby's hand and looked into a pair of moon eyes behind thick glass, blank and unseeing.

'Ow, my hand!' Toby winced with pain.

'Oh, terribly sorry. Don't know my own strength!' George chuckled sympathetically, patted Toby on the arm, then quickly detached himself.

He joined Phil, loading gear at the back of the car. 'Toby!' he hurriedly whispered. 'Can he see?'

Phil grinned and said through gritted teeth that Toby was 'only one of Freddy's weirdos' and wouldn't turn up again.

Forty minutes later we parked opposite the Swiss-style houses in Ilam village. Toby sat on the metal bench at the road side, making a myopic attempt to connect hiking sock with bare foot. Phil, tying his own bootlaces, watched Freddy put on Toby's socks to a chorus of his cheerful burbles and murmurings. Freddy then stood Toby upright, plonked on his sun hat, tucked a loose part of his shirt back inside his trousers and knelt down to shorten his bootlaces.

Phil sighed and pulled back his sleeve. 'Right. Synchronise watches. On my count it will be 10.20. Five, four, three, two, one...10.20.'

'Oh dear.' Toby peered at his wristwatch. 'I missed that. Could you give that again, please?'

'Don't worry, Toby,' said Phil wearily. 'Just stick with Freddy. And Freddy? Don't let Toby, you know. Keep him with you. Ready now Toby?'

'Indubitably,' said Toby. 'Ready for whatever peril we face. Onwards.' He took a step in the wrong direction.

Freddy pulled him back. 'This way.'

Toby pointed a finger, chuckling at Phil's expression. 'Just testing the navigator,' he said.

Phil and George glanced at each other. They reminded me of a couple of drill sergeants, bewildered at being tasked with squaddies who appeared incapable of walking, never mind marching.

'Right,' said Phil dryly. 'Let's go.'

As Toby set off, waddling like a ponderous penguin, I was struck by the realisation that what I had witnessed had been pure onedownmanship. Phil and George's reactions on encountering Toby were proof of its success. Already Freddy had a smile on his face as he steered Toby past the village churchyard. As they did so Toby raised a hand in gesture towards the graves, intoning sonorously, 'Though they go mad they shall be sane, though they sink through the sea they shall rise again, though loves be lost, love shall not, and death shall have no dominion.'

Freddy smiled. 'Easy. Dylan the master,' he said.

'First-class, Freddy. One nil, to you. Now, your turn.'

George stared at Toby as he walked and, for his pains, tripped over a kerb.

Freddy raised an arm, having found inspiration. 'Ah yes. Death.' He spoke slowly, rounding each vowel. 'Thou wast not born for death, immortal bird, no hungry generations tread thee down.'

'Shelley?' Toby asked.

'No, Keats,' said Freddy. 'Two nil.'

'Calamity!' exclaimed Toby. 'I should have got that. My turn, hmm, ha...'

Phil shut his eyes and made a gurgling noise from the back of his throat, blew out his cheeks and marched on. George gave Freddy a disparaging frown, then broke away to quickly join up with our beleaguered navigator. The two stalwarts reached the weir below Ilam Hall to lean over an iron railing. George began talking about the lack of world-class British footballers in the Premiership. Phil, hardly listening, replied in monosyllabic 'Yehs' and ''s rights', while making backward glances at Toby and Freddy labouring towards them.

I joined Phil and George.

Phil gave me an anguished smile. 'Don? Toby. I mean is he... I mean... well... is he... capable of getting round? I mean if he can't...'

George intervened. 'Toby shouldn't go hiking for exercise. What he needs is a damned good brisk sit down.' Again, the staccato chuckle.

'Hiking? Is this what you call it?' scoffed Phil with a grin. 'With these saboteurs?' Phil gave a carefree laugh to impress George.

'Indeed,' smiled George in a grave tone. 'A new breed of terrorist. A Mr Magoo.' He patted Phil patronisingly on the shoulder and wandered along the Manifold river bank, serenely admiring the towering woodland opposite.

Phil grasped his opportunity and turned on me, whispering fiercely. 'It *is* sabotage isn't it! I know what Freddy's up to! He's trying to...' He broke off as the ungainly couple of Freddy and Toby hove into view.

'Now then,' said Freddy to his corpulent charge. 'Look at this.' He ushered Toby to gaze down at turbulent water, close to the river bank. 'It's a boiling hole. It's not a whirlpool. It's water that's run underground from upriver and comes up here. Any good?'

'Er, um…water…let me see…' Toby looked down at the swirling water. 'Ah yes, I have it. One moment.'

He put a hand to his forehead in concentration. 'Light breaks.' His voice resonated with a heavy tremor. 'Where no sun shines, where no sea runs, the waters of the heart push in their tides.'

'Dylan Thomas again,' said Freddy.

'Oh my God,' muttered Phil and strode off along the footpath, leaving behind a quietly gleeful Freddy and a burbling Toby, his mane of white hair floating and sparkling in the sunshine.

Half a mile upriver we stopped to wait by the stile entrance to the short, garden footpath leading to the road. Phil sat on the stile step, sighed, slowly shook his head and looked at his watch. George gave him a seriously sympathetic look. 'I hope this doesn't happen every week.'

'Good God no!' Phil laughed to show he was up with the best of leaders, firm, but good hearted. 'I told you, he won't be here next week.'

Freddy and Toby finally arrived, 15 minutes late. 'I wouldn't send you two blokes out for a takeaway! I'd starve!' said Phil with a ghastly chuckle.

Toby went up to stare into George's face. 'Awfully sorry, Phil, to have kept you waiting.'

'I'm George, Toby, not Phil.'

'Are you?' Toby peered closer. 'Oh yes. My dear fellow. Profuse apologies. Have I caused you a problem?'

'There's no problem, Toby,' beamed George. 'The lesson's simple.'

'What's that?'

'If you keep going to work late you'll end up with a cheap watch. Ha…ha…'

Toby chortled, pointing a finger. 'Oh good one George! Splendid!'

'Freddy?' huffed Phil. 'We really do have to press on, you know.'

'Toby's running in his legs,' said Freddy. 'He'll be faster next week.'

'Unless he's caught your creeping leg disease,' said Phil, heavily ironic.

'No. You only catch it in Greek temples.' Freddy went to crouch down beside a hedge flower. 'Ah, wood aven, also called the blessed herb.'

'I'd be blessed if we could hike,' announced Phil.

'Blessed be the peacemakers,' pronounced Toby.

'I'd say blessed are the pacemakers,' said George.

'Now come on,' Phil said. 'We've a schedule to keep.'

An explosion came from the hedgerow, followed by a flurry of wings. A pheasant flew out across our bows, causing us to step backwards.

Phil made 'sweeping up' motions with his two hands, urging Toby over the stile. 'There's a good Toby. Over you go.'

'Now then,' Toby said, standing on the step. 'Garden, garden. Hah, yes. "I have a garden of my own. Dah de da... and lilies that you would guess, to be a little wilderness."'

Freddy frowned and raised his head in thought. 'Um...er... W.H. Davies? No, don't think so. How about Robert Bridges?'

'Marvell,' said Toby.

'It'll be a marvel if you two could get over the stile!' Phil shuddered at the awfulness of it all, his voice croaking. 'Toby, there's a good chap. Over you go. Freddy? A hand with Toby?' Freddy helped lower Toby on to the garden footpath.

A minute later we assembled at the roadside beyond. 'Right,' said Phil, now back in dignified and commanding mode. 'Listen in. No stops now till coffee break. Don? Stay with Freddy and Toby. We'll be at our usual spot.' He rammed the rim of his red beret firmly down over his forehead. 'And please?' He affected a silly smile. 'Everybody? A bit quicker?' He marched off, followed by George.

En route to our coffee stop Freddy managed to get me in an aside without Toby overhearing. 'I don't like Phil keeping on pandering to George. It doesn't look good.'

'Well,' I said. 'We'll just have to hope and play it by ear.'

Freddy glanced at his watch. 'The longest hike, eh?' He shot me a wry grin.

An hour later we arrived on the ridge above the river to find Phil and George stretched out in the grass.

Phil sat up and saw that George was fast asleep. 'This is crazy,' he rapped out, scrambling to his feet. 'It won't be midnight when we get back. We'll arrive with the milk! George? Wake up.' George came awake and stared upwards, without expression, at the sky above.

Freddy showed Toby the steep drop to the river below. 'The Manifold River. Down there.' He pointed downwards. Toby took a tentative step and peered down. 'River... hah, yes.' Raising both hands to the sky he proclaimed: 'On either side the river lie, Long fields of barley and of rye, that clothe the wold and meet the sky, And through the field the road runs by, to many towered Camelot.'

'Lord,' muttered Phil.

'Correct! Lord Tennyson,' said Freddy. 'Well done Gruppenführer!'

'What?' Phil stared nonplussed at Freddy. 'Coffee break,' he announced. 'Though it's lunchtime,' he added, tetchily. And was George's enigmatic smile that of a king in waiting?

I felt suddenly annoyed. Surely Phil must know his beloved hike was imperilled? Or was he playing a devious game, knowing precisely the score and turning it to his advantage?

Back on the hike we took the road leading to Hope hamlet, Freddy forging ahead to have a few words with Cliff Beloe, an old friend who lived there, a retired drama adviser to the county.

Toby, left alone, trailed further and further behind. The next time we turned to look, we'd reached the bottom of the hill in Hope and Toby had vanished.

'Oh no,' Phil groaned.

Freddy said his goodbye to Cliff Beloe and rejoined the group. 'Where's Toby?' he said.

'It's a valid question,' growled Phil. 'There's the distinct possibility he vanished down a rabbit hole, spouting poetry.'

'Or a boiling hole,' said George and gave a short, dry chuckle.

'Toby in Wonderland,' I said.

'You can say that again,' said Phil. 'I bet he took that turning up the road there. I'll go find him.' Phil ditched his rucksack and set off jogging up the hillside, reminding me of the occasion on Taddington Moor when help was urgently sought for a hypothermic Freddy.

'Madness!' Phil called out to a sheep staring at him from the adjoining field. 'It's all madness. The whole job.' Taking the left turn, he disappeared from view.

We sat on a low stone wall, to await the returnees, Freddy entertaining us with anecdotes from Toby's past. In his youth, conscious of the need to fill his car with fuel, he'd called at the filling station opposite the reference library where he worked, and asked the attendant to 'Fill her up.' 'Fill what up?' had come the reply. Toby had forgotten to bring along his car. On another occasion, said Freddy, Toby had taken his wife into town for her to go shopping, while he went to work in the library. After an hour he had glanced through the window into the deserted staff car park and spotted her inside the locked up car, dementedly banging at its windows.

As Freddy told these tales George tilted back his head, eyes narrowing. 'Hmm,' he said, when Freddy had finished. 'Of all the things he's ever lost, he'll miss his mind the most.' He gave himself a little chuckle.

At last, Phil hove into view, Toby ambling beside him and nursing a bruised arm. 'Collided with a tree,' he jovially explained. 'Got sort of mentally semi-detached. Sort of drifted away, you would have me suppose.' He gave a gentle laugh.

'Toby,' said George, with a pompous grin. 'You are charged with conduct contrary to military discipline and subject to rule 22b of the hike.'

Freddy frowned. 'There's no rule 22b.'

'I've made it up, like you do. Rule 22b: no hiker shall get himself lost. Punishment, loss of drink privileges.'

I noted a very quick and brief exchange between Phil and Freddy. Their various conflicts always lacked malice because, under all the bickering and the chiding, deep down they had respect for each other. What George had said might have been funny, but it came from an unfunny man and was the more unsettling for it.

The hike reached our favourite watering hole, the George at Alstonefield – except it was mid-afternoon. Phil forestalled Freddy's eager interjection.

'Freddy. Let me speak.' Having got our attention Phil, stoic to the end and showing a benevolence rarely seen on the hike, announced his decision. 'Because of unforeseen circumstances we have no chance of keeping to time. So – and Freddy, please take note – I am allowing 20 minutes for a drink.' This met with gentle, happy murmurings from Toby and a 'Bravo Gruppenführer' from Freddy.

George pursed his lips. 'And perhaps those who have detained our leader might be prevailed upon for a tipple to soothe his fevered brow?'

'Certainly,' said Toby. He fumbled in his pocket and brought out a few notes, holding them close to his face for scrutiny.

'I'll pay,' said Freddy and went inside the pub.

We sat down at a trestle table. George looked around him. 'Poetry,' he said. 'I used to write a bit. Let me try and think of something.'

Toby gave him a few seconds. 'Allow me.' He began: 'When the voices of children are heard on the green, And laughing is heard on the hill, My heart is at rest within my breast, And everything else is still.'

George frowned and looked severely at the table top. 'Hmm. Dunno.'

'Blake,' said Toby.

'Hah yes. Know this?' George tilted his chin: 'For they're done with Danny Deever, you can hear the quickstep play, The regiment's in column, an' they're marchin' us away, Ho! the young recruits are shakin', an' they'll want their beer to-day, After hangin' Danny Deever in the morning.'

'Kipling,' said Toby.

'Correct.' George gave Toby a quick, searching look.

*****

Later that evening Freddy rang Phil, inviting him for a drink in the pub. Phil accepted, agreeing that 'certain things needed discussing.' Freddy hung up with a smile.

It was an unseasonable wet and cold night. We sat before the fire in the Red Lion, Phil in his personal winged chair and Freddy on the polished bench at right angles to the inglenook. He looked innocently across the fireside at Phil. 'What would you like to see happen on the hike, then? In the matter of you-know-who.'

'You mean Toby?'

'No, George.' Freddy was biding his time.

'Hah, yes.' Phil seized on this. 'Why George? Why not Toby?' Phil slumped in the Windsor chair, stretched out his legs, held his glass of beer close to his chest and surveyed Freddy with a sardonic smile. 'It was all a wheeze, wasn't it? It was so obvious! That Toby! Hell's teeth, nobody can be that stupid.' He gave a chuckle. 'What do you think, Don?'

Anxious to keep the peace I shrugged as I often do. 'He was...er...'

'A poet?' Phil beamed at Freddy. 'You rehearsed all that, didn't you? All those poetry bits.'

'Oh no! Good Lord no. We play the poetry game all the time.'

Phil chuckled in continuing disbelief, believing he was on top of *this* game. Normally, he was never sure how to deal with Freddy's 'goings on,' as he called them, but this time he had him one hundred per cent, stone cold, banged to rights. As his confidence grew, his chuckle became louder at Freddy's apparent discomfiture.

The irony was that Phil would never know how cleverly Freddy had plotted the wheeze. Even the spectacles that Toby had worn had been borrowed and had such strong lenses that, despite his good eyesight, he'd been made – for the hike at least – genuinely half blind.

And his character and personality had undergone a complete change. He was never the bumbling, genial character who had made his first appearance at the barbecue. Toby's mind was as sharp as a pin. He was never a dreamer, more of a doer. He was an expert bridge player and his walking gait was normal. His stomach was rounded, but not by much. The pillow, tucked under his shirt and strapped in place, had worked a treat. Toby played squash once a week and often went hiking with relatives. The poetry he produced at the poetry group meeting was always humorous, often satirical. Above all, in his youth, he had been a sought-after local thespian, a member of the local Shakespeare society. His acting had been convincing.

The amusing tales of his absent-mindedness had been fictional, but had demonstrated the attention to detail that Freddy put into his wheezes.

'Phil. I've got a proposal to make.' Freddy looked into the fire and paused to give weight to his words.

I picked up a log from the stack in the inglenook and looked at it for a moment before tossing it on the fire, sending up a shower of sparks. This was it. In a moment Freddy would have saved Phil's pride. And Freddy would have won.

Or so I expected.

'Gruppenführer. I'll do a deal with you. How about if I manage to drop Toby – and it's going to be difficult telling him because he's such a nice fellow – I drop Toby and you...'

'And I drop George?' cut in Phil. 'That's the deal?'

'Correct.'

'No deal.' Phil enjoyed Freddy's expression. 'None whatsoever.'

'What!' Freddy stared at Phil.

'Why should I drop George?'

Freddy pulled his eyebrows together in a tight frown.

'Freddy, we know Toby won't go through all that palaver again. It was your wheeze and fair do's. But he's out and George stays. In fact I talked to him about it.'

Freddy glanced at me, then back at Phil. 'You cannot be serious about keeping George.'

'He keeps me away from your peculiarities, Freddy. We talk about proper things, not unanswerable things like the meaning of life.' Phil teased Freddy with a grin and a raise of the eyebrows. Sweet victory.

* * * * *

Freddy returned to the puzzle of why Phil wanted to keep George on the hike. Phil wasn't cutting off his nose to spite his face, was he? That wouldn't be in character, at all. Freddy talked to me about it for hours. Nothing was solved. He mooched about, fixed the iron bell-pull, sat in his shed, went birdwatching, helped Jean with the shopping and thought and thought. Nothing came.

The next hike day loomed.

Freddy called Phil and – yes – George was going on the hike. Freddy would have none of it. 'I'm not going with that man. Anyway, my legorophilia's getting worse. I can't hike without a crutch.'

Jean shoved Freddy out of the house with the promise of his favourite meal when he returned home – royal venison with a rich salad and syllabub to follow. It lightened Freddy's depression not one jot. Freddy was so depressed that he got into the rear seat of the car without noticing anything amiss. Then he saw Phil grinning at him. He turned to me, looked back at Phil and suddenly realised. 'Where's George?'

'No idea,' said Phil innocently.

Freddy paused. 'Has George gone? Left the hike?'

'Yes, Freddy,' said Phil genially.

'What...'

'After the hike last week. He rang me, said his ankle was giving him a problem. It was an old injury, bad enough to stop him hiking.'

Freddy paused, realisation deepening. 'Hang on,' he said accusingly. 'You knew this when we met in the pub! You conniving...scheming...'

'Freddy?' Phil cut in. 'Just a little single wheeze. How many have you perpetrated against me? You pull stunts like nobody's business! Don't talk to me about conniving! Why did you think I brought in George? To escape all that! And I'm bringing in somebody else if you carry on like it.'

I stifled a chuckle.

Freddy looked morosely out of the window. 'I was going to ask for three hikes of my own, all flat, as part of the deal.'

'Okay,' said Phil. 'You can have them.'

Freddy was unimpressed. 'For what kind of pain?'

'No pain! Just for the promise that I'm not going to be subject to any more of your mad wheezes.' Phil produced a smug smile. 'And navigators are allowed to be generous, you know.'

'I'd never noticed,' said Freddy gloomily.

'Well, I am.' Phil paused. 'Look. Do you want those three hikes? Yes or no.'

'The three hikes starting today?'

'Yes. Now let's hear it. Say "I promise no more wheezes on the hike."'

'I promise no more wheezes on the hike. We'll go up the Tissington trail, then off to Parwich.'

'Okay. But I warn you I'm having no more backsliding, wheeze-making or dictators on my hike. So be warned.'

It was a sunny day, but with a wind that had shifted to a cool north-westerly, perfect conditions for hiking. As we set off from the Tissington car park Freddy insisted we celebrate the absence of George with a pint in the pub at Parwich. It was instantly condemned by Phil.

'Hold on!' cried Freddy. 'It's my hike. We do what I want!'

'No, Freddy. Rule 22b states quite specifically that hikers may choose hikes at the discretion of the navigator, but they may not order lunch breaks at public houses without permission. Especially when they got lost.'

'That's scandalous,' said Freddy. 'If we can't celebrate ditching megalomaniacs like George, what's the hike coming to!'

'Freddy. We've been through all this! We have an agreement! Remember?'

'Lors,' muttered Freddy. 'You're worse than George. You're the real megalomaniac.'

Then I remembered something. 'Rule 22b,' I said. 'That was George's. He made it up.'

'It's mine now. Do you think I'd let him take a piece of my hike away with him?' Phil gave an ironic chuckle.

* * * * *

We took Montague for his evening walk, Freddy having come to terms with Phil's counter-wheeze and not begrudging him his moment. 'But we'd still have George if I hadn't done something,' he pointed out.

I agreed. 'By the way, was that poetry rehearsed?'

'Course! We walked the hike two days before. We picked the places, then came back and found the quotations for them.' Freddy snatched a stem of long grass from the hedgerow. 'By the way, I looked up the Royal Marines website. You remember George told us he did commando training in Scotland?' He chewed the sweet end of the stem. 'Well, he couldn't have done. He'd have been far too young. The camp was closed down by the time he was 18. He slipped up on his research that time.'

'Do you think Phil knows he's a fraud?'

'Don't know. But we won't tell him. He's happy and I've got two more flat hikes to go. I've won enough – for the time being.'

We stopped at the five-barred gate to gaze into the field. The mare and foal came happily towards us, jogging my memory. 'What was that we said about needing two acids to neutralise an alkali?'

'Toby and George,' said Freddy. 'The two of them cancelled out the acid.'

* * * * *

The threat to water supplies of continuing dry weather now came from the local water board. 'Typical,' grumped Phil, mopping the sweat from his brow with a handkerchief. 'When it rains for a year the water companies say nothing and ramp up the profits. Then, when we get a few weeks of summer, they want us to stop using the stuff.'

Our leader was now back to his normal, peeved and irritable self. The bickering started again. It was good to be back to the old ways, Freddy sledging Phil and he bearing the burden, not having to impress anybody. We walked across Stanton Moor, west of Matlock, the ground baked and dry from days of constant sunshine, with Freddy stopping every few minutes to take out his water bottle. Phil, in his uniform of khaki shirt and shorts, plus forage cap, gave a groan. 'Freddy, you're stopping every 10 minutes. We'll never get round.'

Freddy looked pained. 'The only reason I came on this hike was because you promised you'd go at my pace. I am not dying again from heatstroke and I have to keep drinking water.'

'But you don't have to keep stopping every 10 minutes for a drink. I've given you hike choices, I've kept my agreement. You...'

'Gruppenführer,' said Freddy, butting in. 'I only came today because Jean insisted you deserved a treat after all the trouble.'

'Kind of you, Freddy, but it's no treat if we keep stopping.'

'It's no treat if insane people take sane people on boiling hikes,' riposted Freddy. 'Aargh!' He threw himself quickly to the ground.

Phil and I instinctively ducked, turning quickly to see the cause of his terror. A 100ft high black vortex swayed towards us, sucking upwards a mass of dust, leaves, twigs, grass and grit. It corkscrewed faster the more it devoured. A roar came from within, like that of a high speed train banging through a tunnel. Phil and I dropped quickly, next to Freddy, each of us clinging to the base of the same stubby dwarf bush, eyes and mouths shut tight against the stinging dust. The ground trembled as the rampaging maw drew closer. And then, to my relief, the racket began to subside as it moved away. I dragged myself upright, spitting out dust. Phil and Freddy joined me to watch the spout move in the direction of Matlock, becoming thinner and thinner. Finally it disappeared – literally – into thin air, leaving us open-mouthed.

'A dust devil.' Phil brushed himself down. 'Mini tornado. Wow, your reaction Freddy, fantastic. You'd have made a good infantryman.'

'I would not,' declared Freddy, taking a sip of water. 'I have no wish to kill anybody, with your exception, of course – ugh!' He spat out the water from his mouth. 'There's muck in it!' he groaned and upturned the water bottle, spilling its contents on the ground. 'That's it,' he said abruptly. 'I can't go on without water. Stevens, I'm suing you for £4 million.'

'I've got plenty of water. You can have mine,' said Phil, staring after the vanished dust devil, his face still lit up with excitement. 'Wasn't that the most incredible thing?'

He turned to Freddy. 'How about that then!'

'Can't hear you. My glasses are covered in dust.' Freddy took them off and wiped his face with the back of his hand. 'Ow!' He clapped his hand quickly against the side of his head. 'What creature's bitten me?' He plucked a sharp piece of bramble from his hair, looked at it in relief, then tossed it away. 'What did you say, Gruppenführer? Something about living? Surely you meant dying?'

'Come on Freddy, you'll never have an experience like that in 1,000 years. Eh Don?'

Before I could speak, Freddy coughed, spat out more dust and intervened. 'Stevens, I shall not be hiking again. It's been a long and painful experience, which I have withstood on account of domestic pressure. But the episodes I remember "living", as you describe it, were near-death experiences, expiring from hypothermia, ditto hypoglycaemia, marooned in a blizzard, lost on a dangerous moor, exposed to thunder and lightning, drowned in mud, drenched with rain, my legs nearly cut off by a mad farmer – and now just missed being sucked into a tornado.'

'But you had good times bird and flower watching, drinking beer…'

'Oh yes,' cut in Freddy. 'Once in a blue moon!'

Phil ignored it. 'And you make jokes about me, but I never mind if it keeps you happy.'

'I don't need to make jokes, I just have to keep watch on you and report the facts.'

I laughed.

Freddy shook his water bottle to expel the last few drops. 'I'm talking about dying in your cause. Maybe I should. Death would be a release.'

'Freddy, have I ever killed you?'

'No, but you will. It's been a succession of near misses, but you'll get me in the end. I know it.' Freddy put the empty water bottle back in his rucksack. 'I have been selected. I am the reason you were sent to earth. That dust devil was your work.'

'Freddy, you enjoy hiking. You know you do.'

Freddy made a short cutting action with his hand extended. 'No. That is the end. That is absolutely and definitely it. When's the next bus?'

Freddy spent the rest of the hike twittering and mumbling, but fell silent as he got into the car and soon fell asleep.

On arriving home he poured himself a fortifying whisky and told Jean what had happened. 'It was just like those twisters in Kentucky,' he said. 'In Alabama and places. I clung to this tree and Phil had his arms round me. Then this great black thing settled over his head, sucking him up. My arms were nearly out of the sockets. Then Phil couldn't hold on any longer and up he went. But I caught his ankle with one hand and just held on. Then the tornado went and Phil fell on top of me. It was incredible. All my past life flashed before me.' Freddy sipped his whisky.

'What was Don doing during all this?' said Jean.

'He was digging himself into a hole.'

'That wasn't what I heard,' said Jean. 'Phil called Ruth on his mobile in the car – you must have been sleeping – and told her what happened. She rang me just before you got in. She said you were the first to hit the ground.'

'You see,' exclaimed Freddy. 'Precisely my problem. I am always the coward, he is always the hero. And you are in league with him in a Satanic pact. Well, I am not hiking with him again.'

Jean, smiling, handed Freddy his daily ration of two squares of Green and Black's chocolate, having heard it was good for the heart. 'You know you love teasing him. I think he's a brick for putting up with it.'

She switched on the oven ready to cook the evening meal. 'It's sad you didn't get a photograph of it, though. Think of the money we'd have made selling it to the press and TV.'

'I don't know,' Freddy said gloomily, popping a square of chocolate into his mouth. 'I shall not fear death when it comes. I think my best plan is to sit in a corner and await the end.'

On our next Montague walkabout Freddy was still in martyr mode. 'The longer I survive on this planet the more I think that anybody who's happy is either a lunatic or blessed.'

'I think happiness is having something to look forward to,' I said. 'Phil looks forward to flying and living longer. That's why he keeps happy.'

'Happiness for him is delusion and a poor memory.' Freddy chuckled darkly.

'But he has got something to pursue,' I said.

'Yes, me.' Freddy tried to prevent a grin breaking out at the corners of his mouth. 'What I need is the American thing, human rights, everybody entitled to the pursuit of happiness in his own way. I'll start a union – the Dead Hikers Society. There must be the dead in life like me, dying in mud like on the Somme, men cut down in their prime by crazed Gruppenführers.'

* * * * *

Freddy was still in rebellious mood when Jean saw him out of the house on the morning of the next hike. 'And make sure you eat the bits of salad. They're good for you.'

Freddy muttered 'Good for me?' as he got into my car. 'Nothing's good for me. It keeps me alive, which is not good for me.'

Phil grinned in the front passenger seat. 'What has Jean done to you now?'

'It's not Jean,' pouted Freddy. 'It's you and her. Even convicts only have to do a few circles in a yard every day. Why must I get more punishment than criminals?' He stretched his legs as far as they would go under the seat in front and, after a pause, sounded tentative. 'Stevens, can you really say you're happy? I mean happy.'

'Absolutely!' Phil was bubbling. 'It's in *The Times* today. Haven't you seen it? It's definite. We can live for ever.'

'Stevens, if you make me live for ever the action's for £5 million. I can't think of a worse fate.'

We drove away northwards, Phil, his excitement undiminished, explaining. 'You see, up till now ageing has been studied by second-rate scientists. But now they've got a scientist chap, Gervais de Phelan, at Cambridge, and he's certain that if we can extend life to 120 we can then live as long as 5,000 years!'

'Catastrophe,' groaned Freddy. 'That's 5,000 years of hiking with you. Fifty-two times a year, times 5,000, what's that in hikes?'

'260,000,' said Phil happily, having worked it out that morning on his calculator. 'We could do the Cairngorms, Canada, the Swiss Alps. There's nothing we couldn't…'

'Hold on,' butted in Freddy, doing a quick mental calculation. 'That's 2,600 new pairs of boots! Times 100 quid, that's £260,000! Where do

I get that kind of money from? Why can't you accept that life is pain? One day you'll see that and opt for the cop out. We should all have that option.'

'No, Freddy, you wouldn't grow old, that's the point,' said Phil. 'There wouldn't be any pain.'

'How many times have we had this conversation?' said Freddy. 'You won't make it anyway because your knees will have had it.'

'Knees? I've no problem with them,' said Phil. 'My Autogenics has cured all that. Plus the glucosamine sulphate.'

Freddy drew out a newspaper cutting from his pocket. 'This is out of the very same paper you get all your information from.' He handed the cutting to Phil. 'It says that walking downhill is better for you than going uphill.'

'Rhubarb Freddy, absolute rhubarb.'

'It says that when you walk uphill – in your case race uphill – you shorten the leg muscles and that doesn't metabolise glucose properly. But if you walk downhill it lengthens muscles and you create energy more effectively. You metabolise the glucose properly.'

'Freddy, what about the cardiovascular system?' Phil was scornful. 'You need to push the heart to keep it fit! How do you do that going downhill?'

Freddy ignored him. 'It says that downhill walks help strengthen the heart and ward off diabetes.'

'Who's written it?'

'An Austrian scientist. Top man.'

'Hmm,' Phil scanned the piece. 'Austrian Society of Cardiology. Bet it's a weirdo nobody's ever heard of.'

'Like your Dr Strangebugger,' Freddy chortled.

'He's from Lichtenstein,' stressed Phil. 'And he's furthest in his field.'

'That's where he belongs,' Freddy said. 'At the far end, in a ditch. Read it, go on, read it. It says that you don't have to kill yourself screaming up mountains. All you have to do is eat dark things, like prunes and blueberries.'

'Oh I know all that stuff,' Phil said, handing the cutting back. 'It's the antioxidants in them that stop cancer. But you have to exercise as well.'

Freddy waved a dismissive hand. 'That Strangebugger turned you from being half mad into 100 per cent barking. Every comedy film I ever saw had mad middle European doctors, hair stuck up on end, with thick glasses, white coats and charging about waving clipboards.'

Phil smiled ironically. 'There's some of us, Freddy, who'd rather rely on doctors, wherever they come from, than Buddhist monks.'

'Well it so happens they are nearer the truth than your Strangebugger ever will be.' Freddy nodded his head. 'Buddhists and people think. They don't grasp at straws like you do.'

'And they don't fart like you do!' Triumphantly Phil held his arms aloft, with a cackle, hands clasped in a boxer's victory salute.

Freddy tightened his lips to stem an involuntary smile. 'Anyway,' he said. 'Which torture have you got for us today?'

'Ashford in the Water,' said Phil.

Dark clouds gathered overhead as we turned off the Ashbourne to Buxton road, on to the twisting B5056, past Grangemill and Winster, then around a succession of tight bends through the green and leafy countryside skirting Birchover and Alport, finally turning left to pass the mediaeval Haddon Hall, through Bakewell to our destination.

As I cut the ignition a few heavy raindrops splashed on the car roof, followed by a heavy drumming noise, forcing us to stay put until the shower died away. Within the time it took to don our hiking gear a hot sun appeared, bringing curls of steam from the hard ground.

We set off through the village. Ashford is a graceful place, sitting comfortably on the banks of the River Wye, having more of the atmosphere of a Cotswold village than an old lead mining centre. It lies on the route of the ancient Portway track, its most attractive feature being the low arched medieval Sheepwash Bridge, overhung by willow trees. In the 17th century it was crossed each week by hundreds of packhorses, often carrying malt from Derby. The bridge is no longer open to traffic and is a favourite spot where visitors can either feed the ducks, or gaze down into the clear waters to see if they can spot a rainbow trout.

As we walked alongside the river towards Monsal Dale, Freddy suddenly burst out laughing.

'What?' I said, smiling.

'Think of the Gruppenführer 5,000 years old. A scabby, leather-faced creature crawling around the hike.' Freddy turned to Phil. 'How old are you now?'

'Fifty,' said Phil.

'Fifty? You were 55 last week!'

'Yes, but I'm now counting each year as 15 months. That makes me 50.'

'So why make 5,000 if you can keep growing younger?'

'How else will I get a pension?' Phil said with a straight face.

I laughed. Freddy put his head back with a big grin. 'Wonderful, wonderful.' He looked at Phil in mock admiration. 'Gruppenführer, where is all this humour coming from? This is the second hike running when you have actually caused my cheeks to crack.'

'Well,' said Phil, 'I got fed up with you talking about drains so I thought up better jokes.'

We always had cause for laughter at some point in the hike. I had always found Freddy's concern about his drains particularly amusing. He had often complained that someone had moved them in the night and had required checking the next morning. Only a fortnight ago he'd lifted a manhole until he was satisfied it was where it should have been. And his search for the meaning of life always kept us entertained, as did Phil's grumpiness about the ills of the world.

No one could call us 'bewildered old men,' *per se*, except when Phil launched himself into his mad and manic moments. It is true that we all remembered the 'foreign country' that had been our youthful England, where authority was respected before the descent into a yobbish culture. And we could list the causes of *that* misfortune. It was also true that the hike provided us with an escape from the ills of the world, but we never fled into the inner world of nostalgia, because Phil, for the most part, would have none of it, always eagerly looking to the future. Freddy and I gave him full credit for that.

But, hey, what was happening to Phil? In the space of two hikes he was no longer a time-driven maniac, but a bloke cracking jokes. As we plodded towards Demons Dell, an archaeological site containing burials of pre-Christian Beaker folk, he kept surprising us. 'So, Freddy, what's the next philosophy going to be? Mine's to dread one day at a time.'

'When I was at university,' I said. 'Everyone who didn't know what to do plumped for philosophy.'

'Well, that's logical,' said Phil.

Freddy whooped. 'Wow Gruppenführer, that is really funny. You know what? You'll live longer with that sense of humour, than by being upset over being a day older. Listen. Don't knock the Buddhists. They could you get you reincarnated, so if you don't live to 5,000, you could survive by coming back in other lives.'

'But I'd come back as somebody else,' Phil complained. 'I wouldn't be me. I wouldn't have anybody to look up to.'

Freddy stifled his laughter to stop in front of Phil to peer, smiling, into his face. 'You know, Stevens, you are the most interesting example of Gruppenführership.'

'Really, Freddy,' Phil smiled and tried to move on. 'That's enough about me, let's talk about you. What do you think of me?'

'Way-hey!' We fell about. Freddy was disbelieving. 'Stevens, where's all this come from?' A sly look crossed his face. 'Have you been reading up joke books?'

'No. I just think of you, that's all I need.'

'You know,' Freddy said, 'I should write your biography. We'd make a lot of money. Except nobody would believe it.'

'My biography?' said Phil. 'What's it about?'

I dug out my pen and notebook, which I normally keep to record events on the hike. I just had to get these one-liners down. Phil was a revelation. I put his surge of good humour down to getting rid of George, plus the latest assurance of his immortality. He didn't have to kill himself racing up and down hills any more. He didn't need a powerful cardiovascular system if he was to live for ever. He reminded me of a restored Scrooge on Christmas morning.

We came to a gated stile with a peculiar catch which proved difficult to operate. 'Look at this,' said Freddy. 'You need a degree in catches to get round the Peak. After your book, Stevens, I'll write a book for walkers, *The Gate and Stile Catches of the Peak District.*'

'Sounds good, Freddy. Best seller. No problem,' said Phil. 'So what have we got? There's the straight drop finger operated variety, the reversible upwards, the reversible downwards, the spring-loaded automatic, what else?'

'There's the sprung lever,' I said. 'Oh, and the hook and eye.'

'And there's the hoop latch with that lump of concrete pulling like a pulley catch,' said Freddy. 'Oh, and don't forget the string loop over post.'

'Yes,' said Phil. 'And the colour of string must be uniform throughout the EEC. A sub-committee reports to the string committee.

They put it to the secretariat. It goes back to the council and after five years it's made law.' We moved over the bright landscape, joshing each other and laughing.

All was right with our world.

That evening, with the western sky rich in red, purple and golden streaks, Freddy and I went on our evening wander with Montague. Coming to the stream near the Red Lion we watched dragonflies flitting over the darkening water, quickly snapping up small insects, a kind of aerial plankton.

Freddy pointed to a dragonfly zipping by. 'They were on earth 300 million years ago,' he said.

We moved on to stop near the forge where we patted and fondled the mare and foal.

The meadow smelt sweet.

Freddy said, 'Why can't every day be like this?'

AUGUST

'Stem cells. I keep telling you,' insisted Phil. 'Infinite bodily repairs equals life eternal. That's the medical philosopher's stone.'

Just then the Land Rover struck a loose rock on the hillside road. 'Freddy, you've just hit one,' he added with a chuckle. Freddy gave Phil a glance, pleased that the humour he'd shown at the end of July had not been a flash in the pan. Since then, Freddy had devised a game he called 'Epitaphs'. Not only would it be a pleasant way of passing the time – Freddy's prime aim on any hike, especially when the going was painful – it might also assist Phil's permanent transmutation from mad Gruppenführer to the wonderfully witty bloke we had encountered at the end of July. Freddy intended to launch the game that day, as soon as the hike had started.

Right now a spot of teasing wouldn't come amiss. 'Know what you are?' he said perkily. 'Dr Faustus.'

'What's his bag, legorophilia?' Phil shot a wicked grin at Freddy.

'No. He sold his soul for immortality, like you,' Freddy said. 'Fancy, you'd never have a tombstone. Nobody knows you ever existed. What price stem cells?'

The hike started at Eyam, the village that had shut itself off from the world after the bubonic plague arrived in 1665. On our last visit here Phil had lingered by the grave of the heroic vicar's wife, Catherine. Today he did the same. Freddy buttonholed him. 'You never go in churchyards. That's twice you've stared at that grave. What is it?'

'Just interested,' said Phil, nonchalantly. 'Come on, let's go.'

'Right,' said Freddy firmly, as we set off through the village. 'Epitaphs. Mine's going to be: "I demand a second opinion."'

Phil chuckled. 'Good one.'

'Now your turn. Oh, forgot,' Freddy said dryly. 'You're not planning on having one, are you?'

'Me? An epitaph?' Phil said scornfully. 'Over my dead body.' He looked surprised as we broke into rollicking laughter. Then, realising, he forced out a chuckle.

'You didn't mean that!' accused Freddy. 'That slipped out!'

'Of course I meant it,' Phil jeered, still laughing.

'Alright,' Freddy replied, placating him. 'Fine. One each. Don's turn.'

I recalled one that had circulated years ago: 'Elvis, accept it.'

Freddy applauded. Phil grinned, raising his walking pole in acknowledgement. 'I've got another. It's for my cryogenic hibernation spot: "Here lies Phil, till further notice."'

Freddy and I clapped. 'Way-hey!'

Pleased with himself, Phil looked up at a passing light aircraft. 'Cessna 152,' he said. 'A trainer, probably going to Chatsworth and back. I've flown that if it's come from our airfield.' He grinned. 'I've got another. He paused while he thought about it. 'Got it. Passenger on a crashed jumbo: "I hated dying in this air crash. To think peanuts was my last meal."' Phil shook his walking pole again, with a victorious cackle.

Freddy did a jig, sharing his delight. 'Incredible! You're not an android after all! You're not only *homo sapien*, you're funny!' He gave Phil an ironic smile. 'I know why you stopped being funny. It's because time passes quickly, isn't it? You're the opposite of me. You'd rather time-stretch and be miserable. If I'm going to stay on the hike you've got to stop that. Understood?'

'If you say so, Freddy,' Phil said equably. 'But, if you want to know, you're funnier than any joke.'

'How?'

'How? Your weird wheezes! Your aunt, the dentist – and that MP job?'

'MP job? Oh yes. That was my first. Long time ago.'

'Since when were you not weird?'

Freddy had chosen his victims from MPs up for re-election, those who held their seats by a tiny majority. He'd sent out the same letter to three of them: 'I am a great supporter of yours and I have thought of a way of increasing your marginal vote. Twenty-five floating voters, friends of mine, say they'll vote for you at the next election if you can get on TV wearing a yellow tie. They will know you've done it for them. And if you can slip in the phrase "as sick as a parrot", it will make their day.' One of the three men obliged. It had been difficult referring to a parrot in a discussion about farm subsidies, but he had managed it without raising an eyebrow. The Red Lion had erupted at Freddy's showing of the recorded video. The MP lost his seat and was last heard of in Australia taking part in a TV game show.

* * * * *

It was late afternoon. Freddy and I trudged behind Phil, the gap increasing, the humour long gone. He turned round, exasperated. 'If you two brought as much water as I do you wouldn't be knackered!'

'We've got water,' called out Freddy. 'It's you. You're insane!'

A formation of swifts flew overhead towards the horizon and then, with the precision of the Red Arrows aerobatic team, wheeled round to hurtle back, uttering wild screams. Freddy stared at them, along with Phil. 'Do you know why they turned back, Gruppenführer? You should if you call yourself a navigator. It means an approaching thunderstorm. But we can't turn back, can we,' he said, mock stoically. 'Because the storm's where the car is. Oh brilliant. Doom.'

'You'll be fine,' said Phil. 'You've got waterproofs and it's not cold.' He kept his eyes on the swifts as they rounded a bend in the hillside. 'Now they're great birds. They eat in the air and doze on the wing. They even mate in the air. Superbirds.'

'How come you know that? You're not a birdwatcher.'

'I'm interested in swifts. Always have been. I'll ask you a question,' Phil said smugly. 'Why do newborn swifts never perch for three years?'

'Because they haven't got bum warmers?'

The three of us laughed, Phil genuinely this time. 'Now that *was* funny, give you that Freddy,' he chuckled. 'Very funny.'

'Much appreciated. A lesson to all Gruppenführers: keep the men happy.' Minutes later Freddy's expression changed as the early clouds of the day began to merge into a darkening haze. Five minutes later came the first drum beats of thunder, rolling towards us, bouncing off the hillsides. 'There you are,' he said. 'What did I tell you? Doom.'

'Never fly anywhere near this stuff,' said Phil. 'Very dangerous.'

'Fly! Stevens, we're walking in it! If only you'd noticed!' Freddy looked suspiciously at Phil. 'How's the Red Baron doing?'

'Fine,' said Phil, looking straight ahead, proudly. 'I've been solo and now I've got my cross country qualifier to...'

'You've what! Solo?' exclaimed Freddy. 'You never told us!'

'Oh, well,' said Phil with a modest smile, 'I didn't want to brag.'

'It's not that!' said Freddy. 'You gave us no warning to take cover!'

Large splats of rain thumped onto the dusty footpath. 'Oh God,' groaned Freddy. 'It's going to chuck it down. I'm not walking in this. I always get wet. Find some shelter. Come on, it's your job. Jump to it.'

Phil sighed, impatiently. 'Freddy. You've got waterproofs....'

'No,' insisted Freddy. 'They don't work in monsoons! They leak! Find somewhere!'

'Barn over there on our two o'clock.' The retired air traffic controller altered his heading, striding towards it.

Freddy was the quickest, scrambling over a fallen section of stone wall, taking care not to step on loose rocks, a frequent cause of sprained ankles. He reached the barn and pulled on the rickety, slatted door. It refused to open. 'Oh no!' he moaned. He took off his rucksack and turned to face Phil. 'If I catch pneumonia, which is about the only malady I've never had at your hands, the action will be for £17 million. Plus expenses.'

The heavy raindrops ceased. There was a pause. Then the waters fell, in torrents. The barn roof thundered to the rain. With a mile of walking ahead of us, crossing the south-west edge of Eyam Moor, the prospect was dismal.

'I don't believe it,' cried Freddy, hardly able to see Phil through the downpour and unable to get his anorak and overtrousers on quickly enough. 'Ow! I'm wet through already!'

'We're all wet. We'll be alright if we walk fast, keep warm!'

'What do you mean, *we'll* be alright?' Freddy adjusted his overtrousers, breathing hard. 'There'll be letters written! Why didn't you get the weather forecast!'

'I did!' Phil set off. 'But it gave this lot for later, tonight!'

We stumbled and hurried our way across the moor, Freddy gasping. 'I've got water in my boots! I'll get foot rot! I'm never ever hiking with you again, Stevens. Never! This time I mean it!'

'It's your fault, Freddy. Look, you've got your overtrousers tucked into your socks.' Phil pointed at Freddy's legs. 'That's how the water gets in.'

'Yow! It's down my neck as well!'

'You should have brought that umbrella, that lady's one,' grinned Phil, enjoying the battle with the elements. 'Come on, Freddy, think how nice it will be after...'

'It will be afterwards,' broke in Freddy. 'If I had a pound for every time you've said that. Well, this is it, definitely it, finally, categorically, it. The end. Finito. Remember this moment. This is the very last hike. No more. This is the last time I set foot in this awful place. The action's now for £19 million.'

'It can't be. It was 17 last time,' said Phil. 'Got to be 18.'

'Hang on! I'm the plaintiff! I can ask whatever I want! It's now 20. £20 million. If I live to collect it,' he added glumly.

When Freddy arrived home, damp, soggy and gently steaming after an hour sitting with the car heater on, Jean told him to undress in the shed. 'Frederick. You can't take that lot off in the house. They smell awful!'

Freddy, banished to the shed, chose a hard centred personal chocolate and began to peel off his clammy layers of clothing. There were times for jokes, he thought, and times for action.

Later, warm and dry he tucked into his meal, fortified by a glass of merlot, but resisted the impulse to exaggerate his experience. It was dispiriting as Jean never paid much attention to his near death experiences. He remained in a thoughtful mood all evening.

* * * * *

From an upstairs window, Freddy carefully watched his wife drive her car on to the road and turn in the direction of Derby. She had left him in no doubt that his latest attempt to quit the hike was based on nothing more than sheer laziness. 'All these little tribulations never harm you Freddy,' she'd said, taking out the medical report from her desk in the hallway. It was the result of Freddy's recent check up. 'You see here? Your good cholesterol outweighs the bad. Your overall score is 3.4. Your blood pressure is 130 over 85. You've no diabetes. And your chance of a heart attack in the next 10 years is virtually nil. It says it here. Read it again. This is the latest Framlingham Scale. Go on.'

Freddy released the curtain, sat down on the adjustable chair and meditated on the loneliness of the long-distance hiker. Ah well. He switched on the computer to look up 'last minute Buddhist holidays'.

He was disappointed that the euphoria evoked by eliminating George had soon palled. And the brief interlude of Phil as humorist, so welcome, had also come to a stop. 'He's still on that dark angel's mission,' he told me. 'You only have to look at the last hike, that drenching he gave us. And that dream I had!' Phil, 'The Ghost of Hike Future', had whipped Freddy all the way up Kinder Scout, then back down to the pub at Edale, where a waiting beer had eluded his grasp. Up and down he was driven, on a never-ending cycle of pure torture.

When he told Jean of his nightmare she'd laughed. 'Oh come on! Phil's not like that. Cheer up. I do believe there's a Magnum left.'

Freddy was determined to escape the next hike, not only to re-establish his status as resistance fighter under Phil's jackboot, but also to give him more time in which to work out plans for a permanent exit from all hikes. But he'd used an old excuse, saying that the forecast heat was above his 'fainting level', a temperature likely to 'fry eggs on stones'. 'I got it from a farmer,' he protested. 'He's a naturalist clairvoyant. He uses pine cones and has visions. The Met office uses him. He's never wrong.'

Freddy told me later that Jean had stuck the *The Times* weather forecast in front of his nose. And Phil had referred him to the relevant website on British weather. 'They're in league you know,' said Freddy. 'Of course Phil's in with her,' he protested after I'd doubted it. 'Jean's making my favourite gooseberry tart and Phil's offering me two more hikes. What more evidence do you want?'

Jean gave him more ammunition. She followed up with a lecture. 'Freddy, hiking does you good. It's been scientifically proved. More wine, love?'

Freddy scowled at the screen. He disliked it even more than bum warmers, afraid of its hi-tech link with the outside world, a spy that could filch his credit card and refuse to offer much-needed information out of spite and malice. And, yes, here was confirmation as it blinked defiantly, refusing to show Buddhist holidays anywhere other than in India, depressing news. India was too far, too hot and there was always the possibility of picking up Delhi belly. The only option, and so convenient, was the local Tara Buddhist centre, which ran such courses. But his unfortunate and embarrassing indiscretion of two years ago – a prize fart – had put paid to that. It was a pity, as Buddhism at Tara was all about sitting on chintzy sofas in a Victorian drawing room, sipping tea out of china cups, after which the chief monk would stretch his legs then clear off to his bedroom for a spot of meditation, leaving guests to their own devices.

It would be easy to bunk off on some bird or flower expedition. You could get up to all sorts of things without them getting suspicious. 'And they don't even make you sit cross-legged if you don't want to, as chairs are provided,' Freddy told me in the Nag's Head, a location safe from Phil's eavesdropping. Without Phil and Jean on his back, he said, a Buddhist retreat might give him the time and space in which to get lucky and stumble across the 'meaning'. In any case, wasn't he due some payback on account of getting rid of George?

As Freddy stared, stone-faced, at a pop-up advert telling him to invest in chest expanders, a crying noise drew his attention. He looked through the bedroom window and saw a large formation of birds wheeling and gathering, the signal for their imminent departure from these shores. Swifts again. They might please Phil but to Freddy they were harbingers of doom, signalling the fag end of summer and approach of winter, which meant cold, wet and miserable hiking. He brooded on his predicament. He needed a proper ailment. He should stop teasing Phil with legorophilia-type illnesses. He jotted down 'Death by hiking', then scribbled it out. Another phrase jumped into his head. He printed, in block capitals, his epitaph: 'A hike too far'. Then he added, 'and steep'. It would bring remorseful tears to the eyes of his oppressors. He would go down heroically. Outdo Phil in the heroism stakes. Yes, in martyrdom he'd show them what he'd gone through.

In this determined mood he clicked into his 'secret drawers', bringing up his 'Wheeze' file, and tapped in a note, 'Do real illness research'.

He came back to Google for inspiration and searched for university sites, adding the word 'Buddhist'. The screen flicked to a brilliant display of red, saffron and gold around the caption of 'Buddhist summer school at the University of Cambridge'. A further click brought him the sub-heading, 'Immediate vacancy due to cancellation'. Hurriedly he checked out the syllabus. He read that the 'course will examine some of the extraordinary qualities of the Tibetan lamas, or civilised shamans'. Studying 'their visions, dreams, deaths and rebirths, it would assess their encounter with modernity in the years since the Dalai Lama led his people into exile in 1959'. It was ideal. It was actually perfect. He would even enjoy it. The course would begin the coming weekend and last five days, accommodation provided. He noted with delight that he would have to travel the day before the course began, glory be, hike day.

Freddy let out a whoop and eagerly tapped through the logging on process, entering his details, including credit card number. He clicked 'Pay' and went to 'Confirm'.

His right index finger paused one inch above the mouse, withdrew, went back into hover, quivered slightly and, after a minute, slowly retreated, allowing his hand to settle on his lap. He looked through the window. The swifts were still out there, reminiscent in their black gatherings of Hitchcock's *The Birds*, an ominous sight. He turned back to the screen, staring at it for a whole minute, then logged off and went downstairs into the back garden to stare at the dark, damp patch where the coal bunker had stood and where now nothing grew. A bit like his mind, he thought, blank and depressed. He went into the shed and sat down in contemplation. What an idiot he was. Jean checked their internet bank account each day, didn't she? There was no chance she'd miss a deduction of £555 pounds, naming Cambridge University as the payee. He could imagine her calling him. 'Frederick? What on earth's this?'

He stepped out of the shed and looked up, shielding his eyes with one hand against the sun. The swifts had multiplied into a huge vee formation, sweeping overhead on a final circuit, at the end of which they made a sharp right turn and raced towards the southern horizon. They were soon out of sight.

Freddy lowered his gaze from the empty sky. He had never really liked the month of August. It had an elegiac feeling about it, a staleness in leaf and grass, the lush green of spring all gone. The telephone rang from inside the house, disturbing his steady gloom.

'Hello?' Freddy was just in time.

'Freddy? It's Graham. Any chance of you dropping by? Usual problem.'

'Of course, Graham. We're hiking...' He stopped abruptly and, after a pause, said calmly, 'We're hiking on Thursday. What time?' Saving Graham had priority. The man who'd saved his life came before his own concerns. Ah well. There was always the next hike to miss.

He made himself a nice mug of lemon and ginger tea and sat in the living room, listening to Bach's Goldberg Variations. But as soon as he relaxed to concentrate on each pure and perfect note, an idea struck him. He got up to gaze out of the living-room window at the house opposite, an elegant, square-shaped building with a Georgian-style portico, owned by a couple in their late 40s, Richard and Muriel. The design was quite out of keeping with the village character. Freddy wondered if Richard's uncle, a member of the local planning committee, had anything to with it. The couple had recently retired by selling Richard's double glazing company and Muriel's three hairdressing shops. They had then bought a villa on the outskirts of Marbella, where they spent a lot of time. Breakfast would be taken by the pool (overlooked by a number of flats) both adorned with gold dripping from fingers, wrists and around necks. After that came subjection to an hour of sun, still sporting their essential accoutrements. Then they would make their trip into town, first destination being Orange Square, there to sip cocktails and exhibit their bling-bling.

Their next duty was a stroll around the marina, admiring the luxury boats. They would pause to gesture favourably at any feature that caught their attention – a gently knowledgeable nod of the head here and comment there – and always with a critical poise. Then, if their energy levels would permit, they would go for a glitzy wander around the fastidiously cleansed and brilliantly lit 'Corte Ingles' store. The afternoon would be spent back at the villa, sunbathing and swimming. In the evening they would revisit the town and sit at an alfresco bar, to watch the Ferraris and Porsches cruise past – and most importantly, to be watched themselves. They would never be seen at the weekly street market as many items were offered at bargain prices.

As Freddy looked through the window he noted that the house had two cars parked outside, a Mercedes S430 saloon and a Golf GTI. It meant that Richard and Muriel were both in residence.

Freddy, thinking no evil, went to queue in the post office for a book of stamps and found Muriel in front of him. She wore a white dress, emphasising the leathery texture of her dark brown skin, in places almost black. Around her neck was a chain of brass, plated with white gold. On her wrist was a gold chain and a hip-hop watch, but with a woven golden strap instead of the usual red leather variety. From her ears dangled large, golden hoop rings. Across the fingers of both hands were spread batteries of gold sovereign rings.

On arrival home Freddy poured out a whisky and sat motionless, in deep thought like Sherlock Holmes, but chewed a stick of gum in the absence of the sleuth's little helpers, cocaine and tobacco. By the time Jean had watched *Celebrity Big Brother* and *Deal or no Deal*, he had the answer. The thought of seeing Graham the next day added to his bonhomie. Perhaps tomorrow's hike wouldn't be too bad after all.

* * * * *

As we strapped ourselves into Freddy's Land Rover – Freddy had volunteered again for driver duty as he intended to collect a load of muddy potatoes from a friendly farmer – Phil outlined the itinerary for the day. 'First, Youlgreave, then walk through Lathkill Dale and over the fields back to Middleton. Graham will be there around four o'clock. Not that I like Lathkill Dale, but it's the nearest. Any questions?'

Just then a wheel dropped sharply into a pot hole.

'Ow!' I exclaimed at Freddy.

'Hell's bells, Freddy!' said Phil.

We had never come to terms with Freddy's ancient Land Rover, in which the ride was a cross between horse riding and crashing along in a flat-bottomed speed boat. Then we hit a sunken drain.

'Freddy,' said Phil, recovering from the blow. 'Any chance of getting a proper car?'

'Gruppenführer. You like it tough. You weakening?'

Phil scowled, widening Freddy's grin. Yes, there were always diversions on the hike if only he took the trouble to think them up. The hike planned – Lathkill again – was very helpful in this respect. Freddy could enjoy the multiplicity of wild flower and bird life in this, one of English Nature's finest reserves and, at the same time, be kept amused at the sight of Phil stumbling and clambering along a tortuous footpath which, for part of its length, was littered with fallen stones and the exposed roots of trees. That was why he didn't like it. He couldn't walk quickly enough, which did not fit in with his cardiovascular aspirations.

Freddy also liked the Lathkill lunch stop on warm days. It would be spent sitting on a stone outcrop by the wooden footbridge, close to the remains of the mediaeval sheep wash. It was best in spring when orchids and cowslips dotted the rough sides of the dale. But it was nice on this day, too, just to munch his Cornish pasty while watching brown damselflies dance over the shallow water trickling through the thick reeds. He glanced up and saw a little owl motionless on the cliff top opposite, keeping watch for mice below. He closed his eyes as he ate, savouring the blissful calm.

A young man and woman walked towards us from the Youlgreave direction. Both wore rucksacks, the man cradling something in cupped hands. They stopped at the stile on the bridge. The precious handful was taken carefully by the woman to allow the man to step over the style. Then it was transferred back in the same delicate manner.

The couple climbed the steep footpath that passed us close by. As we exchanged polite greetings I caught a glimpse of something brown in the man's hands.

He noticed our curiosity. 'It's a bird,' he explained in a north Derbyshire accent. 'We found it flapping around some stones back there. Do you know where we can take it?'

'What kind of bird?' Freddy went to take a look.

'We don't know. Don't know about birds.'

'It's a kestrel,' Freddy said. 'A male. See the black spots on the brown colour? And the head and tail are both blue and grey. What are you going to do with it?'

'Dunno. I was just keeping it warm,' said the man. 'Then ring the RSPB or somebody when we got home.'

'Have you tried to examine it?'

'No.'

'Good, because they might get traumatised if you handle them. It needs somebody who's trained. If we empty my rucksack and Don? Phil? Put my things in yours. I'll make a nest for it in mine.'

Freddy is normally clumsy, so I was impressed by the deftness with which he emptied his rucksack, making a nest out of a spare pair of hiking socks. 'Can you put it in gently?' The kestrel was laid carefully into the bottom of the rucksack. 'Now we've got to keep the top open. It's got to be ventilated.'

'What will you do with it?' said the man.

'We'll take it to a friend,' said Freddy. 'He lives in Middleton. We're going there next. No problem.'

The man pointed at the rucksack. 'A bird in there's better than one in the hand. Gosh, what a relief. Thanks.' He laughed and walked away with the woman, both wishing us luck.

We took it in turns carrying the rucksack, 15 minutes each. It was difficult walking over rough ground while, at the same time, trying to keep the rucksack stable.

'He's wrong,' I said, easing my back from tension. 'One in your hand's got to be better than one in the rucksack.'

We arrived at Middleton. As we entered the yard by the five-barred gate, the twin geese scurried towards us, hissing hostility. At the last minute they veered towards Freddy as the choicest of the three burglars.

'Yow!' Nervously he backed between the bust of Queen Victoria and the East German patrol car, last seen in action on the other side of the Berlin Wall.

'Shoot!' The shout came from Graham, who stood in the open doorway pointing at the geese. They hesitated at the command, giving Freddy time to nip round them and make for the house. Once again the pirate-bearded man, black patch over one eye, had come to Freddy's rescue.

'My friends. Feldschlossen!' Graham exclaimed, then noticed me fussing over the rucksack. 'We've got an injured kestrel in there,' I said.

'Mein Gott!' Graham took out his mobile. 'I know just the folk.' He made a call. 'Pollyanna? It's Graham Goodall. I've got a damaged kestrel. Yes. Can I bring it over? Okay will do, bye.' Graham switched off the phone.

'It's Bird Rescue near Matlock. I'll take it over when you've gone.'

We sat in the front garden, among the hollyhocks. An intermediary fence made it impossible to see any of the Trabants parked in the rear garden. I thought what a peculiarity it was that villagers should complain when the only way of seeing them was by helicopter.

The twin geese singled out Freddy, surrounding him. Graham dismissed them by the raising of a finger. 'After you'd been last time,' he said. 'I remembered something. I didn't get the order to remove the Trabbies because I was in Germany when it came. When I got back I was out of time, and because of that I've got a £1,000 fine and I've still got to get rid of them.'

'You need a lawyer,' Freddy said.

'I can't afford it.' Graham looked sadly at the geese. Although they no longer threatened Freddy, they were now staring up at him in begging mode. 'And how do you get rid of 40 Trabants? Take them to the council dump?' He laughed and puffed furiously at his black pipe, stuck in the corner of his mouth, reminding me of Popeye.

'Why don't you appeal?' said Freddy.

'Appeal? Can I?' Graham looked surprised.

'Anybody can appeal against a court order,' said Freddy.

'Appeal.' Graham puffed out a smoke ring. 'Right,' he said crisply. I'll look into that.'

* * * * *

'Where is this, Burma?' Freddy stood in the doorway of the Red Lion, grimacing at the torrential rainfall bouncing off the terrace slabs. 'I'm not going home in this.'

'Don't worry Freddy, neither am I.' Phil was the first to walk back to the snug, Freddy and I following him.

'You amaze me,' said Freddy. 'You love getting wet through on the hike.' He picked up the half-nibbled pork scratching that he'd left on a plate.

Phil lowered himself into the Windsor chair and stared into the dying fire. 'It's your knock Don.' He looked up at Freddy with a patronising smile. 'Okay Freddy, you've not told us about your latest onedownmanship effort. Who's the lucky lad this time?'

I looked at Freddy, waiting for his reply. He sat down inside the inglenook, savouring the pork scratching, examining it, being deliberately provocative. 'Nice these. Not a word to her majesty.'

'Come on. Who's the victim this time?'

'I don't have victims,' said Freddy, aloofly. 'Only converts.'

'Ayatollah Freddy. Come on, who is it? I need to know to take out insurance.'

'It's not you,' Freddy said airily. 'But I can't reveal targets. It's classified. Else they'd be taken into protection and I'd lose them.'

'Them? More than one?'

'Yes. I can say no more. I'll reveal all when the operation's complete. End of statement.'

'Onedownmanship,' scoffed Phil at Freddy. 'All that crap about getting the meaning! It's a cover story for a lunatic's practical jokes!'

'Takes one to know one,' said Freddy, po-faced.

The next morning Muriel took a 'withheld number' call from Freddy, who posed as a rep for *Expat*, a new Costa del Sol English magazine. Had they received a letter in Spain, he asked, saying they'd reached a photo final with another couple for their outstanding 'dress and accoutrements?' Muriel said no, but then they had recently returned and presumably had missed it. 'I see,' said Freddy. 'Well, the winners get free delivery of the magazine for the next two years and will be featured in the first edition, front page, with their photograph.'

'Oh, terrific,' said Muriel, who was chewing gum and had taken to mangling her vowels, a bit like an American. 'But I can't remember going in for it.'

'You wouldn't,' said Freddy. 'It was just a photograph. You gave your name and address to be sent on.'

'Oh yes,' Muriel said vaguely, not calling it to mind. She added that Richard would 'most certainly cooperate'.

'Could we do the shoot at your house, say tomorrow at 11am?'

Muriel readily agreed.

'Oh, one last thing, please don't skimp on the accoutrements, you know, the gold earrings and so on? They'll show up wonderfully.'

Muriel's smile widened, a shade seductively. 'And we have the perfect spot, you know, on the deck by the hot tub.' She added a high-pitched giggle.

'Oh, good,' said Freddy. 'Oh, sorry – I should have mentioned it – but this other couple. Do you mind if they join you for the shoot?'

Muriel paused, her face dropping. 'What, the…?'

'You're both finalists,' said Freddy. 'The winning couple's decided by who looks the most fashionable tomorrow.'

Muriel's smile betrayed some bewilderment. 'Oh, I see,' she said. Her smile turned to a twitchy frown as Freddy said his goodbye.

He made another call. 'It's on,' he told me.

* * * * *

The next morning, after a spell of rain, the weather brightened and with it Freddy's spirits. The shoot would take place, as arranged, at 11 o'clock. He positioned himself at the bedroom window to get the best view. As the hall clock struck the hour, Toby and Angie – the lady with a knitting needle through her hair – arrived outside Muriel's house, driven by another member of the poetry group, posing as a photographer.

Toby wore a dark suit, white shirt and blue tie, looking nothing like the shambling 'Mr Magoo' of July. His mane of white hair had been neatly cut back, the overall effect giving the impression of an insurance broker. He had volunteered to wear his Longines watch, a model with a slim plain dial, but Freddy had deemed this too subtle. Apart from the knitting needle, Angie *was* dressed in fashion – years old fashion, a multi-coloured kaftan, Jesus sandals and friendship bracelets. Freddy could see the hot tub and eagerly watched through binoculars as Richard and Muriel stepped on to the decking beside it. Richard looked magnificent, with gold glistening from both ears, bared chest and both hands. He wore a deep open-neck cerise shirt and white jeans, with a Diesel belt. Muriel gleamed likewise, dressed in a frilly, white, low-plunging top and silky black trousers.

Freddy's grin widened as he observed the couples being introduced to each other and then directed to stand on the decking. Noticeable were Muriel's body movements as she glanced in perplexity at Toby, even more so at Angie with the knitting needle. The photographer took his 'shots' at speed, calling out to them to make various poses. Freddy, later, said he had briefed his team to perform as in an SAS operation, in fast and out fast. The shots were rapidly taken, 30 in all, and the photographer was away, thanking them with a wave of the hand. Toby and Angie followed in a hurry, explaining they had a train to catch. Freddy watched Richard and Muriel, still rooted by the hot tub. Muriel had a blank look on her face and a hand at her chest, opening and closing her mouth like a fish. They stood there for some time, without speaking.

* * * * *

That night, in the Red Lion, Phil shook his head at Freddy's report. 'That is just seriously insane. Two people photographed with another couple who happen to be dressed differently. Not grunge, like your dentist with his car. Just ordinary. I don't get it.'

'Exactly,' said Freddy. 'They don't get it either.'

'So they don't get it, so what?'

'That's it. They don't get it.'

'It's nuts.' Phil drank some beer. 'You know what you are? You're a...' He quickly broke off to jerk away from the open doorway leading to the terrace, splashing some beer down himself as he did so. He was just in time to avoid a plume of cigarette smoke drifting in from outside.

Freddy laughed. 'And you say I'm nuts.'

'Freddy, I just saved 10 minutes of my life.' Phil wiped foam from his shirt with the back of his hand.

Freddy grinned. 'Don't tell me. Another equation.'

'Yes. It is as a matter of fact. I got it from a scientific report on the web. You make up a life chart.' Phil took a piece of paper out of his wallet. 'See that?' We stared at an equation that looked like something out of Einstein. 'At the moment I'll live till 93. But with all the stem cells, all that stuff, I should make 102. By then we'll have cracked immortality. If not, I'll go in the deep freeze.' Phil opened his wallet to tuck the piece of paper away.

'Hang on.' Freddy took the paper from him, staring at it. 'What's this?' He pointed to the written word, 'aviation'.

'That's right.' Phil was open and forthright.

'Any moderately stressful activity is good for the body and mind,' he assured Freddy. 'Flying does that. Keeps your brain working. I've got my qualifying cross-country soon. I reckon I'll have my licence by October.' He wore a frank and disarming smile.

Freddy directed his anti-con laser straight between Phil's eyes. 'I am not going in your aeroplane,' he said. 'Not in October, or ever.'

The next day Toby drove round to give Freddy copies of the shoot. In terms of onedownmanship they were actually better than his pics of the deranged dentist. Freddy beckoned Toby into the hallway. 'Come on, got something for you,' he said conspiratorially, tapping the side of his nose. 'Not a word to senior management.' Opening the cellar door, he switched on the naked light bulb and tiptoed down the narrow, red-brick staircase. 'Mind your step.'

Toby followed Freddy down into the small, damp-smelling cellar. 'Aren't these places wonderful?' Freddy enthused. 'Think what you could get up to down here. But just look at it. Jean's wines.' He tutted at the stack of B&Q collapsible wine racks that left little room for manoeuvre. Shuffling past, he crouched down in the darkest corner and pulled out three loose bricks, placing them on the floor. Then, brushing away a cobweb and spider, he drew out from its hiding place – oh so carefully – a bottle of whisky and held it up to the light. 'Ardmore. Single malt.' He pointed a finger at Toby and then himself with a wide grin, mouthing the words: 'just for us'. He glanced at his watch. 'Oh lors, she'll be back.'

They returned to the kitchen and hurriedly downed their drinks, after which Freddy quickly rinsed out the glasses and put them away – just as the front door opened to reveal Jean with the shopping. Freddy went to give her a hand.

'Hello Toby.' Jean's smile wasn't that enthusiastic. She rather suspected Toby encouraged Freddy's odd leanings.

'Hello Jean. Just going. Bye.'

Outside, Toby hesitated as he was about to get into his car. Muriel was staring at him from inside her stationary Golf, opposite. Toby got into his car quickly and set off. Muriel's stare now swivelled to pinpoint Freddy. He gave her a neighbourly smile of acknowledgement, half raised his hand in greeting and then went back inside, closing the door.

* * * * *

'You see, it's not as if I'm a sadist,' Freddy said. A light drizzle had started to fall as we trailed behind Montague sniffing through the wood. 'You don't think I am do you?'

I said, after a pause, that I thought his mission to create a 'Jungian subconsciousness' among the masses, leading to overall enlightenment, might take for ever. But I did think he was in the league of genuine practical jokers, somebody who's an outsider. I went on to point out that Leonard Cheshire VC had been such a joker and nobody could have been more sincere and unselfish than him. I also suggested that Freddy, even in his Beatles days, wearing winkle-picker shoes and Teddy Boy drainpipes, had paid good money to learn transcendental meditation. And what did that indicate, somebody who was not serious?

The next morning Freddy made his routine 8am call to Phil, but not complaining, since he still had choice of hike. He said he wanted one that passed near the cottage of his 'guru', Bernard the Bodger, the Cambridge-educated philosopher and maker of wooden furniture by primitive pole lathe. Freddy had spent a lot of time learning 'at his knee'. It would be a speculative mission, he said, as he didn't have Bernard's phone number.

'Oh Freddy,' sighed Phil, reaching out for the waffle dripping with honey, to be washed down by Ruth's killer coffee. 'Okay,' he said, 'I'll do a deal. We go to see Bernard and you lose one of your hikes. It's a rule, 1d, remember?'

'No, I don't. There isn't a 1d. It ends at c.'

'No. There's always been a 1d.'

'Right. I lose one hike. Just one. Note my tolerance of your wiles – I'm making a note of this conversation timed at 8.03am.' Freddy put the phone down, pleased with himself. In order to clinch the deal he'd been prepared to lose two of his flat hikes. In his resistance to the occupying power it was a small, but significant, victory.

* * * * *

'Peregrine!' called out Freddy in excitement, pointing into the sky. We were on Curbar Edge, above the Derwent valley, washed in mellow sunlight. Above us, gliding in a slow circle at 1,000 feet, was the bird that had been almost extinct 25 years ago. Now the most protected of predators, which had once provided great sport for Henry VIII, it fixed its beady eyes on the lower sky beneath. Its scrutiny paid off. A wood pigeon fluttered alongside the gritstone edge, 800 feet below. The next few seconds were astonishing. The peregrine falcon snapped back its wings and, like the terrifying Stuka dive bomber of World War Two, plummeted in seconds to smash into the pigeon, its feathers exploding, bringing gasps from the three of us. Phil could not stop talking about it, even when the hike had ended. Swifts may have been top of his bird list. But this…!

The sky was darkening and the air was humid as we left the car and approached the wood where Bernard lived. But there was no welcoming smoke this time. And no sound. I was apprehensive lest Freddy's day came to an abrupt and disappointing end. What if Bernard no longer lived here? What if he'd died? What if he didn't want to meet Freddy and talk about stuff that he'd gone over before? Freddy, as a wannabe philosopher, surely couldn't interest the man who had once studied under Bertrand Russell and Wittgenstein, the Austrian genius.

We walked on a cushion of leaves, crackling the odd twig underfoot as we entered the clearing. The place looked not much changed from when we were last there, at Hallowe'en two years ago. The kitchen garden looked much as before and the work area was still occupied by the pole lathe, wicker baskets, sawing-horse and piles of wood. Most encouraging was the litter of freshly-cut wood shavings close to the sawing horse and lathe. The sound of a man talking came from the white painted cottage, with its wavy roof tiles in terracotta. A few seconds later Bernard stepped out of the cottage, a mobile phone to his ear. Seeing us, his bearded face did a bungee jump of surprise from raised eyebrows down to a big smile across his cheeks and back again. He put up a hand and went back into the cottage to quickly finish the conversation, then came outside again with an even brighter smile. He wore much the same working clothes as before, a faded cherry waistcoat and a pair of white braces holding up calf-length, baggy trousers. A large red handkerchief was slung around his neck. In a memory flashback I saw him at work in this clearing, two years past, holding lump hammer and splitter, caught motionless in time, like an old woodcut. In that moment I had understood what he meant about being at home in his 'universe of nature'.

'Ha, my philosopher and friends,' Bernard said in his educated voice. We shook hands and asked how he was progressing. 'Well, did you not see me on *Heart of the Country*?' He mentioned the regional TV programme. No, we had not, unfortunately. 'Oh, it was quite good. I managed to get across that I was a bodger who made a good bodge.'

We laughed. 'Now then,' he said, turning to Freddy. 'I can assume what brings you here. Now, I've just got to fix this billet.' He sat on the sawing horse and clamped the length of wood in the vice. Using a draw knife he peeled back the outer layers of wood towards his crotch, fashioning it into a rough cylindrical shape. The billet was then transported to the lathe, the cord of the pole wrapped around its centre and secured in place using a screw clamp. 'Right, that's that.' Bernard left the contraption ready to be worked by the foot-operated lathe the next morning. 'Do you like herbal tea or coffee?' he said, going into the cottage.

We drank herbal tea, with Freddy and Phil sitting on tree stumps, while Bernard and I were slumped in rickety deck chairs of a dubious vintage, threatening to collapse if we moved.

'Be still like a mountain,' Bernard said, with a twinkle in his eye. 'What comes next, do you know, Freddy?' We stared blankly at him. 'Flow like a river,' Bernard answered his own question.

I confessed to having heard the saying somewhere before.

'It's my new philosophy,' said Bernard. Freddy nearly fell off his tree stump with excitement and asked him to explain. Had it anything to do with Wordsworth, Freddy's favourite poet philosopher? Freddy repeated the phrase that he knew so well, 'The whole world in a flower.'

'Partly,' said Bernard. He outlined it as simply as he could. It had all started in the sixth century. Based on traditional Chinese ideas, the brand of philosophy was known as Taoism. The guiding philosopher was Lao-tzu, meaning the 'old master'. Unlike Confucius, who believed in the importance of convention, Lao taught that convention was not always a good thing, as it interfered with man's natural ability to live in harmony with the world. 'They have no gods,' said Bernard. 'They seek answers to life's problems through inner meditation and outer observation.' As he spoke his chair gave an ominous creak.

Freddy wanted to know how different Taoism was from Buddhism. 'It seems the same to me.'

'Hah, well,' Bernard murmured with a smile. 'Not really. Buddhists aim to rise upwards spiritually through meditation to enlightenment.'

At that the chair collapsed and Bernard lay on his back. 'Did I say rising?' We helped him to his feet, laughing. 'And I make chair legs. I told you I was a bodger! More tea anybody?'

We stayed for a second cup of tea. Bernard continued his lecture, saying that Taoists were concerned with their bodies as much as their minds. For them time was cyclical, not linear as in Western thinking. And Taoists had an interest in promoting health and vitality.

Bernard wiped a film of perspiration from his forehead using the red handkerchief. Freddy began to fidget nervously, watching the sky and feeling the same prickly damp as the humidity level continued to rise. Over the trees the southern sky was a thick grey-black. The weather forecast had cold Polar air meeting warm air from North Africa, always a volatile concoction. On any other occasion Freddy would have been on his feet, urging us to find shelter. But he still felt the need to learn more at the feet of his master.

I smiled to myself. If this didn't prove Freddy was serious-minded, what did?

Bernard went on to say that Taoists recognised five main organs and orifices of the body, which corresponded to the five parts of the sky: water, fire, wood, metal and earth. Each person must nurture the Ch'i (air, breath) that was given to them. Development of virtues was one's chief task. The three most precious were compassion, moderation and humility. Taoists recognised all gods as mere human constructs, placing their trust in the Tao so that they lived in peace and balance with the Universe in this life and beyond.

'Now this is where your understanding of Wordsworth ties in, Freddy,' Bernard said. 'Taoism believes in a power that surrounds and flows through all of nature, as does Wordsworth. As you said, "All the world in a flower".'

Freddy said he understood but didn't sound convincing, and Bernard became sympathetic, even gentle. 'Look,' he said. 'Us westerners have great difficulty in our competitive consumer society. I'm lucky because I'm not part of that. I am developing those virtues, or trying, and I am trying to work and live accordingly.' Bernard turned to Phil. 'If I remember rightly, you had a problem with longevity. Or was it immortality? Philosophy deals with that, as well.' He indicated Freddy. 'You know, you two are searching for the same thing.'

It was dark inside the wood as we walked back to the car, the air damper and heavier, laden with the rich and musty aroma of rotten leaves. Phil waited until we were well out of Bernard's earshot before he spoke.

'Me?' he said tetchily. 'Going in for Asian sixth-century philosophy?' He made a backwards gesture with a disparaging look at Freddy. '*I'm* looking for the same thing as *you* are? He's out of his tiny mind.'

Freddy beamed. 'Surrender yourself to the force, Gruppenführer. Amid all your pills, Autogenics and Strangebuggers you might find enlightenment yet.'

'Hmm,' grunted Phil. 'Weirdos.'

We reached the Land Rover just as the rain started, drumming on the car roof, rapidly increasing in intensity. The windscreen wiper was not as old as the vehicle but it was just as slow, unable to shift the continuous buckets of water hurled down from the sky. Visibility was nil.

'Now I don't blame you for this monsoon, Gruppenführer,' said Freddy.

We waited for the deluge to pass. But there was no sign it would relent – if anything the downpour was even more intense. We waited another five minutes.

'Oh my God!' Freddy exclaimed, pointing out through the side window in horror. A wave of water tumbled and flowed down the adjacent hillside and flowed over the low, dry stone wall to surround us in seconds. An iron manhole cover rose out of its key slots from the pressure in the main drain. 'It's coming down the other side as well,' said Phil crisply. 'It's a flash flood. We're in a Land Rover. It's built for it. Go on Freddy, move!'

'I don't believe this. Every time I go out with you I'm drowning! Oh lors....'

'Freddy, go straight ahead and don't panic,' said Phil commandingly, chin tucked into chest. Such windiness from his own troops. 'I'll look out this side,' he said calmly. 'And Don that one. Move off, slowly. Go on.'

With water topping the wheel hub caps, Freddy put the Land Rover into a low gear and moved away, rounding a bend to descend into a hollow, now being transformed into a rising lake. Three cars were stationary ahead facing us, each on the verge, the highest point. But even there water was up to the doors.

'It's your doing, Stevens. This is the end, I know it. That clairvoyant told me to stay clear of water and madmen.'

'It was you who wanted to see Bernard. We'd have been home by now if we hadn't! Keep driving. Stay in low gear. Go round them.'

'I can't go round them! Look how deep it is!'

'Overtake on the verge then. To the left of them!'

'I'll hit the wall!'

'No you won't. I'll tell you if you're going to hit the wall. Get moving, go on!' Phil waved at Freddy. Freddy uttered a nervous moan and drove on to what would normally be described as a grass verge, but was now a fast-flowing stream. The Land Rover tilted with the banking. 'Is there a ditch?' Freddy cried. 'I'll go in the ditch!'

'No you won't. There isn't one. Promise! Keep straight as you are. That's it. You're okay. That's it. Keep going!'

We trundled past the line of cars, their occupants staring out at us with pale, frightened faces.

'Good grief. Look,' said Freddy.

The car in front had its bonnet up, a man leaning underneath trying to fix something. Hearing the Land Rover approach he withdrew his head to look at us, water cascading from the sides of his trilby hat. Around his neck was a white clerical collar.

Freddy overtook him, hauled the Land Rover back on to the road, selected reverse gear and backed slowly towards the stricken car, stopping a few feet away. Freddy got out of the Land Rover, went to the back, opened the doors and took out a length of rope.

The priest saw his intention. 'Thank God,' he said, in an Irish accent. 'A Samaritan. Bless you!'

In times like this Phil could not sit by and watch acts of heroism taking place without his involvement – especially by Freddy. He clambered out to join him. 'I'll do it, Freddy.' He waded towards the car.

The priest looked at him in amazement. 'Another one? I'm surrounded by good men.'

Phil took the rope to lower himself down in the water, struggling to keep his head clear and, at the same time, feel for a secure anchor point for the rope. 'The poor man,' said the priest. 'Is he an angel?'

'No. He's a masochist,' Freddy said. 'He loves getting wet.'

Phil stood upright, water oozing from every stitch of clothing. Holding the loose end of the rope he sloshed through the water to tie it firmly to the Land Rover's tow bar.

'I just don't know what to say,' said the priest. 'You're a godsend. Bless you, bless you.'

'Get in, father,' said Phil, dripping. 'And make sure the brake's off.'

'Oh it is. It's off, it's off.' Bestowing more thanks and blessings, the priest banged the bonnet down and got back behind the wheel.

Freddy and Phil climbed back into the Land Rover, Freddy muttering the word 'doom' three times.

'Freddy?' cautioned Phil. 'Take it gently. Take up the slack first.'

Freddy obeyed. I heard the creak of the rope under tension. Would it snap? We pulled away, Freddy driving gingerly.

'Well done,' I said, feeling worthless. I followed it up with an instinctive 'What's that smell?' Then I realised. The water had come from manure-covered slopes and possibly from an overflowing main sewer or drain. Windows were opened. Rain splashed inside, but it was preferable to the stench.

Freddy pulled in at a small garage about two miles down the road, where we delivered the priest and his car. He bade us farewell, subjecting us to varied and multitudinous blessings. Freed from bondage, and with the ever-pressing need to escape the foul smell, Freddy gave the Land Rover its head.

Phil, on arriving home, clambered painfully out of the vehicle. 'I never thought I'd say this,' said Phil. 'But I need a hot bath. And a rubber cushion.'

'Hah!' exclaimed Freddy. 'Did you hear that, Don? You see? He's not immortal. He's human, after all!'

Phil slapped the side of the Land Rover and said, 'Well, the old banger came up trumps, anyway.'

'Oh, be'jeez,' exclaimed Freddy, imitating the priest. 'Don, did you hear the good man? After all these years?'

A couple of minutes later he dropped me off, proudly. 'What car could have done what we did today?'

I said I could think of none. It made Freddy very happy.

Freddy entered the house and found Jean in the lean-to, sorting out freshly picked apples. He beamed at her and threw his arms open wide, as if inviting praise. Jean stared at him. 'Freddy? What on earth…you're wet through again! It's twice in a fortnight! What happened?'

'I had to save a priest in a flash flood,' said Freddy, aloofly. 'I had to lie in the water and fix a rope underneath the Land Rover for a tow. Otherwise he would have drowned.'

'A priest?'

'Irish.'

'Where? How? Where was Phil – and Don, in all this?'

'Don stayed inside the Land Rover because it only needed one pair of hands. And Phil had a chill. I made him stay inside as well.'

'Is this one of your fishy stories?' Jean cocked her head to one side. 'Are you sure, Freddy?'

'Yes. You ask Don. Phil said he needed a hot bath. Gospel truth.'

Jean stared dubiously at him, then wrinkled up her nose in distaste. 'What's that smell? Freddy!' She drew nearer and recoiled. 'Oh, you stink!'

'It's hiking. It might be better if I didn't do it any more.'

'Oh Freddy. Off to the shed. Go on with you.' She shook her head. 'I don't know. You do some peculiar things.'

SEPTEMBER

'But it's a long, long while from May to December
And the days grow short when you reach September.
The autumn weather turns the leaves to flame
And I haven't got time for the waiting game.'

Freddy sang softly, gazing down from the hilltop over the canopy of
woodland above Matlock Bath. The leaves, however, were not bursting in
New England 'flame', but instead looked tired in their old England green.

'That's true, we haven't,' said Phil, picking up on Freddy's lyrics. 'We've
no time at all. Whatever it is, we've got to do it now.' He'd been edgy all
morning, frowning and shaking his head, adding nothing to conversation
except giving out grunts and sighs. It was the same every September, of
course, with his birthday looming: 'another nail in the awaiting coffin.'
Normally, Freddy would have a gentle, malicious reply at the ready, but he
was in no mood to chide Phil this day, having heard news that shattered
any lingering notion that our beloved Peak was pure and untouched by the
outside world. It was a river bailiff we had encountered, in the depths of
Cromford, who had given us the awful news. The extremely rare white-
clawed crayfish of the River Dove was no more.

The story, apparently, had surfaced in our morning newspapers, but
none of us had seen it, as we were too busy getting ready for the hike.
I recalled the moment when the old bailiff, Harold Barker, had stood in
the doorway of his river cottage, calling out that the battle continued to
save the relatively unknown fish. At that time, nearly three years ago,
all had seemed right with our idyllic world. Harold, the big man with
his corduroys held up by a wide leather belt, had symbolised a steady
and purposeful guardianship. He wouldn't let us down, we felt, and
neither would the world scientists, who descended annually upon the
Dove to record the continued existence of their prized crayfish. Freddy
had called them 'Gaia men' after Lovelock's theory, which held that
planet Earth was made fit and comfortable by the presence of life itself,
rather than the generally accepted converse. Freddy had neatly summed
it up: 'What he's saying is that living things produce and remove gases
from the atmosphere so as to keep themselves alive.' Lovelock had
posited that life was not sustained by virtue of the Earth having ready

in its possession the life-supporting mix of air and water, but had emerged in tandem with the developing planet. The beauty of the notion lay in its concept of our world as one organism, each living creature within it interacting with the environment in a perfect cycle – a cycle that human beings were doing their best to break with each passing day.

The white-clawed crayfish could hardly compete with the white rhino in nature's beauty stakes, but was equally important. The monitoring of the river had taken place between Hartington and Milldale, the same stretch immortalised by Izaak Walton in his 17th-century book *The Compleat Angler*. In our first year of hiking we had encountered the scientists at Milldale hamlet, watching them step, bare-footed, into the shallow, crystal clear water to lift stones and reveal the presence of these small creatures. The news of their extinction was truly depressing.

'Oh well,' I said, in an attempt to alleviate our gloom. 'Nothing stays the same. Everything changes, given time.'

'That's precisely why we shouldn't be moaning about crayfish,' huffed Phil. 'We're still here. We've got a duty to sustain ourselves.'

'Oh!' Freddy turned upon Phil. 'Do you realise what you've just said? That's the whole point! We can't sustain ourselves if the environment that we sustain – and sustains us – is being poisoned by us!' Normally he would have put such a reproof in a way that raised a laugh, but it seemed inappropriate.

* * * * *

Phil had complained for some time about a pain that he felt in his back and went to see a chiropractor. Freddy said it was proof that Phil was falling apart, his attempts at 'personal bests' being no more than 'personal stupidities'.

Apparently the cause of his problem was named the serratus posterior superior muscle, which, in ageing, can tighten up to cause discomfort. The chiropractor had laid him flat on his stomach, asked him to breathe out, then had thrust both hands down upon his spine, causing it to crack. 'I could actually hear it,' said Phil in the Red Lion. 'I thought she'd broken my back.'

Freddy said he wasn't surprised. 'You're cracking up everywhere. Cracked up top as well. Time to grow old gracefully, Gruppenführer.'

Phil pooh-poohed this and said that Freddy would benefit from a spot of weightlifting, the art of which Phil would happily teach him. He had bought an exercise bench and a set of dumb-bells, saying that it was 'dead easy, progressive and safe'. To his surprise Freddy had accepted the offer, surprising me as well as Phil.

After Phil had diverted from our path to go home, Freddy chuckled to himself. I looked at him enquiringly.

'Bet you I can get Phil to do something, though he knows it's a wheeze.' I looked at him. 'What?' I said. 'A wheeze against him? And he knows it is?' I looked at Freddy in rank disbelief.

Freddy chortled.

The next day we walked into Phil's garden, Freddy licking an ice-cream. Phil, wearing tracksuit bottoms and his red 'para' tee-shirt with its distinctive Pegasus logo, had placed the exercise bench on the patio, a set of dumb-bells at its side. Then, in army-speak, he instructed us to 'listen in'. 'You sit down, like this, back straight.' Phil demonstrated the exercise position. 'And you finish with the palms facing out. Got that?'

Freddy nodded, being careful to lick up the runny bits of ice cream before they streamed on to his wrist, a distraction that served to peeve Phil. 'A pity about Freddy,' he once said to me. 'For years I've put up with his mockery at my attempts to get him fit. You'd think he'd be grateful.' He was constantly irritated by Freddy's oft-repeated theory that the more exercise you did, the less strength you possessed, maintaining that the body was a battery, charged up at birth and run down over 70 years, give or take a few, until you were 'ready for the knacker's yard'. Exercise was 'for the birds,' he always said.

'Freddy.' Phil began toughly but then softened his tone, not wanting to upset his trainee, especially if this was the day when some of the 'right stuff' might be injected into him. 'Remember not to lock out your elbows, alright?'

Freddy nodded obediently.

I noticed Phil hesitate and frown, no doubt thinking this was too good to be true. Since when had Freddy shown any cooperation where physical exercise was concerned? Or was Freddy taking a real interest – at last – in his own physical welfare as the years advanced? If so, then Phil would do his level best to help him. 'Yes,' he said. 'What we've got to do is stop you licking ice cream. Instead lick you into shape.'

As Phil spoke Freddy was examining the dumb-bells, apparently not listening. Phil breathed hard, but again showed restraint, particularly as Freddy appeared to be interested in the apparatus. 'And as you get stronger you do more reps,' he said lightly.

'What are reps, Gruppenführer?' said Freddy, dutifully.

'Reps, Freddy, are repetitions.' Phil stood up with head erect, took a deep breath and flexed his biceps.

'Superman,' I said, grinning.

'Well, he does look fit,' said Freddy innocently.

This drew another suspicious look from Phil. 'Hmm,' he murmured and pursed his lips. He had the feeling – he *always* had this feeling – that Freddy never took him seriously, about *anything*.

'When you're ready,' Phil said, waving at the dumb-bells and trying to sound casual. He didn't want accusations afterwards that he'd forced Freddy into straining himself.

Freddy stood upright and took deep breaths as he stared at the dumb-bells, like an Olympic weightlifter psyching himself up for the 'big one'. 'Bet I could do 20 reps faster than you.' Freddy remained focussed on the dumb-bells, rubbing the palms of his hands together.

'What do you mean you could do 20 faster than me?' Phil put on a tough grin to cover up a sinking sensation.

'Bet I could. A fiver I can beat you. 20 reps.'

'Oh yes.' Phil nodded cynically, staring at Freddy the joker – Freddy, the mental slow bowler, one who would deliver the unexpected ball, one which sprang to the left when you, the batsman, thought it would come from the right. 'You can do 20 reps faster than me. Impossible. It's a wheeze. Come on Freddy, what is it?' He sounded matter of fact, wanting to get rid of any silliness.

'No, I'll time you,' said Freddy, happily. 'Go on, sit down. You do them first.'

Phil sighed. 'What's the point? This is a wheeze, isn't it?'

'No. How can it be? It's a simple challenge. You do 20 reps and then me. Don will take the times.'

Phil was all for packing it in there and then. It was a wheeze. Of that he had no doubt whatsoever. He tutted and puffed and sighed. 'I know you're up to something. It's no sweat from me. I can do them. You can't. So whatever the wheeze is, I *know*. Okay?'

Staring heavily at Freddy, he sat down on the bench and reluctantly picked up the dumb-bells. 'Don't stand near me. And don't say anything. And Don? Watch him. If he does anything funny tell me and I stop. When I say "now" start counting.' He held the dumb-bells in the start position. 'Ok, ready…now!'

I snapped the timer button of the watch Liz had bought me some years ago, but which had never been used in anger until today. 'Five seconds, 10, 20,' I counted as Phil, veins standing out on his forehead, grunted, panted and heaved.

'25…30.'

Phil stopped the exercise, gasping for breath.

Freddy stared over my shoulder at the stopwatch. 'Thirty-one seconds! That's fantastic Gruppenführer!' Freddy shook his head in admiration. 'That's a time to beat. Well done!'

Phil stood upright, chest heaving, took a deep breath and pointed to the bench. 'Go on then. I bet you can't do more than two.'

Freddy sat on the bench, put a hand in his jacket pocket and brought out a miniature set of dumb-bells, in reality an axle with wheels attached, taken from one of his grandson's toy cars, about four inches in width and weighing about an ounce. He pumped his wrist up and down, in jerky fast movements, then stopped. 'That's 20. What in, five seconds?' He raised his eyebrows at Phil in a big grin.

Phil shook his head, threw his hands in the air and went into the house for a drink.

'Absolutely pathetic,' he said.

Although the days were cooler Phil insisted it was not summer's end, anxious to stretch time, as always. Freddy, over a pint in the Red Lion, disagreed, saying that his 'aches and pains' were exacerbated by autumnal dampness.

'Oh yes,' said Phil dryly. 'But you had them with summer dampness and spring dampness. Since when have you never had them?' He picked up a log and tossed it on the fire, still smarting from the latest wheeze.

'Rule 93c.' Freddy nibbled at a pork scratching. 'Every hiker has the right to opt out of hiking if it hurts.'

'Get out of it,' Phil said scornfully. 'I looked up legorophilia. There's no such thing! How you think you can get away with something…'

'I haven't got long,' Freddy cut in, martyred. 'I'm on the way out. I won't be here for much longer. I've hardly used my pension. All hiking does is hasten the end.'

'Cobblers. If you hadn't hiked and listened to me you'd be in a wheelchair or six feet under by now.'

'Ask Jean if you don't believe me.' Freddy knew that Phil would not ask Jean. There were things she wouldn't discuss, not even with him.

'You might do yourself a favour by packing in those scratchings,' said Phil. 'The amount of cholesterol in them...'

'Wonderful,' said Freddy, taking another nibble. 'It's my intention. Can you think of a nicer way to go?'

The next morning Jean gave Freddy a plastic bag and told him to pick some blackberries on the hike.

'I can't do that. I've got a Gruppenführer on my back,' he hotly declared. 'You think Phil's the best thing since sliced bread when he's really one whip short of a slave driver. You should come one day and see what I have to go through. Anyway,' he added. 'I can't walk properly with my hips playing up. I've got to go for an X-ray.'

Jean was unimpressed. 'You can't be ill, Freddy,' she declared. 'You haven't got rid of all the bits of that concrete bunker yet.' She stood in the large Victorian kitchen with its 'servant summoning' bell still in its original position above the pine door leading to the Minton-tiled hallway.

On the worktop were assembled the ingredients for a Bakewell pudding, or tart, one of the gastronomic glories of the Peak. Jean's family claimed to possess the secret ingredient that had made it world famous. She had acquired it via a family connection stretching back to a misunderstanding between a Mistress Graves and her pub serving girl. It was such a prize that not even Freddy was allowed to know the secret. But he had no objection to that. Covert operations always enthralled him.

He sat on the Windsor chair by the Welsh dresser, waiting for Phil and me to arrive in the hike car, gloomily watching Jean assemble the ingredients, butter, eggs, sugar and jam, after which she brought out the white oval pie dish reserved for the ceremony. Then, unlocking an antique corner cupboard, she reached in and drew out a black-painted jar labelled 'do not throw away'. It did not contain almonds, which some people thought the secret. No, they were used merely to flavour the custard before cooking. The secret ingredient was special, so special that, in the event of Jean's unexpected death, Freddy was to be charged with handing the recipe – always kept in the jar together with the secret ingredient – to the family solicitor, who would then place it in a locked vault, to be brought out only when Jean's will was to be read.

Freddy was always amused whenever Ruth or Liz made tentative queries about the pudding, always probing for a clue that might lead them to the holy grail. But Jean never gave anything away. She remained, as always, a giant clam.

On the hike-bound journey Phil was bubbling with his news. 'You'll both be pleased to know that I've done my qualifying cross-country.'

'Oh really, Gruppenführer,' said Freddy. 'You know I hate cross-country. I was the fat boy, remember?'

'Freddy.' Phil tried very hard to be patient. He still felt a remnant of peevishness over the dumb-bells wheeze. 'I'm talking of my *flying* cross-country. I had to fly from Derby to Wickenby. It's near Lincoln. I had to land there, then take off again south to Peterborough. Land there, then take off back to Derby. I had to do it solo.'

'And who did you fly with?' said Freddy and, before Phil could blow up, followed up quickly with, 'but weren't the populations of Derby, Lincoln and Peterborough warned you were coming?'

Phil glanced at Freddy in the rear-view mirror. 'For your information,' he said. 'I am judged by the Civil Aviation Authority, GA division, to be as safe and competent as anybody.'

'But you're old, Gruppenführer. You might collapse at the joystick.'

'Column.' Phil maintained his calm. 'I have a medical every year. I have my blood pressure taken, an ECG – that's electrodes all over my body – tests for diabetes, hernia, eyesight, hearing – the lot. And the doc says I'm as fit as any commercial pilot he checks flying out of East Midlands.'

'But when you were an air traffic controller, people who knew you always booked flights on your day off. Now you're up in the air – on your own – that's even more dangerous. Don, we'll have to do a course in plane recognition so we can take cover when he comes over.'

Phil huffed, but soldiered on. 'For your information I'm buying a Bulldog. Well, a share in one.'

'Which part? Its teeth? Or its legs?' Freddy nudged me with a cackle.

Phil sighed. 'It's an ex-RAF trainer. There's a chap at the airfield who's got one and wants me to share it and go 50-50 on costs. He works all week so I can fly almost whenever I want.' Phil paused as he reflected on the dream, his tone softening. 'And it's still got its RAF markings and the name of the squadron leader who flew it painted on the side.'

'Oh Lord,' Freddy groaned, the spectre of Phil crouched behind RAF roundels alarming. 'When will this horror take place?' he said.

'Soon as I get my licence,' said Phil. 'Two or three weeks.'

'Oh dear.' Freddy pursed his lips. 'You'll be doing personal bests. Like how low you can dive on my house before pulling out. And I wanted to sit out in the sun for my aches and pains.'

'Freddy, I'm not allowed to fly over any settlements below a height I can't glide clear from if the engine fails.'

'Oh cripes,' Freddy said gloomily. 'I can see you now. You'll have a white kamikaze headband round your head, the rising sun painted on it. You'll have a fur-lined jacket and thick goggles on. And you'll grin as you come at me. Hold on,' his tone changed. 'How many seats do Bulldogs have?'

'Two,' Phil said.

'Glory be. There's three of us. We're saved!' Freddy cackled in delight.

'But I can hire a Cessna 182.'

'What?'

'It's got four seats. It's a good weightlifter. It will take your lump Freddy, no problem.' Phil allowed himself a smile.

'It will not take me,' Freddy said. 'I have a medical certificate to prove that I cannot go above 100 feet off the ground on account of my vertigo.'

'You flew to Spain last year with Jean.'

'That was in a pressurised aeroplane.'

And there the matter rested – for the time being.

The hike began at Great Hucklow, not far from Chapel-en-le-Frith, once a lead mining centre, one of a number in the Peak District. Apart from its gliding club the village used to boast 'The Great Hucklow Village Players', a drama group under the direction of L. du Garde Peach. It was quite famous in its day, with performances attended by people from far and wide. The playhouse was set in a converted lead mine building (known locally as a 'cupola' from the lead smelting furnace). Its first production was in 1927, *The Merchant of Venice*. The theatre closed in 1971 due to economic problems.

Freddy coined a new epitaph for hikers as the car drew up in the parking spot. 'I died with my boots on, but I'd already lost my sole.' As he tied up his bootlaces, Freddy glanced up at Phil. 'And no talk of gliders or aeroplanes, over and out.'

'There's no "over and out" anymore, Freddy,' said Phil, grandly, sniffing the autumnal air. 'To acknowledge a message you receive over the radio you give your call sign. Mine will be Golf Hotel India Kilo Echo.'

'What's that?' Freddy said, then looked at me in alarm. 'He just said Golf Hotel India Kilo Echo.'

'Yes.' I said, puzzling over the implication. Then I had it. '*Hike!*'

Freddy nodded ominously and turned to Phil. 'That has to be a joke,' he said.

'Yes,' Phil replied – and added deliberately, for revenge – 'just a small wheeze.' He put on his rucksack, stamped his feet to settle them into his boots, picked up his stick and set off, pleased with himself.

'This is a bad day, mark my words,' Freddy muttered. As we toiled up a hillside to the north of the village he spotted a large bird circling overhead. 'That's a raven,' he said. 'Another harbinger of doom.'

An hour later, as we walked along an east-west ridge, an idle thought struck him. 'Stevens,' he called out. 'You still haven't told us why you stared at the vicar's wife's grave in Eyam.'

Phil turned round. 'Talking to me?'

'It would appear so, leader, as I can't see anybody else for miles. Why? You never go into graveyards on account of your fear of dying.'

'I'd heard there was a mistake on her tombstone, Freddy,' said Phil, grinning smugly. 'You didn't notice it?' There were times when Phil had the better of Freddy and he liked to enjoy them for as long as he could.

'Mistake? What mistake?'

'Her name was spelt wrongly. The stone mason had to make a correction. You could see the chisel marks. Didn't you spot it?'

'Was that all it was?' Freddy sounded disbelieving. 'There was Don and me thinking the Gruppenführer had some human sentiment, never before witnessed, a weakness in accepting his mortality, and all he went to look at was a spelling mistake?'

'Get away!' Phil gave a chuckle. 'It was the poor old stone mason I was thinking about. Imagine how you'd feel if you'd made a mistake on something that had taken you days to make!'

185

'A grave mistake,' said Freddy.

'Exactly,' said Phil, missing the witticism.

'Hmm.' Freddy nodded. 'You know what you are. You're the kind of chap who'd watch a woman being rescued from a burning building and be more concerned about her watch getting scratched.'

Phil shook his stick. 'Look, I read of a poet – can't remember his name – but he said that he went to Wordsworth's cottage in the Lake District. And the only thing he remembered about it long afterwards was – guess what?'

'The central heating didn't work? No idea. Tell me.'

'There was a mistake, just like in Eyam churchyard. Wordsworth had printed the letters of his name, in ink, on his leather school case. But he ran out of space and had to put the 'h' above the 't' right on the edge.'

'Fascinating,' said Freddy. 'The great Wordsworth reduced to a spatial error of judgement.'

'Precisely,' said Phil, not detecting Freddy's note of sarcasm. 'It shows you just how fallible he was. And you tell me he's a genius.'

'Gruppenführer.' Freddy waved a hand about in despair as he tried to think up something devastatingly witty, but gave up. 'You are past redemption. Phil the Phillistine. What can be done with you?'

We followed the edge with Phil waving his stick into a cool westerly. 'You can forget all this arty-farty stuff. Live in the real world! Hike the best country in England. Close to nature. Think of all those poor devils in factories. Your factory Freddy, the sulphur mines. And think about the future, what that holds.'

'Future?' said Freddy, wryly. 'Oh yes, you're 68 next week, aren't you?'

'Talk about birthdays is banned,' Phil snapped. 'Rule 55, para one.'

'So tell us about the future.' Freddy spoke slowly. 'Tell us about flying to Canada.' He gave me a meaningful look.

'What are you on about?' Phil frowned heavily. 'I said nothing about Canada.'

'Come on. You've been on about it for a year now. Oh yes. I have looked at the map. Faroes to Iceland, Iceland to Greenland, Greenland to Hudson Bay. You can make it in a Cessna 182 with long-range tanks. I checked on the internet.'

'Sounds wonderful.' Phil gave me a grin. 'Good of you to do the flight plan. We should try it.'

'No. Let's not. I can see the headlines. "Geriatric pilot crashes in north Atlantic. Last words on voice recorder. This is Golf Hotel India Kilo Echo. A posthumous knighthood would be welcome. Give my dumb-bells to Help the Aged."'

Phil gave a tired chuckle. 'Good one, Freddy. But for your information, I have no intention of dying in an aeroplane or out of it.'

His words would come back to haunt him before the year was out.

* * * * *

Freddy did his best to give the next day's hike a miss. He told Jean he'd been asked by 'Friends of the Peak District' if he could take part in a bird survey in the area.

'Never heard of them,' said Jean.

'Precisely! They asked for Lottery money to get known and they didn't get it. Tomorrow's the day set aside for the bird watch. I can't do that hanging on rock faces by my finger tips and Phil dragging me up.'

'You do say some daft things. Before you use up all your energy you can shift those bits of coal bunker. They're still lying there.'

'They're only tiny bits.'

'But bits. Max is dropping in tomorrow.'

Freddy felt his stomach shrink. 'You didn't tell me. Oh lors.'

'You're alright. It's hike day. He'll be about to go when you get back.'

On the Montague walk that night Freddy told me he now had a suitable illness. His vague complaint of 'aching all over' had been intended as a precursor to something horrible, but he had now found this was a symptom of a disorder in its own right. Fibromyalgia was a condition affecting the muscles, ligaments and tendons. All it needed was a certificate from his doctor. It would be impossible for Phil to deny Freddy with that stuck in front of his face. Freddy said he would proceed slowly with his symptoms, so as 'to avoid suspicion.'

I didn't tell him that however slowly he proceeded, Phil would never believe it.

The next morning, as Freddy was about to call Phil with his medical report, the phone rang.

It was Phil. 'Freddy. I've got toothache. Have you any Nurofen?'

Freddy adopted a cod Indian accent. 'Thank you for your call. To cancel the hike press one. To…'

'Alright Freddy.'

'To deal with the hike leader's toothache press –'

'Freddy! We're hiking. All I need is a painkiller for God's sake!'

'Toothache? Where's the triumph of the will you SS go on about?'

Jean took the phone out of Freddy's hand. 'Phil. It's Jean. Oh, hello Ruth. Sorry, it's Freddy with his usual – what did you say?'

'He's hiking,' said Ruth. 'It's just a painkiller he needs and we're out of them. No, of course he will. You know him.' She glanced at Phil, who was holding his jaw while sipping a mug of coffee. 'He'd hike on one leg if he had to. He'd go on a pogo stick! Hike hopping!' She gave a screech.

'May I have a word?' Freddy put out a hand. Jean handed him the phone.

'Ruth. There's a danger here. No, it's called navigational toothache. Driven mad the hike leader with toothache often mistakes his south for north and sufferers have been known to walk off cliff edges.'

'Aagh!' Ruth cackled in delight. 'Freddeee! You're so wonderful! Phil? Freddy says you'll walk off cliff edges! Aagh!'

* * * * *

The hike started at Taddington post office, from where we trudged through pasture land and old lead mine workings towards Flagg. These two villages owed their presence to the availability of spring water during the late Saxon period. The name 'Flagg' indicates a place where 'turfs are cut', from the old Norse expression 'sod of the earth'.

Phil was in high grump mode on a range of subjects, including train information. 'Why do we have to ask somebody in Bombay about the 10 o'clock from Derby to London? They tell me the price and then I find I could have got it cheaper…' He broke off, raising a hand in a 'stop' manner. 'Listen. What's that?'

A tinny but tuneful melody came from somewhere, but from what distance and direction it was difficult to tell. And there was no human being to be seen on the landscape. Phil turned from looking round to peer at Freddy with a thin, knowing smile.

'What are you looking at me like that for?' Freddy spread his arms wide. 'It's not me.'

'Let's see it,' said Phil patiently, as the music stopped. 'What is it?'
A tinny, robotic voice spoke. 'You walked one point two miles.'
Phil lifted the overhang of Freddy's shirt to reveal a small aluminium
V-shaped instrument clamped to his belt. 'Oh yes. An all singing, talking
pedometer. And who doesn't go in for hi-tech?'

'Evidence,' said Freddy challengingly. 'For my lawsuit. £21 million.
My QC said I've got to get a medical certificate proving what you've put
me through. I ache all over. He thinks I've got fibromyalgia.'

'Fibro what? What happened to legorophilia? Oh don't bother,'
sighed Phil. 'No, come on. What's it really for?'

'I've told you, evidence. I have to take it down to his chambers in
Lincoln's Inn Fields.'

The truth, as usual, was somewhat different. Freddy had told me
that Max was coming. He would almost certainly ask Jean if Freddy
had ever used his Christmas gift. And knowing Max, he would probably
demand proof and read the instrument's mileometer. Freddy had resisted
but finally agreed to wear it for the sake of peace and quiet.

We walked through Flagg village, once plastered with placards of
doom. 'Welcome to Chernobyl' one had screamed. The protest had arisen
from the Government's decision, at the time of the BSE crisis, to turn the
local abattoir into a national cattle incinerator. It was still working as we
crossed the driveway entrance. It may have been cremating far fewer cattle
than in years past, but the chilling boom could still be heard from the
after-burner. I noticed that Phil, as usual, held his breath as we passed by.

* * * * *

Soon the hot days were memories and the cooler air, tinged with the
sweet smell of wood smoke, slowly filled with gatherings of lapwings,
starlings and swallows. The huge migration had begun, part secretly, as
though in shame, the birds surreptitiously filtering southwards at low
level through woods, dales and gardens. Others, including some
thrushes and many warblers and starlings, chose the dark night sky as
their cover for escape. Swallows, like the swifts of August, chose to
brazen their way south in daylight, first gathering squadrons into
groups, then joining up with other formations to create an aerial armada
breaking out over the Midland plain.

Freddy praises the brave birds that refuse to migrate. Among their number was the blue tit, he said, as it refused to panic as soon as the temperature dropped a degree or two. Emitting a characteristic churring note, it showed contempt for those fellow creatures that had departed by enriching its plumage, demonstrating its defiance. 'That's what you should be eulogising about, Gruppenführer. Not your mad physical romps but steadfast courage.' Freddy had written to newspapers and Government departments requesting that a law should be passed forcing farmers to leave barn doors ajar so that swallows could re-enter to nest on their return. Also required would be weed-covered edges surrounding ploughed fields, to keep the swallow population stable.

Phil might complain about the rapid passage of summer, but Freddy had a sensual appreciation of the changing countryside. He enjoyed the sharp aroma of manure mingling with the smell of damp leaves. But there was sadness, too. Autumn was always associated in his mind with Keats. 'Where are the songs of spring,' said Freddy, looking soulfully into the dark days ahead.

But September always gave him great compensation – mushrooms.

As soon as a likely field is spotted on the hike he hurries ahead, plastic bag at the ready, eager to pull up autumn's treasure. His mood is always enhanced by the sight of fungi. And Phil, knowing that Freddy is happy mushrooming, allows it under rule '33a sub-para 1'. It provides 'a spot of relief', he tells me, not that he suffers at Freddy's hands all the time, but there is often tension in case he *might*.

In this matter Phil regretted his choice of fourth hiker. Someone less arrogant than George would have served his purpose. But he knew that if he tried to secure another Freddy and I could justifiably turn him down. The debacle had weakened Phil's authority, something that Freddy had spotted and exploited with his peculiar brand of humour.

I noticed that Freddy had suddenly switched his gaze from the grass to the sky high above his head, attracted by birdsong. I could hear it if I cupped an ear, the trill of a lone and reluctant skylark. But the song soon ceased, having been no more than a brief phrase from its earlier rapturous hymn to high summer. But, being so short and solitary a sound, it was all the more poignant.

Freddy stood in the bathroom staring at the common English house spider, black against the white bath. He had a fondness for spiders and resented anyone who washed them down the plughole. If blue tits were brave, well, spiders had a sense of adventure. The resourceful creature had probably crawled many a spider mile after a bout of mating – September is when they first feel the urge – for a refreshing drink at a watering hole. Freddy made a point of informing people that flushing them away was pointless, as the spider would remain in the neck of the plughole, forming a bubble of air around its body, shielding itself from the torrent of rushing water. It would wait until the enemy had departed, then crawl back into the bath. But Freddy was not the enemy. He picked up his hero in cupped hands and took it to the lean-to, where it might dine on lesser insects crawling over Jean's apple tray.

*****

As usual, on or around Phil's birthday we do the Ilam hike, my favourite and Freddy's number one, as we stop for lunch at the George at Alstonefield. Sue and husband Richard had not retired as we had been led to believe (glory, as it restored some of the lost fabric of our hiking lives) but had stayed on to allow their daughter and husband to take over from them in retirement, whenever that was to be.

It was an Indian summer's day, the trestle table warm to the touch as we ate our lunch and drank Burtonwood ale as permitted on, or around, birthdays. Phil rested his elbows on the table, cupped his head in his hands and stared morosely at a group of teenagers who sat or stood around the green, some listening to a young skinhead teacher as he showed them how to fill in their environmental study papers.

It was the day after Phil's birthday, a time when allowances had to be made for his depression. His mood wasn't helped by watching some of the kids lark about, no attempt being made by the skinhead to get them to pay attention. Phil meditated darkly, as he poured out the dregs from his coffee flask. Since his 65th birthday he had received an annual battery of revolting mailshots. The first, this year, had been the offer of a 'friendly, ecological cardboard coffin'. Then came the chance to take out insurance to guarantee nursing home fees. Added insurance for a longer pension was also thrust at him and, finally, a brochure with illustrations outlining the benefits of travelling upstairs in an inexpensive chair lift. It was, in short, 'damnable and offensive'.

'I shouldn't worry,' said Freddy. 'You're going to die soon, aviating.'

Phil made a clicking sound with his tongue and stared into his beer. The resident pair of Muscovy ducks approached, eyeing Phil carefully, at which he desultorily tossed them a few crumbs from his lunch box. The whole world was batty, he'd earlier complained. It was now impossible to catch a bus or a tube train without some twit offering him their seat. It never occurred to him that kindness was being shown. Phil was more concerned with his self-esteem. Why couldn't the idiots see what he saw in the mirror every morning, a fit and biologically 50-year-old? He was prey, along with many of his generation, to feeling like an alien in his own land. 'And what about that school where they said the lessons weren't "interesting enough"? The kids were bored.' We had all laughed at this. 'Shouldn't lessons sometimes be boring?' he said. Shouldn't education prepare kids for the real world and not a socially engineered society? Hadn't the current lack of discipline in schools started with the dropping of traditional methods for the new 'child-centred' teaching of the 1960s, all stemming from the 'let it all hang out' flower power children of post-austerity Britain? Phil had written down a whole host of facts supporting his thesis. 'Everywhere you look,' he said, 'duty and responsibility have been replaced by selfishness and rights-obsessed individuals.'

'It's not all bad,' said Freddy. 'We've had some progress. Compared with when we were young there's a lot of caring going on.'

'Yeah,' said Phil. 'Caring for criminals. You think there's progress if a cannibal starts using a knife and fork.'

Freddy gave a chortle. 'Good one. Did you rehearse that?'

'No I did not.'

'Good,' said Freddy. 'I tell you, humour is your only salvation.'

But Phil, who felt no humour at all, said nothing and resumed his gloomy surveillance of contemporary youth. He envied them one thing, their age. They had no need of time-stretching, their years extending ahead into infinity. A verse from the poem *For the Fallen* came to him, for what reason he had no idea:

'They shall not grow old,' he murmured. 'As we who are left grow old: age shall not weary them, nor the years condemn. At the going down of the sun and in the morning, we shall remember them.'

'What's that Gruppenführer?'

But Phil fell silent and watched a spotty youth hiss nastily at one of the Muscovy ducks as it waddled towards him. 'Do you remember what that school kid said here last year?' asked Phil. 'This is a National Park so where are the swings?' He gave a contemptuous 'tch.'

After lunch Freddy irritated Phil by stopping to examine wild flowers and lecturing him on them. 'That's a hemp agrimony. And look, there's a small tortoiseshell butterfly on it. Can you see?'

I left the footpath to look, but Phil remained where he was. He took an acorn from his pocket, one he'd picked up earlier. It was smooth and shiny and had come from an ancient oak that was still green in leaf. When Freddy and I rejoined him he was still staring at it. 'That tree's 300 years old if it's a day. If it can do it, so can we. We're all in it together. Spaceship Earth, Freddy, what you keep going on about.' But Freddy wasn't listening. He'd spotted treasure ahead and shot off with his copious bag at the ready.

'You see,' Phil said, contemptuously. 'Look at him. Legorophilia, my backside.'

On Freddy's return Phil recalled that, earlier in the month, Freddy had sung a verse from *September Song*. 'You missed a line, though. *The days dwindle down to a precious few*. Well, every day's precious,' continued Phil, his jaw jutting out. 'We've got to make more days, stretch more time.'

On the way home from the hike, Phil fell asleep for a while, nodding and grunting, a wisp of grey hairs bristling out from under his red beret. Then he came awake and began to rail against receptionists and shop assistants who called him 'darling', a term used in our locality for addressing either an infant child or a senior. He quoted from Dylan Thomas, the only poem that he remembered. 'Rage, rage against the dying of the light.'

On the last hike of the month, circuiting Chatsworth House, Phil returned to the great subject of time and immortality. That morning, he said, his electric toothbrush had once more been deployed in his on-going check on time: time perceived, compared with time measured by the clock. The toothbrush always stopped briefly after two minutes of use, reminding the user that operations should now be terminated, lest it wear away too much of the tooth enamel. During the last two years Phil had produced a graph, illustrating his findings.

Every month he would test himself. Each time his idea of two minutes *as experienced* fell short of clock time. Extrapolated, applied to his overall life span, it reinforced what he'd maintained years ago, that he was losing one third of his life.

Freddy said, 'You should read Jared Diamond's book, *The Third Chimpanzee.*'

'Don't tell me a chimp's lost a third, Freddy.'

'He says if you're a westerner, and you own a Mercedes, you service it to prolong its life. Correct?'

Phil nodded, giving his cautious approval.

'Right,' Freddy continued. 'But if you're in Papua New Guinea there's no point. Before cars can be serviced they're wrecked in crashes. No amount of servicing is any use. Your genes do the same thing. They ditch the ageing body and produce new ones through procreation. It's illogical that you can service your brain and heart and liver for ever.'

Phil grunted. 'Well, that's why we have cryogenics. And stem cell technology. I told you. It's a matter of clinging on until we can get our hands on them. Just because it's traditional to regard ageing as a dying process it doesn't mean we can't reverse it. The medical profession's only concerned with disease-based models. Now what we've got to do is eat beans, dark fruits, vegetables and drink red wine or beer and we can get there.'

'Get where, exactly, Gruppenführer?' asked Freddy.

'To long life! What else? Do you get your daily dose of cod liver oil, both of you?'

'Yes,' said Freddy, in falsetto German. 'Vee haf your orders mein Gruppenführer, but I am at vaw mit you! I refuse to be poisoned!'

Phil had handed us each a list of food to eat, marking all the dark fruits and vegetables, including broccoli, avocado, prunes, blueberries, blackberries, kale and spinach, all of them producing polyphenols, strong anti-cancer agents. He had no idea that Jean was already dosing Freddy with these highly effective juices, including nuts, but Freddy enjoyed Phil baiting and so continued his tease.

'If you don't take them the hike will fall apart,' Phil snapped.

'Wonderful!' exclaimed Freddy. 'What could be better? No hiking! If it's freedom from Nazi rule then its ice cream and doughnuts for me!'

Deep down, hidden beneath the repartee, Freddy had concluded that his fears were confirmed. He saw himself as a condemned man, forced to walk until he dropped. It was all the more necessary to push on with his 'get-out-of-hike' strategy. He told me he'd every justification now there was no doubt that Phil was completely nuts.

*****

We sat on a bench overlooking the great Chatsworth House, our backs to the Hunting Tower built in 1582 for Bess of Hardwick, ancestress of the Duke of Devonshire. It was originally used as a viewpoint for ladies observing the hunting dogs as they worked the surrounding woods and fields. At our side were three cannon, each facing outwards, all of which had taken part in the Battle of Trafalgar.

Phil looked upwards as he heard the drone of a light aeroplane. 'That's a Lycoming engine,' he said. 'Can't mistake it.' Then he spotted the aircraft passing southwards over the valley. 'There it is. And I do believe it's a Cessna 182 or 172. Difficult to tell.'

'Polluting our atmosphere,' said Freddy, biting into his Cornish pasty.

'Polluting?' Phil was indignant. 'I'll tell you what polluting is. It's the Tourist Board. Do you know what they're putting on? The first ever Peak District Walking Festival.'

We knew of it. It had been advertised in the local press. Set amid the peaks, moors and gentle rolling valleys of the High Peak, Derbyshire Dales and Staffordshire Moorlands, the two-week festival was to run from next April to May and offered a huge programme of guided walks.

'We should sabotage it,' said Phil, tapping his stick on the ground. 'They've given up Dovedale to trippers with ice cream vans and built-up footpaths, now they want to give up the rest of the Peak. Doesn't this worry you, Freddy? You of the flora and fauna? All those yoicks tramping everywhere?'

'The Peak doesn't just belong to us,' said Freddy.

'It's only for a month,' I said.

Towards the end of the hike we passed through a wood. The only birdsong we heard was that of the robin, marking out its territory for winter. In August its twittering sounded wistful. In September it was more rousing. Leaving the wood by the footpath we heard the drone of another light aircraft. Phil, looking up, watched it on its way north.

'Hmm,' he murmured thoughtfully. A little later he said, 'Yes,' as though satisfied with a secret idea.

On the way home, having thought carefully about how to secure Freddy's cooperation, he gave up any notion of being devious and came straight out with his plan. He announced that one of the tasks set by the CAA prior to issue of his licence was to fly solo to – and identify – a small airfield sandwiched between Chesterfield and Sheffield. He proposed to fly the approach via the Derwent Valley, making Chatsworth House a way-point en route. He said he would like us to be there, to take a photograph of the aircraft passing over. It was set for Thursday, which was hike day. Freddy shouted 'Yippee!' when he thought he would have a day off.

Phil had a finger raised. 'This is not an excuse for a lay off. The hike must always be done if any personnel are fit for the purpose, rule 1a.'

'That's fine, Gruppenführer,' said Freddy. 'I shall come along with my ground-to-air missile and bring you down in accordance with rule 17c.'

'Rule 17c?'

'Any hiker caught flying, instead of walking, shall be shot down. You should like that. No old age and infirmity. You go out a crashed hero, what you really want. What are the photos for?'

'I've got a nephew in Kamloops who'd like to see them.'

'Kamloops?' Freddy's eyes narrowed. 'That's in Canada!'

'Yes, the Rockies.'

'There you are!' exclaimed Freddy triumphantly. 'There he goes again. Canada! You see, Don? You see what we're up against!'

'Freddy, you have nephews all over the Peak. So I can have one in Kamloops.'

'Prove it!'

Phil said his word was his guarantee. Freddy was unimpressed.

That evening Freddy and I took Montague on a stroll by the old mill stream, bathed in the red and yellow rays of the dying sun. 'Canadian Rockies,' said Freddy, darkly. 'Notice how he drops facts, or so called facts. They settle in your head for a bit and then he goes for the kill. If he's got a nephew there I'm a...'

He broke off as Montague suddenly dashed into the hedgerow with an explosion of crackling twigs, then emerged empty-pawed. 'Silly dog,' said Freddy and then fell into deeper thought. 'Trouble is,' he brooded, 'Jean's his fellow conspirator. She'll want to go with us. She likes flying. Don? Whatever happens, I want your promise, no flying with Phil to Canada in a light plane. Yes?'

I nodded. 'Only on scheduled.'

'What? That means hiking with him in the Rockies! No way! Canada is *verboten*!'

Freddy grinned mischievously. 'Next week's hike. No rushing around, no Gruppenführer with a whip. I'll take the camera so I can snap wild flowers. We can nab an ice cream at the car park. We'll have a pint in Bakewell! Luxury hiking. And then the *coup de grâce*.'

Freddy made the guttural 'ack-ack' noise of a gun. 'Gruppenführer shot down. Hiking partners witness tragedy. Then celebrate.' He let out a low whoop.

The next Thursday morning Phil downloaded the latest nine-hour aviation weather forecast from the Met Office website. It promised a base cloud level of 3,000 feet, a gentle westerly wind and visibility of 20 kilometres, ideal for flying.

Freddy met me with his camera and an air band receiver in his rucksack, the latter lent to him by Phil in the hope we would hear him talking to East Midlands Approach. This call would take place, he said, when he was over Carsington Water, a reservoir en route, close to Wirksworth and Matlock. The time we would hear his call – and Phil gave us the East Midlands frequency of 134.17 VHF – would indicate he would be approximately seven or eight minutes from his ETA over Chatsworth.

All the way north, winding and diving through the soft green hillsides of the White Peak, Freddy hummed and sang. Ten minutes later we arrived at the car park on the southern side of Chatsworth Park. It was 10.30am. Phil's ETA was around noon. Freddy was all for buying a Magnum ice cream there and then, but I persuaded him to wait. The treat should come later, I said, and Freddy reluctantly agreed. 'We'll celebrate when we've shot him down,' he said. 'I've got the SAM missile in my rucksack. Won't take five minutes to assemble.'

We walked the first section of the hike in a southerly direction to swing right past the 'Russia House,' a building where you might expect to meet Dr Zhivago, then through a small copse to enter into the many acres of sheep grazing land with Chatsworth House a mile away. As on other visits, its numerous gold-edged windows were struck by the sun, so that even the stonework seemed to glisten.

Freddy took out the air band receiver, switched it on and fiddled with the knobs. But all we could hear was a steady crackle.

Trapped in a valley, as we were, was not the best of places for VHF radio reception. Freddy looked at his watch. 'He should be at Carsington in two minutes. If I can get this thing to work.' We listened to white noise and crackling sounds for five minutes. Then suddenly came a tinny male voice. 'East Midlands Approach. Golf Alpha Romeo Foxtrot Bravo is overhead Trent at 2,300 feet. Request Flight Information Service.'

There was a pause. Then the air traffic controller gave information which we now heard Phil reading back. 'Q-N-H one zero one eight Golf Hotel Bravo.'

We looked at each other. It was impossible to tell if it was Phil's voice, but the word 'Trent' referred to a radio beacon of that name on the western side of the Carsington reservoir. It fitted Phil's briefing. Freddy took out his camera as we walked down the sloping parkland towards the house.

Staring southwards down the valley there was nothing to be seen except a hawk circling high above the hillside on our left. But wait… Freddy touched my elbow and gestured towards the southern horizon. There was a dot in the sky, framed between the eastern and western hill sides. I put a hand to the side of my face as a blinker to shield my vision from the bright sun. Minutes passed. The dot grew larger, unmistakeably an aeroplane. It was high winged as well, a feature of a Cessna. As it drew closer I could see it was white, with red markings – exactly as Phil had described. Then came the engine note, that of a Lycoming, a steady-pitched growl. Freddy got ready with his camera. The Cessna lost height and fell below the eastern skyline, heading for the great house. Freddy planted his feet apart to ensure balance, aimed the camera and waited. The aircraft levelled out and passed over our heads.

Freddy clicked the shutter button, once, twice, three times, then lowered the camera to watch the Cessna waggle its wings. It then went on in a northerly direction.

'Good Lord,' said Freddy, in awe and trepidation. 'That was him.'

On the journey home the implications of what had occurred were still sinking in. Phil was a pilot. It wasn't a joke any more.

'What we mustn't do,' said Freddy, 'is panic. What he's done is amazing. We have to grant him that.' There was a pause and his voice dropped a level and became almost sepulchral. 'But it is the end of civilisation as we know it.'

I laughed.

'What are you laughing at?' cried Freddy, his voice half strangled with a wild laugh. 'It's doom. Can't you see! Doom! Wait till I see the doctor! Fibromyalgia, here I come!'

OCTOBER

Freddy stared at the list stuck magnetically to the fridge door. One of his daily orders issued by Jean was printed in capitals, followed by an exclamation mark. 'What's this?' he asked, pointing to COAL BUNKER!! 'I've done it.'

'No, you haven't,' said Jean, chop, chop, chopping away at apples. 'It's still there, in bits, under the shed. What a mess.'

'But you can't see them.' Freddy looked aggrieved. 'They're hidden.'

'But I know they're there, Frederick, and that is too much.'

'No it isn't. Bertrand Russell said a hippopotamus wasn't in the classroom if no one ever saw it. He said…'

'That's stupid. I've seen it. I know it's there.'

'But if it's covered up with that tarpaulin?' Freddy gave a helpless gesture with his hand.

'Frederick,' Jean sounded firm. 'Aunt Cynthia will *root*.' She dropped a handful of apple slices into the fruit juicer. 'She always goes rooting. You know it's the first thing she does when she gets here. She remembers where everything was from every last visit. You know she does. And she'll tell Max and they'll have a snigger as they always do. It's awful.'

She turned to Freddy with a grimace. 'They do laugh at you, you know. And I don't like it. I'm fed up with it.'

'Well don't invite them then!' Freddy exclaimed.

'Don't be stupid. They invite themselves. Why do you rile them both? Why? I don't get it at all.' Jean wrinkled her snub nose and blinked a little.

Freddy stared gloomily through the window. A light rain had begun to fall, darkening the white slabs of the patio. Aunt Cynthia and cousin Max would arrive in a couple of weeks for a short stay, dreadfully long by Freddy's reckoning. He made a mental note to inform Phil that this was the best way to stretch time – invite the evil enemy. Soon they would rise from a well of darkness to wrap their dreadful selves around him like a voluminous black cloak. Jean was right. Aunt Cynthia would check if the coal bunker had gone, as she had done each year ever since the arrival of North Sea gas. Freddy had described her to me, a crone with a long, thin nose, wearing perished weeds of green and blue chiffon and large pendulum ear rings of cut glass that tinkled as she moved. There she would go, sniffing around the place, like an old fox. She would, almost certainly, find the rubble and then come inside to make one of her caustic comments about Freddy's total lack of responsibility.

Freddy yawned, a sign of stress. The terrible two were so evil that upsetting them could be considered the duty of any upright citizen. 'A consummation devoutly to be wished,' he murmured.

'What did you say?' Jean dumped more bits of apple into the juicer and then carried on before Freddy could answer. 'I don't want them sniggering behind your back.' She turned to give him a light, pleading smile. 'Just do it for me? Please, Freddy?'

Freddy sighed. His magnificent lottery wheeze of long ago had led him into a wonderful year in which he believed he had set himself free. But Aunt Cynthia and her gross son, Max (Freddy described him as a dead ringer for Martin Bormann, Nazi party chief) had returned by the following Christmas, making snide remarks and drinking litres of wine that he and Jean had hauled all the way from Bordeaux and which had very nearly been confiscated by Customs. It had been galling to watch the pair glugging away at his hard-won bottles.

As the juicer machine started its wail Freddy stepped out of the back door. It was true what Jean had said, of course. Aunt Cynthia believed, without any doubt, that he was insane. If she found out about his art of onedownmanship it would give her all the proof she needed that he was one pip short of an orange. How could he explain to Jean that he was really a secret agent, fighting an underground battle on behalf of humanity? He couldn't, of course. His was a lonely path, as with all missionaries.

He stood at the back of the garage, gazing at the covered mound. He decided that the single breezeblock that trapped the tarpaulin was insufficient. He bent down to drag another breezeblock from under the garage floor, and heaved it on to the cover for more security. He rubbed dirt and grit from his hands. It was high time he took the initiative again, he decided. Why not go on the attack? He had the armoury, the place and the time. The lottery wheeze had taken place long ago. Wasn't it time he had some recompense for all the misery they'd inflicted upon him since then? It wouldn't all be revenge. Most of it would be pure onedownmanship. He decided to go to his upstairs study and meditate on his peculiar art.

* * * * *

The Wye Valley, viewed from the high viaduct of Monsal Head, three miles north-west of Bakewell, is a most spectacular rural scene. It is this view that provides the most popular Peakland image chosen to impress tourists in calendars, glossy magazines or guide books. The Monsal hiking and biking trail, of which the viaduct is part, follows the line of the now defunct Cromford and High Peak Railway, which opened in 1830. Freddy, a steam buff, had demanded this hike as payment for the aerial photographs of Phil's aircraft in flight. Today, Freddy insisted we stopped to take in its majesty. Where engines once chuffed, now cyclists pedal and hikers walk. As we gazed out over the landscape a man walked towards us, then stopped nearby to lean against the viaduct railing and gaze down the valley. He looked about 80. He wore a black waistcoat with a shiny back, heavy grey trousers and polished boots. He possessed a body that spoke of manual work in his younger days, still square, compact and broad-shouldered. We exchanged greetings, after which he volunteered that he was an ex-steam engine fireman and had been on the footplate when the last train ran on the Cromford and High Peak Railway on 30 April 1967. For 137 years the line had carried goods by wagon 'across the top' to the Peak Forest canal at Whaley Bridge, from where the rest of the way was made by water haulage to the markets and factories of Manchester. 'Aye, I were on the last train, right n' all.'

'Incredible,' said Freddy, enthusing. 'I'd have given anything to have been on it.'

'Aye, it were pretty sad though,' the man said. 'My name's Charlie by the way.' He stuck out a hand and as I gripped it felt the coarse and roughened skin, betokening years of toil. 'First time I've bin 'ere for years. I'm from Halifax, stoppin' with my daughter. She's in Bakewell.'

Charlie quickly dispelled the idea that being a fireman was just a job of tossing coal into a firebox. Steam pressure had to be regulated ahead of its need, he said. The adjustment of the fire height was critical. Air flow had to be carefully adjusted. Anticipation of steam demand was vital. 'Aye,' he continued. 'But yer could have yer back froze while yer front burnt. Mind, yer could fry an egg on back of shovel in that firebox. And we did. Toasted the bread and fried the egg.' He gave a chuckle.

'It was hauling goods,' said Freddy. 'So you never got any thanks. No passengers.'

'No, not until last one. It were last day in April, 1967. Yer couldn't get a ticket fer love ner money. Every last soul wanted be on that last train. I were treated like a king. Everybody wanted to shake me hand. Everybody. I got home and I cried a bit. Aye, it could be scary, mind. There were a brake man once 'ad to jump for 'is life when wagons ran off down Sheep Pasture. Took off at bottom at a 'undred and twenty mile an 'our, wagons goin' so fast they jumped right across canal. Aye.'

'You miss those days,' commiserated Freddy.

'Eh? Oh no! I don't. It were graft. Yer couldn't in them days do what folk do today, walk it, this wonderful track. Ain't it grand eh? Just look out there.' He cast a hand indicating the view. 'Ain't that summat?'

We agreed, then said our goodbyes, leaving Charlie staring into the valley.

'Sometimes,' said Freddy, 'you, Gruppenführer, can't be blamed.'

'For what, Freddy? Blamed for what?'

'For taking me hiking. I would never have met that man, would I?'

'Freddy,' said Phil, with a grand air. 'That's the first time you've thanked me. That will get special mention in my hike report.'

It prompted me to ask Freddy about 'the meaning'. 'Any latest news?' 'Yes,' said Freddy, 'I've come to nothing.' He gave me a grin. 'What if they're right, scientists?' said Freddy. 'What if life's a dream or a computer programme? We're not here.'

'Oh Freddy,' sighed Phil. 'You're not here, we know that. You never are. Can we talk about something more interesting?' He sighed and called lunch break.

As Phil and I took out our bum warmers Freddy, the Puritan, blew out his cheeks. 'You two,' he groaned, as he always did on sight of the NASA-like material. He shook his head in sorrow as Phil and I produced our stainless steel, hi-tech flasks, as we had done every hike for the last three years.

Phil carefully opened his lunch box and poked with a plastic fork at the assembly of raw carrot, celery, cherry tomatoes, avocado and kale, but delayed speaking until he had poured out his coffee. When he spoke his voice was a degree higher in pitch (it always rose whenever news of great import was about to be announced). 'Something happened yesterday that changed my life. Come on you two. What was it?'

Freddy, who knew what it was, refused to give an inch. 'You've come to your senses and abandoned the hike and we're all going to grow old gracefully and die without being stuffed with stem cells or packed in ice at Grimsby Docks.'

'You know what it is, Freddy. I told you.'

'Hah. You've turned your life round. Instead of being mad and daft you're now daft and mad.'

Phil sighed heavily. 'It was my skills test. You knew that.'

'Was that skills in putting up bivvy tents? Oh I know! You put a ship in a bottle and you managed to squeeze yourself out.'

'No.' Phil took a deep breath, about to lose patience.

'Something to do with an unnatural act?'

'Flying.'

'Precisely.'

'I'm trying to tell you,' Phil snapped. 'I am now waiting for my pilot's licence to come through. I've got my PPL.'

'PPL, what's that for? Prattish pompous lunatic?'

'It stands, Freddy, for Private Pilot's Licence. I get it by post in about three weeks. I think I did pretty well. At my – chronological – age?'

There was a pause. Freddy sniffed and bit off a chunk of his Cornish pasty. It was quickly devoured. Freddy, as a child, had three bread-snapping brothers and so had developed a cast-iron stomach and rapid-fire eating to keep up with them. He pouted his lips and sipped some coffee. 'Well, you'll be shot down before you can do any damage because they've already installed it,' he said in a casual tone.

'Installed what?'

'The early warning system in the village. For when you come over.'

Phil shook his head, 'I know you don't want to fly with me, but...'

'Really?' Freddy's eyebrows lifted in mock astonishment. 'A most remarkable deduction Holmes. From what quarter did that evidence arrive? Was it you Don?'

Phil was careful to moderate his tone. 'Freddy. Okay. You won't fly with me, but my instructor would take you up this weekend. He has 20,000 hours of flying in his log book. He used to fly jumbos.'

'Yes, well, I suppose those big ears make good wings. But isn't the trunk a bit of a drag?'

I laughed briefly, which annoyed Phil. But he kept his patience. 'I'll pay for the flight. All you do is sit back and enjoy it. If you don't like it I swear I will not bother you again.'

Freddy bit into an apple. 'There is always some machination dedicated to my downfall. You never do anything without an ulterior motive and on those grounds I warn you that anything you say may be taken down and used in evidence.'

Phil put up both hands as a disclaimer. 'I promise no more talk of flying if you don't like it. There's no plot. All I'm asking is you give it a chance. That's all.'

'Hmm.' Freddy grimaced and packed away his flask. 'I know all about Gruppenführers, remember. Every little move is planned with Teutonic efficiency. I can tell you now the answer is no. *And* Aunt Cynthia and Max are coming this weekend and Jean certainly won't let me off playing aeroplanes. So there.'

'I thought you hated Max and...' Phil was interrupted by the London Symphony Orchestra playing *La Donna e Mobile*. Freddy, all fingers and thumbs, unclipped his mobile from his trouser belt. 'Hello. Oh hello! Yes... oh wonderful! Great news!' He turned to us. 'Graham's won the right to appeal against kicking his Trabbies out. He wants to show us something.'

* * * * *

An hour later we arrived in Middleton. Graham was there to greet us with his usual cry of 'Feldschlossen!' We sat in the living room in front of a log fire as a video ran of a recent *Midlands Today* television news programme. As the newsreader talked a cartoon showed Graham's head poking out of the roof of a Trabant, as large as the car itself. For Midlands television news to take the trouble to caricature him reflected his growing status. He had taken on the might of bureaucracy. The little man with a fleet of communist two-stroke bangers had triumphed in adversity.

'You're a folk hero,' chuckled Freddy.

'Well.' Graham got up to switch off the video then bang out his pipe in the chimney hole. 'I didn't set out to be anything. All I wanted was to keep my collection. And they're still hidden in the back garden. Nobody can see them. They don't smell or smoke or make a din. So what's all the fuss?'

Freddy noticed an envelope with an address printed in block capitals. 'One of your fans?' He pointed to the letter.

Graham picked it up and handed it to him. It was addressed to 'Mr Trabant, Middleton, Derbyshire'. 'You see,' Graham said. 'That letter would never have reached me six months ago. Now I'm famous.' He jogged Freddy's elbow. 'Eh, do you think they'll make a TV series out of me?'

More laughter. The log fire crackled in the wide fire basket. I stared into it, lost in reflection. When I was young Britain had lots of eccentrics. An art lecturer, at Borough Road Teacher Training College, waxed his hair into a spike reminiscent of a Kaiser helmet. He found his way on to the front page of *The Daily Express* by plodding barefoot along Bournemouth's beach, selling his paintings, which he kept tucked under his arm. There were many such 'odd men out', beloved of the newspapers. The British film industry thrived on eccentric characters. But, of late, I had come to the conclusion that the mass media and the 'wiring up' of the population by means of computer and mobile had flattened out our British individuality.

Graham pulled the video out of its player. 'So what do you think?' he asked.

I said I thought it significant that a regional TV broadcaster with a low budget should create a moving cartoon as visual back-up to a news item. It had worked and was pleasing. BBC Midlands Television now had a newsworthy eccentric, with an ongoing news life. There seemed no doubting that they banked on future stories about 'Mr Trabant'.

'I might become a character in a kid's comic,' said Graham, lowering himself back into his deep leather armchair. More laughter as Freddy and I relaxed, taking in the pleasant odour of Dutch aromatic tobacco. But Phil rose to his feet, time impatient, anxious to be on the move.

'Freddy? Don? Come on, we're behind schedule.'

As we made our last goodbyes, Graham reminded us that his 'victory' was only partial. His next – major – step was to appeal to the High Court, even though the Peak Park Planning Board would oppose it. We left him with a final wave of the hand to plod down towards the

River Bradford. Halfway down the rough track Freddy stopped suddenly, hushing us with a raised hand. We could hear birdsong.

'Look!' hissed Freddy in delight, pointing. 'Look, see there? It's a nuthatch.'

A bird walked down a tree trunk head first. It was blue-grey on top and had a black stripe on its head and a long black pointed bill. 'It's off to find acorns and hazelnuts.' The sight pleased Freddy. On the journey home he soon fell asleep. But, before he did so, he said that today had been a special day. He wasn't in favour of praising any hike. All of them were essentially painful but, in the general order of things, the hike of this day would go down as, well… 'tolerable'. Phil was very pleased. As soon as he arrived home he opened the safe and took out his hike reports to add notes on today's hike, writing 'Freddy grateful – at last.' This prompted him to think. As he thought he doodled a little and, without realising it, saw that he'd drawn the outline of a Cessna 182 aircraft.

*****

The 'season of mists and mellow fruitfulness' had begun. Across the Peak the first leaves had begun to drift from the trees, though the horse chestnuts bravely refused to wilt by turning their leaves into a challenging red or a cautionary yellow. Along the hedgerows bramble leaves became crimson and black bryony was lit up by brilliant necklaces of bright red berries.

As the countryside began to change, so did Phil. He became more purposeful, striding out with lengthier steps. With cooler weather he intensified his physical training, aimed at breaking his 'personal bests'.

Freddy was merciless in his expressed disbelief. 'Stevens, you're pushing 70. That's enough exercise for you. You want to do my type of early morning exercise.'

'Oh yes,' said Phil, dryly. 'What's that – sitting down?'

'No. I go up, down. Up, down. And then the other eyelid.'

Phil laughed, coughed, shook his head. 'Freddy, do you rehearse these jokes?'

'No, I've told you. All I have to do is look at you.'

The first of Phil's targets was the ascent of K9 – his code for Shining Tor, the steep hillside opposite the river bailiff's house in Mill Dale. He had failed in last year's attempt to beat his record time by two seconds, which, in his book, meant he had aged. Oh the calamity!

Determined to reverse this awful performance he had trained fanatically, racing up his staircase every day for the last three weeks, 100 times per session and wearing the carpet at such a rate that Ruth forced him outside to do hill running. One morning Freddy looked out of the window and watched Phil labour up the steep incline, then jog slowly downhill to repeat the climb again and again. After an hour of this exercise Freddy went outside and held up a white sheet of paper, on which was written, in felt-tip, 'Come in number 1, time is up.' Phil liked being called 'number 1', but objected to 'time is up', as he knew that Freddy meant he was 'past it'. Most of his training was carried out in the garage, employing his 'devil's machine' in various roles, stretching, pulling and testing each sinew and muscle. His diet of carbohydrate and lots of starchy vegetables and wholegrain bread was supplemented with cereals and pasta. Baked potatoes got the nod instead of chips. Some vitamins had been cut back in favour of more dark fruit. Ruth, laden with them, bumped into Jean in Tescos. Explaining the excess of fruit in her trolley, she screeched with laughter.

The hike from Ilam to Alstonefield – which would take in Shining Tor – passed quietly. Freddy said little, preoccupied with the arrival the following morning of 'Mistress Dracula' and 'Monster Max'. He still had no cunning plan with which to 'onedown' them.

We left the footpath outside the bailiff's house at Mill Dale. Freddy and I crossed the pack-horse narrow, hump-backed bridge to stand on a grassy patch by the old mill house. I dumped Phil's rucksack on the ground and, with Freddy, watched our stalwart prepare himself. Phil looked up at the 150-foot ascent, spat on his hands, took deep breaths and flexed his knees.

'Just look at him,' scoffed Freddy, then shouted at Phil. 'Stop looking at it, get on with it! Don's cold and I'm bored!'

Phil ignored him, mentally working himself up to a peak of aggression. Then, clicking his stopwatch, off he went, scrambling and flailing his arms while stabbing his feet into the grassy hillside.

'Good grief,' murmured Freddy. 'Totally, 100 per cent, raving loony.' He turned to me. 'But what do we do for fun if he dropped dead?' He cupped his hands to his mouth and shouted. 'Gruppenführer, we don't want you dead just yet!'

Phil continued his assault on the hillside. But now he was slowing down, using his hands as well as his feet to scrabble to the top. As soon as he got there he rose, like a sprinter from the blocks, to launch himself at the marker stone, which he'd placed there years ago to act as his finishing line. As his hand touched the stone he snapped his stopwatch and collapsed, lowering his head to the ground, his body heaving. After counting 30 seconds in recovery mode – fitness, he said, was all about recovery time, the faster it was the fitter you were – he got to his feet and took his pulse rate over a period of 15 seconds. The result was pleasing. He walked back to the edge to stare down at his troops. First raising two Churchillian fingers in victory, he spread his arms wide to exalt in his glorious achievement. Then he took his pulse rate again. It had lowered by 15bpm in less than 30 seconds. Brilliant.

'How old are you now then?' Freddy asked as we joined Phil at the summit, handing Phil his rucksack. 'Don't tell me, 52.'

'No, I'm still 50!' Phil protested. 'That time's better than three years ago! I haven't aged at all.'

At Milldale hamlet, shortly after lunch, Freddy took off his boots and socks and stepped into the babbling, shallow river, to carefully turn up stones to see if the white-clawed crayfish really had disappeared, as stated by the world scientists. They had.

As he poked about in his rolled up trousers, a solemn-looking couple in their 50s came to sit on a bench and, in unison, placed blue tartan rugs neatly over their laps. Sitting ramrod straight, without so much as a flicker, they watched Freddy return to dry land.

Later, as we walked into Dovedale, a raven passed overhead, muttering to itself. 'Definitely doom,' said Freddy, glancing at his watch. 'D-Day minus 19 hours,' he sighed. And still no plan of action.

* * * * *

'Frederick, have you been in there?' Jean pointed to the corner cupboard in the kitchen. 'Somebody's moved my Bakewell pudding jar.' It was D-Day minus one hour.

'Not me,' said Freddy. 'How do you know anybody's been in?'

'I know because I always put the jar in a certain way.'

'Mice?' Freddy grinned nervously.

'Mice? I'm not joking. This is serious. It's secret Freddy. The recipe is secret.'

'I know that.'

'Frederick?'

'What? Scouts honour.' Freddy opened his arms in a gesture of pure honesty.

Jean sighed. 'I can't bother with this. They'll be here in an hour. Try to behave.' Jean opened the back door to call Montague. He had to be kept on a lead while Aunt Cynthia and Max were around. They had a dislike of animals. What they didn't know was that he had an even greater dislike of them.

The moment Jean stepped out of sight Freddy shot out of the kitchen, dodged through the hallway and out through the front door, guilt chasing him like the devil. He had lied, of course. But his motive had been altruistic, not espionage. He would never betray the secret. All he had done was open the cupboard and handle the sealed jar. Was there anything he could use against Mistress Dracula and Monster Max? It had been an instinctive act as he searched for something – anything – he could use in his battle with the people of the night. Thinking logically, he wondered now why he'd done such a thing. But a drowning man grasps at straws. And that's what he was, about to be drowned. He would walk, he told himself, until he found an answer.

Phil was driving past the Post Office when he saw Freddy walking towards him, head down, looking troubled. It gave Phil an idea. He waited until Freddy had passed by without noticing him and then set off.

Moments later he parked outside Freddy's house, walked up to the front door and pulled the black knob that caused the Victorian doorbell to jangle.

Jean came to the door. 'Oh, Phil, come in. Freddy's around somewhere. Freddy?' she called upstairs. Jean waited, but no reply. 'Well he's not in the garden,' she said. 'I don't know where he is. Do you want a coffee?'

Freddy, oblivious, passed the church and then walked down the footpath at the side of the cricket field, deciding to walk the old railway line – yet another trail – until he found the answer. He left the footpath by a stile which led on to the lane. Hands in pockets, a picture of gloom, he stopped suddenly to stare at the ground. He remained like this for a minute, then resumed his walk, passing by the old gamekeeper's cottage to reach the small railway bridge surrounded by tall, closely planted, pine trees. At the side of the bridge was a sloping set of wooden steps that led down to the trail. He stood at the top, hesitated, then faced the truth. The lottery wheeze had been top class as it had brought out the worst in the diabolical duo and had even forced them to suck up to him. How could that wheeze possibly be equalled? It couldn't. At this miserable conclusion, he turned back.

Meanwhile, Phil and Jean were swapping anecdotes over cups of filter coffee.

'Oh, I love flying,' said Jean. 'My father was a navigator in the war. And I flew round Blackpool Tower once. Five pounds, that's all it was. And the queue! So long. My father thought we were idiots for giving the jet engine to America. And he was always saying how precious small airfields were.'

Phil nodded in sympathy. 'General aviation the Government doesn't understand. Not interested. And we've got British Airways saying their pilots aren't initially trained in light aircraft. Well, lots of BA pilots were first PPLs from airfields like ours.'

'That's right. Oh yes.' She nodded her head. She and Phil were soulmates when it came to flying.

At the other end of the village Freddy sat on a chair in my kitchen. With Liz out shopping he had found in me a ready counsellor. 'I just can't face them,' he said, sighing deeply. He spread out his large hands to waggle his fingers in a show of muddled thinking. 'I just don't know,' he grimaced. 'What I really want to do is escape the horrors. But how do I do that?'

I thought about it. 'You could pretend you're ill and spend the weekend in bed,' I suggested.

'No. Jean would see through that.' Freddy shook his head in dejection.

On his way home he noticed that the silver birch trees in the locality of the cricket ground were now dotted with yellow leaves. It reflected the way he felt, melancholic. As he turned the corner at the top of the hill he saw Jean waving away Phil in his car.

'I'm glad you've come,' said Jean, poised over an enormous black jam kettle on the stove, a family heirloom. 'I've got a little surprise for you.'

Freddy stared at her. 'Surprise?' he said, suspiciously.

'Nothing less. I know how you hate Cynthia and Max coming. So I'm letting you off for the day.'

Freddy blinked hard. 'Letting me off for...'

'Stop repeating everything I say and listen,' said Jean, not unpleasantly. 'Phil's just left. He called to say he's bought you a half-hour flight at the airfield. Then he wants to show you round. He said it would take the rest of the afternoon. I said yes, you would go. I'll tell Cynthia that it was booked a long time ago. Well, look pleased about it!'

A fruity, sweet smell of apple and blackberry juice rose from the jam kettle as Freddy dumped himself on the chair by the Welsh dresser, stunned, caught 'between the devil and the deep blue sea.' Of course he would grab at any excuse to get away from the dreadful pair but – do it by flying? Freddy pondered. It was obvious that Jean and Phil had banked on his dread of Aunt Cynthia and Max exceeding his fear of flying. But, he told himself, if he chose flying today then he lost his moral ground when it came to fighting off Phil's attempts to take him to Canada.

Jean read his thoughts. 'You're not flying with Phil today,' she said. 'It's an instructor. So you'll be safe.' Realising what she'd said she added hurriedly, 'You'd be safe with Phil, course, but... you know... just to give you confidence. I should look sharp. Max rang on his mobile. They're making better time. They'll be here in about 20 minutes.' She bent down to give him a smiling kiss. 'Now off you go. Go on, off. Let me concentrate.' Jean stirred the bubbling concoction with a ladle. As soon as all the sugar was dissolved, she would keep the jam at a rolling boil until the setting point was reached. Jean was a perfectionist when it came to making jam. 'And a black belt at landing me in it,' thought Freddy.

'Well? Are you going or not?' Jean sounded exasperated.

Freddy shook his head, looking mournful, and got to his feet. Anything was preferable to spending the afternoon in the company of the monsters from Market Harborough. Problems with Phil and Jean could be dealt with later. And he'd make that 'later' infinitely long, if he was given a sniff of an opportunity.

He drove to the airfield where Phil sat in the club hut wearing a blue peaked cap and a leather flying jacket, a goatskin replica of that worn by US Army pilots in World War Two. The gold wings and green laurel wreath of a current PPL adorned his chest. He greeted Freddy enthusiastically. 'Knew you'd come,' he said. 'But there's a change of instructor.' Freddy was introduced to a slim, dark-haired woman in her 30s called Sam. She had a pretty face and wore a white shirt with epaulettes and black trousers and rose from a table, popping the last remnants of a sandwich she was eating into her mouth. She shook Freddy's hand. 'Have you flown before?'

'Only to Spain and Italy,' said Freddy.

'Sorry, I meant in a light aircraft.'

'No.' And then he added, 'I don't know anything about them. In fact I'm a bit nervous.' Freddy tried to think of something else to say to help spin out the time.

Sam smiled warmly and said 'ah,' in sympathy. 'Don't worry, you'll be fine.'

Freddy felt a wave of charm embrace him. As Sam led the way out to the aircraft he thought it might not be so bad after all.

He was taken to a Cessna called 'Alpha Charlie', a small aircraft with high wings, standing by a red fuel bowser. The pre-flight 'walk-round' was unsettling. Split pins had to be in place. Were nuts in their right places? Were the brakes leaking fluid? Had a spider got into a torpedo-shaped tube under the wing? He found it difficult to concentrate, his mind occupied by imagined events two and a half miles away. Around now the 'terrible two' would be sitting in the kitchen drinking coffee, after which M. Dracula's 'walk-round' of the premises and garden would take place. Any faults found would be alluded to in comments intended to shrivel, depress and generally undermine Freddy's ego. He tried to shut out the images and concentrated on helping Sam to apply his safety harness. Her proximity, her thigh touching his in the narrow cockpit, and the gentle and solicitous manner in which she talked reduced him to a state of feeling happily drugged. There was a brief stab of fear as they tore down the grass runway, but they were quickly aloft and soon he found himself searching below for familiar landmarks.

On landing, Phil was waiting. As soon as Freddy had disentangled himself from his headset wiring and safety harness, Phil stood under the wing, keen to query the result of his investment. 'How was it?' he asked.

'Okay,' said Freddy lightly, never giving Phil any encouragement.

'How did he do?' Phil asked Sam.

'Fine. He held the controls. Kept it straight and level. You enjoyed it, didn't you?'

'Oh yes. I did,' said Freddy and smiled – he hoped – enigmatically at Phil. Back at reception he received his signed 'I flew a Cessna aircraft' certificate, thanked Sam and was about to give himself up to Phil for the rest of the afternoon, when he remembered something. 'Flu jab,' he announced suddenly. 'It's today.'

Phil spoke scathingly. 'Flu jabs? That's for geriatrics who're knackered. You don't want a flu jab.'

'Yes I do. I'm old. And it doesn't matter how fit you are because it's free. So why not have it? I promise I'll come back here with you, if you come with me for my jab,' Freddy said. 'I may have a reaction. I might need somebody to drive.'

Phil grunted and tutted and looked irritable. 'It's against my religion, you know that,' he said. 'A flu jab? Never. I can fight flu, any time.'

Ten minutes later Freddy and Phil walked through the double doors of the village hall to join a small queue at a desk manned by a portly woman with sheets of names in front of her. She looked up at the next customer. 'Name please?' As she ticked the name off her sheet, Phil looked around the large room at the abundance of grey heads, all of them chinwagging away. 'What are they all sitting round for?' he whispered, as he gazed at the appalling sight.

'In case they have a reaction,' Freddy stressed. 'I told you. They have to sit for 10 minutes after their jab.'

'God, in case they collapse. I can't stay here!' He turned in panic. 'Not with my flying jacket on!'

Phil spent the next 10 minutes outside the hall watching a squirrel run to and fro along a wooden fence. He puffed and sighed in impatience. He had great plans for his men. Adventure was in the air. It was corrupting and demoralising to have to spend time with defeated and decrepit wrinklies.

'There's a new rule,' he told Freddy as he came out of the hall. 'Rule 19d. No hiker shall indulge in flu jabs without permission of the navigator.'

'And there's another one,' said Freddy. 'Appendix C1. It states quite clearly that no navigator shall connive or plot with a hiker's wife to force that aforementioned hiker into the air.'

Phil gave Freddy an odd look as they walked back to the car. Five minutes later Freddy crept sneakily into the house by the front door, closing it oh so gently. He intended to bunk off to his study and stay there in hiding for as long as he could. He tiptoed to the stairs to begin his careful climb. The lower step creaked.

'Is that you, Freddy?' He froze at Jean's voice coming from the living room. Drawing a deep breath, he steeled himself to enter, forcing a smile for the awful encounter.

There they were, Mistress Dracula, her thin and bony body coiled up in his personal armchair, and Monster Max, gut bulging above his trouser belt, a roll of fat hanging over his collar. They smiled at him in disdain. 'Hello Freddy, wasting our money on planes now, are we?' droned M. Dracula with a twisted smile.

'Oh no,' jumped in Jean. 'A friend bought him the half-hour flight. We didn't pay.'

M. Dracula ignored her. 'And what's that mound of stuff I saw at the back of the garage?' The sardonic smile widened on her thin, red lips. 'What's hidden under that tarpaulin? Eh? I hope it's not that coal bunk...'

'Explosives,' said Freddy suddenly, without thinking, staring in disgust at the three black hairs that grew out of her chin.

'What!' Max launched himself to the edge of his chair. 'Explosives!'

'Yes,' said Freddy, his mind madly racing. 'I was digging and found some old grenades, er... mortars... bombs...'

M. Dracula and M. Max looked at Jean for a reaction. She nodded quickly. 'Yes. Freddy was digging at the bottom of the garden and found them.' She held her breath.

'Have you told the police?' asked Max sharply.

'Yes.' Freddy spoke abruptly. 'But the Bomb Squad are out on an exercise and said to leave them where I'd put them.' He hesitated. 'Till Monday. Nobody must even look at them.'

Max held Freddy with a dark, piercing look, then turned to Jean. 'It's rubbish, isn't it? He's having you on.'

'No,' cut in Freddy. 'They told us not to tell anybody.'

'In case of panic,' added Jean, still holding her breath.

'Sounds fishy to me,' said Aunt Cynthia, looking suspiciously at Freddy.

During the weekend it was surprising the number of walks demanded of Freddy by Montague. I joined him on one of them, walking round the lanes in mellow sunshine. The blackthorn was now a watery yellow, the hawthorns either purple or red. Freddy was surprised to find one bush still displaying a lone white flower at this late date, even though it was in a sheltered spot. 'The last flower of summer,' said Freddy, in genuine sadness. He looked at his watch. 'The grotesques go in three hours,' he added. Just then the London Symphony orchestra struck up. Freddy drew the mobile from his pocket and answered it. 'Hello? Oh Graham!' He broke off to listen. 'Oh dear.' He gave me an aside. 'Graham's had another enforcement order.'

On his return home Freddy announced that he had 'a friend in need' who required immediate help. He would be away for three or four hours and was thus saying farewell and wishing the vampires a safe journey home. 'Friend in need?' Aunt Cynthia echoed sarcastically. 'Money grabber. Stay clear.' Then she cackled. 'Somebody's got your number. You know what you are, Freddy me lad? You're a softie,' she grinned. 'It'll be somebody after your money. Tell them to take a running jump.' She chuckled even louder as Max joined in with a sour laugh. 'Friend in need!' They were still laughing scornfully as Freddy shot out of the back door and into the shed. In the corner, a dark place, he lifted a bunch of oily rags to reveal his personal box of chocolates. After the dreadful duo had paid their last visit, he had found four of them missing. He opened the box and counted them – 14, correct. He popped one into his mouth in relief.

Graham was in surprisingly good humour when we arrived in Middleton by Youlgreave. We sat outside in the autumnal sunshine drinking tea and reading the enforcement notice. It was from the planning authority, giving him three months to remove 40 of his 49 Trabants or 'face further legal action'. But what about his leave to appeal, which was granted? 'That's still there,' said Graham. 'I'm going to the High Court. Good news is the planning authority says they won't challenge it. Too costly for 'em. But what do I do with this order? I can't just ignore it.'

We cogitated and ruminated. More tea was drunk, plus a glass each of Feldschlossen. Then Graham started to chuckle. 'Just remembered,' he said. 'I told the planners last week I'd not got just 49 cars. I said I had

533! I told them over the phone. Chap at the other end screamed "What!" Then I told him they were in my model collection!'

Freddy had a bright idea. 'What about this?' he said, causing us to quieten down. 'Doesn't it all revolve around the word "storage?" They use that word, it's here, look.' Freddy showed us the relevant line in the notice. 'They say you're storing cars. But you're not, are you?'

It took a little time for the subtle implication to penetrate. 'You mean,' said Phil, 'he's not storing them?'

'No, he's not,' said Freddy. 'He's keeping them. He owns them.'

'Hah,' said Graham. 'Not a storage depot. Good one Freddy.'

'Good one,' we all agreed.

* * * *

October drew to its darkening end. Soon we would be in the lonely, misty and cold world of November. Phil continued flying on good days, mainly around the Peak District, circling Chatsworth again and then further up the valley, to view the great dams of Ladybower, Howden and Derwent. But local flying soon began to bore him and he thought ahead to the longer days of the following spring. Phil remained optimistic about Freddy. 'We'll reel him in sooner or later,' he confided in me. All it did was make me feel guilty; I was a fellow conspirator, guilty by association. I did, indeed, welcome the idea of the three of us taking to the air. But I was not keen on Phil's obsession with Canada. The dangers and logistics of such a trip were legion and not suited for elderly mortals, but for experienced young pilots in a well-equipped aircraft. Could he be serious? Yes, in his own world. But flying was done in the real world and it was beyond imagination to conceive the journey as a possibility. And, surely, official bodies such as the Civil Aviation Authority would step in and prevent such foolhardiness. Or would they?

But one project, mentioned by Phil, did catch my imagination – flying to Le Touquet for lunch and back. That sounded possible – and fun.

But all our hopes and expectations for whatever we sought as individuals were thrown into disarray by a discovery that I made in November.

NOVEMBER

Phil sat in the conservatory, its windows plastered in wet leaves from yesterday's gale. He picked up his knife and fork, drew in a deep breath and exhaled in great pleasure. Facing him, as on all hike days, sat the big breakfast. Bacon and eggs, combined with black pudding and sausage – plus Derbyshire oatcake – was the main course, followed by a grand buttered muffin laced with honey, kept warm on the kitchen Aga. A mug of Ruth's killer coffee steamed at his side. All considerations of calorific consumption and arteriosclerosis were set aside this one day of the week. On the other days his breakfast was fit for a monk, a tiny amount of porridge and fruit.

The phone rang. It was 8.03am, Freddy of course. 'Gruppenführer, do you realise that we shall encounter severe fog today?'

'What fog? Where? I see no fog.'

Freddy was unbending. 'The fog is in the Peak, where I suffer pain and anguish, that's where. You can't see a hand in front of you.'

'Who can't? Now let me guess. A nephew in Bakewell, perhaps?' Phil smiled cynically. 'Freddy, you must come up with a new fib. This one's so ancient it's fossilised.'

'Hah, got you!' triumphed Freddy. 'I haven't got a nephew in Bakewell. It's my maiden aunt in Parwich, so there. She telephoned…'

'No, Freddy,' Phil interrupted. 'You have no aunt other than the one in Market Harborough. I've seen the forecast. What bit of fog there is won't trouble us.'

'I do not wish to walk in thick fog. We shall get lost and being lost with you is pain.'

'Freddy, will you let me eat my breakfast?'

'Be it on your head, as always. My solicitor has your address.'

'Okay, Freddy. See you in court. Now off you pop. Oh, you're driver today, don't forget.' Phil switched off and piled into the meal with gusto. Could he be happier? He doubted it. He was younger, fitter and, now, a fully fledged pilot. But, he reminded himself, best not to toss ideas around without caution. His plans, if they were to succeed, had to be concrete and unassailable. It was a case of 'slowly slowly catchee monkey…'

An hour later we had just cleared Ashbourne with a shake, bump and rattle of the antique Land Rover, when Freddy braked and came to a halt. He took out from his pocket a plastic bag, got out of the vehicle, opened a field gate and walked towards a horse chestnut tree.

Minutes later he returned with a bagful of conkers, each of them still shiny after spending a month in the damp undergrowth.

Phil blinked hard. 'What are you up to?'

'What am I up to? Stevens, you pledged your troth to this. Last year, remember? Time to face up to your obligations. Both of you.' Freddy climbed into the driver's seat.

Phil and I looked at each other. Then it came back to me. A year ago Freddy had asked us to join him on a visit to Ashton in Northamptonshire, where the world conker championship was taking place. It was an international event, with Russians, French and Germans, as well as the English, competing to see how much of the opposition their individual, heroic single conker could destroy. But Freddy had found no enthusiasm for the pilgrimage from either Phil or myself. I had been too busy writing my book and Phil had pretended that he'd strained his right wrist, the one that would have to be flexed sharply in delivering a conker blow. In reality, of course, he was secretly undertaking his pilot's course. Freddy had moaned at our lack of spirit. In his childhood, he said, he had a 'beauty of a conqueror' with over 400 victims to its credit. Why couldn't we indulge him once in a while, given that he risked life and limb each week walking over wild and dangerous places, purely to humour a mad navigator?

As a pacifier Phil and I had offered to attend the competition the following year, this October. But again we had managed to cry off, displeasing Freddy. If he was incapable of looking jaunty – oh, those peculiar, sagging trousers – there was a confidence about him, almost a challenge, in the way he walked back to the Land Rover, perhaps not 'John Wayne' exactly, but an indication that he had a wheeze in mind, some fitting punishment that would have something to do with his bagful of conkers.

Phil frowned at him. 'What are you up to?' he asked, yet again.

'You'll see. You won't escape retribution,' said Freddy aloofly, placing the bag under his seat. He drove away, our destination Longnor, a village five miles south east of Buxton.

Half an hour later we pulled on to the small, cobbled market place, dating back to 1225, since then becoming famous for its numerous fairs, all of which had their origin in mediaeval times. The rugged, stone-built market hall has a character of its own and is now a thriving craft centre, but it still exhibits the ancient table of tolls for buyers and sellers, covering everything from livestock to eggs. The village, in the 18th and 19th century, had its own beehive-shaped lock-up. The hard-working community boasted brick and cheese factories, saddlers, eight boot and shoe makers, two mills, two bakeries, a candle factory and quarries producing lime, millstone grit and lead.

What other English village could surpass Longnor's list of trades and professions? In its heyday there had also been several butchers, masons, wheelwrights, tailors, auctioneers, blacksmiths, joiners, a surgeon, a gentleman's outfitters, a registrar of births and deaths, a druggist and a watchmaker – varied skills by which to service a town, let alone a village. Phil noted, with relish, that oatcake making had been an important cottage industry in Longnor. Rarely is he interested in local history, but study of the origin of Derbyshire oatcakes, clearly, is an exception.

Freddy's interest, in contrast, lay in the relatively large number of inns and beer houses that had flourished during the 19th century, today whittled down to four. 'You, Gruppenführer,' said Freddy sitting on a bench in front of the market hall and struggling with his socks and boots. 'Coming from Munich, as some of you Huns do, should be keen on ale. Why aren't you dressed in lederhosen and conducting drinking songs instead of being a purveyor of pain?'

'Not in hiking hours, Freddy, rule 26b. And leather shorts are banned.'

'Appendix B,' quoted Freddy.

'Appendix B not permissible,' said Phil, stamping his boots. 'Navigator's privilege. Onwards.' He pointed his stick towards a narrow stone passageway that led off from the market place.

'You see,' puffed Freddy, as we plodded up the incline. 'I'm already in agony. I'm not even run in. If you had my pain, Stevens, you'd stop!'

Phil gave a derisory cackle and put on a spurt, waggling his elbows with the effort, pain not his enemy, but his friend. 'No pain, no gain,' was his motto. Hadn't he proved that he could withstand almost anything? Sir

Ranulph Fiennes was his hero, a man who had run seven marathons in seven days on seven continents after a triple heart bypass operation.

Freddy shouted after his charging leader. 'I invoke Appendix D. You didn't know we had an Appendix D, did you? Do you hear me, Stevens?'

But Phil ignored him. He was in serious training for another attack on two 'personal bests', the ascent of K7, as he termed a hillside near Hartington, followed by K3, his code for Thorpe Cloud, at the entrance to Dovedale. He hoped to have them both in the bag by Christmas.

'Oh the fascist buggerance,' grumbled Freddy, bringing out from his anorak pocket a hunk of chocolate wrapped in silver foil, his instinctive response to Phil's reckless behaviour. As he savoured his Thornton's special he fantasised about a suitable demise for his tormentor. 'You see, Don,' he said. 'Killing him's no problem. He's always in front so we can get him from behind. We could drop him in the Bottomless Pit. The Peak's full of holes in the ground.' He sighed. 'Pity they haven't got gibbets any longer. We could have strung him up, his boots round his neck, as a warning to others.'

'The best way to knobble him,' I said, 'is to sabotage his aircraft.'

'Hah!' Freddy seized eagerly on the idea. 'Yes! Poetic justice. They tried to blow up his Führer Adolf on a plane, didn't they? We'll succeed where the plotters failed. What do we call it? Operation...?'

'Downfall?' I suggested.

'Hmm, what about "Operation Nutcase?"'

I laughed, always amused by Freddy's ability to counter physical distress by plunging into fantasy. The thought of Phil's untimely loosing from earthly shackles fired Freddy's imagination and provided him with a degree of comfort on the wearisome climb to the ridge top.

We found Phil staring out over the Dove valley, misty green in its wintry panorama. 'Look at that,' he said sharply, pointing to a hilltop in the distance.

'Don't give me that,' huffed Freddy. 'You do not like views. It's a diversionary tactic, designed to free you from my retribution...'

'No, over there!' Phil almost shouted, keeping his finger pointed. 'That's a Lancaster bomber, for God's sake, look!'

We followed his gaze. An aircraft, black against a sky of slate grey and deep lilac pink, flew slowly over a northerly ridge. It had four

engines and had twin upright tail fins, unmistakably a Lancaster.
'Listen!' hushed Phil. 'I can't hear it, can you?'

'No,' I said. 'I can't.'

'Look,' Freddy pointed to a flock of jackdaws cackling overhead.
'That's bad, very bad. Jackdaws mean death.'

'What are you on about?' Phil stared at Freddy. 'Whose death?'

'Yours. They only fly over mad people. You won't have time to get
your affairs in order.' He took off his rucksack. 'As it's unlikely you'll
reach home alive, I propose a coffee break, now.' He sat down on a
rock, dumping his rucksack in front of him.

'We've only been walking 40 minutes, Freddy. You know the 10 minute
rule, either side of the hour.' Phil tried to look and sound reasonable.

'Yes, I do,' said Freddy. 'But there's another rule – I can't remember
its number but it certainly exists – "any hiker who suffers pain and
distress on any section of the hike can call for a break after 40 minutes
of the first hour."'

'Call, yes. But not order.' Phil gave one of his irritating smiles, for a
moment reminding me of George. 'The only person who gives orders is
the navigator. Come on, let's go.'

'No.' Freddy remained stubbornly seated. 'This is the Alamo. I draw
the line here.'

Phil paused. 'Freddy, this is mutiny, again, you know. Action can be
taken against…'

'Gruppenführer,' broke in Freddy. 'If you observe the sky you will see
that there is a storm brewing. All the more reason to have coffee break
now – in the dry.'

'Hmm.' Phil stared at Freddy. Then, surprisingly, he took off his
rucksack. 'Alright, this once,' he said lightly. 'Never let it be said the
navigator doesn't humour his backsliders occasionally.'

'Oh yes?' Freddy looked at Phil in deep suspicion. 'Why are you
being nice?' He unscrewed the cap of his flask. 'What torture is in store
now? How do we pay for this privilege, in blood?'

'Freddy, you've got your way. Now drink your coffee and eat your
banana and be thankful you have a lenient navigator.'

'Thankful,' echoed Freddy. 'Since when did a condemned man thank
his executioner?' He continued with his low-grade grumbling, talking
more to himself than Phil. But he still downed his banana in seconds.

After the break Phil led us down a footpath that led to the base of the hillside, at the top of which the Lancaster had appeared. Freddy, deliberately unobservant and muttering, went through a catalogue of barbaric practices he had been forced to endure under Phil. 'But,' he said, his voice becoming loud and clear. 'There will come a time when justice will wield its trusty sword. The night of the long hiking sticks. That's when your regime will end, Stevens. Stabbed in the back by a long, pointed hiking stick.'

Phil turned off the footpath to climb towards the hilltop. Freddy began to follow and then, realising, stopped to look around. 'Hold on,' he said in a warning tone. 'This is not right.' He raised his voice. 'Stevens, I am not following you up K10. The way back to Longnor is not up there. It's down here. This is a hill too far. Are you listening to me?'

But Phil continued the climb and then stopped, his head raised towards the skyline, exclaiming. 'Good grief! It's back!'

Above the ridge the Lancaster bomber, the mainstay of Bomber Command in World War Two, made another appearance. In silent majesty it turned through 180 degrees to disappear back over the skyline.

'That's impossible,' said Phil. 'Lancasters are noisy.' It was an understatement. One Merlin engine makes a noise, a deep-throated roar – witness the Spitfire fighter's single engine. *Four* Merlins firing in unison, as fitted to the great Lancaster bomber, would make such a howling wail as to raise the hairs on the back of a pig.

'It's another sign, Stevens,' called out Freddy. 'Another sign. Collect your stake, crucifix and garlic, or die.' Then he fell silent, standing still, a frown on his face as he turned to look at me seriously. 'It *was* a Lancaster, *wasn't it?*' he stressed. 'We did see one?'

I nodded. Freddy nodded. We shared the same thought. Most local hikers had heard the stories of doomed aircraft in these hills. A number had crashed during World War Two. The Dark Peak, to the north, has been dubbed a 'Bermuda Triangle' as 50 air crashes occurred there in just 30 years. Tales of the aeronautical paranormal were legion all over the Peak. Was this the apparition of one such wrecked aircraft? And a ghost of a machine would not make any noise, would it? Intrigued, I plodded after Phil, up the metalled track that was hardly a road, but able to take light vehicles. Freddy followed, panting and coughing with the effort. We reached the hilltop to find Phil, his back towards us, in conversation with a couple of grey-haired men, one wearing a padded quilt jacket and jeans, the other a combat jacket with numerous pockets. Three cars were parked in a row near the edge, their boot lids open. A much younger man, dressed in a huge sweater and woollen hat, stood in the centre of the hilltop, a small black box clutched in both hands. The Lancaster had been flying downwind but we now watched it turn 90 degrees back towards the plateau at a height of 50 feet, descending steadily, still not a whisper of a sound coming from it. At a height of 20 feet it levelled out, entering the flare. Touchdown was completed with immaculate precision and the model quickly rolled to a standstill.

We approached, admiring the 12 foot wingspan and the realistic gun blisters protruding from the black-painted fuselage. Along its side were painted small Nazi crosses, each one representing fighter aircraft shot down by the gunners. This aircraft's number was 'AJ-G for George', named after Wing Commander Guy Gibson's Lancaster that had led the raid on the great dams of Germany in World War Two.

'We thought it was a real bomber when we first saw it,' said Phil.

'Yes, you would,' agreed the enthusiast, nodding his head eagerly. 'You had nothing to scale it against. But you must have known it was only a model when you couldn't hear its engines. Didn't you?'

Freddy looked wryly at Phil. Our leader hesitated. 'Oh yes, it was obvious. You'd hear four engines a mile away!' he said with a false laugh. Freddy gave a sigh. As we took our leave he gestured towards the model. 'Why aren't all aircraft like that?' he said. 'Silent with electric motors. No pollution.'

On that regretful note we thanked the members of the High Peak Model Aero Club and left their High Edge site, descending the way we had come. 'You should see our Spitfire perform,' the Lancaster man called out after us. 'Come and see that fly. That's something special.'

Freddy waited until we were out of earshot to give Phil a wigging. 'You didn't know it was a model,' he said accusingly. 'You thought it was real.'

'Well it obviously wasn't a spectral aircraft was it? What else could it have been, if not a model?' Phil marched on, sound in the knowledge that he was the least likely of us to believe he'd seen a ghost. Freddy tried to think of ways of unsettling Phil further, but gave up. Needling the Gruppenführer was occasionally a failure.

Later, near lunch time, we walked down the hillside towards our precious dell. Freddy was in happier mood as the minutes passed, progressing ever nearer to the stream that tumbles under the tiny packhorse bridge, reached by an old drovers' way of flat stones and cobbles, edged by watercress, marshy flowers, trees and an old stone sheep dip. This perfect place is like stepping back a millennium. Some years ago we had sat here for lunch when the idyll had been rudely disturbed by the arrival of a scrambler motorbike. Today, we were met by the equally disturbing sound of childish giggles and shouts. An entire class of school children occupied the bridge and the banks of the stream, in the company of two teachers, a man and a woman. They chomped at their bags of crisps and drank litres of Coke in the spot where we hoped to sit in silence, having lunch and saying little, absorbing the peace and tranquillity of an age-old place that bore no disfigurement from the hand of modern man.

'Lors,' groaned Freddy. 'I like kids – one or two. But this…!'

We greeted the teachers and fled the scene, crossing a stile to walk along a muddy footpath, broken occasionally by boggy ground. Time passed, our progress slow and laborious as we carefully skirted what Freddy described as 'the Grimpen Mire'. He had a permanent scowl on his face. 'I should be eating my Cornish pasty. Letters will be written,' he said. 'A good Gruppenführer would have checked with the National Parks school programme.'

'Beyond his remit,' said Phil.

'A good Gruppenführer,' repeated Freddy, 'has the welfare of his men at heart. He should always have a fall back if the place for lunch has been compromised. The only reason I undergo pain is to eat my Cornish pasty. That's all that keeps me going. This grave error will be logged in my personal diary and may be used in evidence at your court martial.'

'Freddy,' said Phil. 'All diaries are personal.'

'Not like mine though.' Freddy nodded his head to emphasise the point. 'Mine is full of evidence, dates, times – as well as torturous and life-endangering events inflicted by an insane leader. Oh yes, your time will come. Justice will prevail. It may not be a hiking stick. It may be something far worse – aaargh!' Freddy's right boot, placed on what had looked like firm green ground, sank into glutinous, sucking mud.

As he pulled his foot free, the boot remained in the grip of the bog. Phil and I broke out into spontaneous laughter. Freddy was seriously unimpressed as he dug into the mud with his hands, while trying to balance on one leg. He failed.

'The claim now is for £8 million – and rising. Oh lors, my hands are frozen – and look at my sock,' he said in anguish. 'I do not like hiking. I shall never, ever allow you to navigate me anywhere in the world.' Freddy found a dry tuft of grass, sat down on it, opened his rucksack and took out a roll of kitchen paper that he kept for emergencies and began to clean out his boot. Then he turned his attention to his foot, peeling away the slimy sock. 'Oh, smell that,' he said in disgust and dropped his head on to his hands. 'My life as I knew it is over. I am prisoner of the foulest terror known to man,' he murmured.

'Freddy, the good news is that the bog ends here.' Phil sounded jolly and sympathetic.

'Do not humour me!' Freddy cried.

'Okay, but it's dry the rest of the way. Come on, put your sock back on again. It will get warm again as you walk. Soon be over. You'll be home in no time.'

'What?' Freddy raised his head to stare at Phil. 'I shall not be home for hours. I demand a bus or a taxi. A helicopter. Call mountain rescue. All at your expense. Tell them that I am one-legged and dying. Tell them…'

'Yes Freddy, we'll do that when you're on your feet.'

From overhead there came the cackle of jackdaws and a flurry of wings, drawing our gaze. The birds were performing aerobatics, riding the wind, chattering 'jack jack jack', toppling madly, then sweeping, milling and racing towards each other in astonishing arabesques and subtle changes of wing angle, all in a truly avian Battle of Britain.

'Oh my God,' Freddy said, miserably, staring upwards. 'Look at them. When that happens, it's the end of all of us. It's doom.'

Phil took a deep breath. 'Freddy, come on. You'll be better walking…'

'No,' Freddy was adamant. 'You are the worst Gruppenführer, not just in Britain, but worldwide, do you know that? No navigator could be as bad as you. You are the very worst. Has anyone got a sweet?'

There was no storm that day and the skies were clear during the dark journey home. Near Osmaston village Freddy suddenly stopped to point into the western sky. 'Good God, look at that!' I caught sight of a green light with sparks falling from it as it swept across the heavens.

'That's from a comet called Encke,' Freddy said. 'It happens every year at this time but I've never seen it before.'

Phil, in the front passenger seat, looked impressed. 'Since when were you an astronomer as well as everything else?'

'I'm not. I just saw a programme about it.'

Freddy arrived home to catch a whiff of the richly alluring smell of ginger. He hurriedly ditched his boots – Phil had not allowed him to take them off in the car because his feet smelled, and he didn't want to contaminate his shoes – and went via the back door into the kitchen. Jean, wearing a pinafore and surrounded by pots and pans, worked the ingredients that made up that most scrumptious of all cakes, the Peak's delight, the sticky ginger. Freddy drooled. 'Oh, smell that,' he murmured.

'And smell that!' exclaimed Jean in distaste, staring at his feet. 'What a stink! What have you walked in?'

'A bog. I nearly got sucked under. It was touch and go.' He nodded at the cake mix. 'Will it be ready for tonight?'

'This isn't for you,' said Jean. 'I'm making it for Phil.'

'You're...' Freddy fell into a horrified silence.

'Ruth's paying me for it. It's for their wedding anniversary. It's stem ginger, tea-soaked sultanas and orange zest.'

'Do you know he nearly killed me today and you're making him my special, personal cake! I should have one for having had courage in the face of his attack!'

'Freddy, I'll make you one tomorrow. If you go and have a shower! Now go and get clean!'

Instead of going upstairs to the bathroom, Freddy went outside, muttering about injustice.

He entered the shed, removed the oily rags hiding his personal box of chocolates, opened it and took the hardest he could find, its sweetness lasting longer than the soft ones.

* * * * *

Phil ate his breakfast in the kitchen, not the conservatory. His fare was not the splendid repast of a normal hike morning, but porridge, with honey and a mug of coffee. *The Times* newspaper lay at his side. He read the words but failed to digest them. He looked at the kitchen clock. It was 7.55am.

7.56am. Holding his anorak, Freddy stared out of the watery window. The conifers at the bottom of the garden swayed in a strong wind. He examined the frayed zip, which had partly detached itself from the anorak, grounds for cancellation on a day like this. And the village library was more inviting than ever, with its newly created and comfortable reading zone. But he knew that Phil would lend him his spare anorak. No, that wheeze was a non-starter. He opened the back door and stuck his head outside, testing for temperature. It was cool, but not as cold as that grim February day when he had contracted hypothermia. Anyway, Jean would only push him outside with, 'You've been hiking on days like this for years and it hasn't killed you yet.' He picked up his second mug of tea of the morning.

The library pictured bright and warm in his imagination, as comforting as the tea he was drinking – he still followed the Buddhist instruction of 'feel, observe and taste'. He decided he should read Philip Larkin again, maybe have a new look at his poem about dying. But it was a few lines from John Betjeman that sprang into his head as he looked out at the swaying conifers: 'The Advent wind begins to stir, with sea-like sounds in our Scotch fir, it's dark at breakfast, dark at tea, and in between we only see, clouds hurrying across the sky, and rain-wet roads the wind blows dry.' He thought that Betjeman would never have allowed himself to suffer under a Nazi Gruppenführer. Freddy went into the hallway and opened the cellar door, switching on the light. His mobile still worked halfway down the red brick steps and Jean, getting up to make breakfast, never heard him from there. A damp, musty odour met him as he descended. The notion struck him that the cellar floor, easily dug out, would make an excellent hiding place for an assassinated Gruppenführer. The only problem was the crates of wine that Jean had acquired over the years, stuck over much of it. It was about time, he thought, that he fired his local resistance cell into action. He pressed the button on his phone and stared at the illuminated picture of a bushy-tailed squirrel, his index finger poised over the digits beneath.

What should he say? Should he just go for bad weather? Or should he merely point out that he had no intention of suffering again from hypothermia, thank you very much? As he started to tap numbers on his mobile, the hall telephone rang. He went back up the steps into the hallway and picked up the receiver. It was Phil. 'This makes a change,' said Freddy. 'I was just about to call you.'

'Well, I've beaten you to it. Afraid I've got to rest up today.'

'Oh,' said Freddy. 'So we're going to the George to sit in front of the fire. And have toast and honey and drink Burtonwood.'

'No, 'fraid not. I've called to cancel.'

Time stood still. Freddy wondered if he'd heard correctly. 'What do you mean? You never call to cancel.'

'I have this time.' Phil sounded flat, almost detached.

'Why, what's happened?' It could be a hoax call, of course. Big Fred, part-time ruffian and champion darts player in the village, specialised in taking off local people. 'Can you identify yourself? If I'm speaking to the navigator please will he tell me the code word that I call him?'

'It's me, Freddy.' Phil sounded tired. 'Your Gruppenführer.'

'Has your house caught fire? Has Ruth thrown you out? Has war been declared? Has the plague struck?' As he spoke Freddy felt a warm feeling flooding through his chest.

'No, I'm not too good today.'

Freddy dropped his banter. 'Oh, sorry to hear that. What's wrong?'

'Something I ate, I think. So why were you calling?'

'Oh, nothing. I was... I was hoping I could borrow your spare anorak. My zip's bust.'

'Well you can, if you and Don are going.'

'Ah yes, I'll speak to Don.'

'I've called him already. I expect you both to go. The hike must be kept up.'

'Absolutely,' agreed Freddy. 'Absolutely. See you. Look after yourself. Bye.' Freddy put the phone down and jumped up and down with glee. 'Ha ha!' he cried, nearly cannoning into Jean as she came down from the stairs.

'Freddy, what's going on?'

'Phil. He's cancelled. Yippee!'

Freddy rang me to discuss the astounding news. 'Yes,' I said. 'He just called, sounded dodgy. Not like Phil at all.'

'Anyway,' Freddy was anxious to secure his freedom. 'You don't mind missing the hike today, do you? Not in this weather?'

'No,' I said. 'Poor old Phil.'

'Yes,' said Freddy. 'I hope it's nothing trivial.'

* * * * *

Freddy went to the library. Ditching Larkin, he decided to trawl through the early 20th-century Georgian poets, Gibson, Sassoon and so on, but found it all a bit depressing, especially when it came to World War One. T.S. Eliot was next on the list, but was difficult to understand with all his classical allusions. The meaning was nowhere. Eliot was a man inside himself, trying to break out, Freddy thought. Was he searching for the meaning also? Freddy gave up and went for Ted Hughes, but he was out on loan. W.H. Auden was 'difficult', like Eliot, so Freddy decided to revisit the death poem by Larkin. Two lines of *Audabe* sprang out from the page. 'Most things never happen, this one will,' and 'Death is no different whined at than withstood.' It was all true, Freddy realised. Being brave or cowardly in the face of death made no difference. Death will happen however you approach it. Phil, of course, had no such belief.

Freddy's thoughts transferred to Phil. What if his violent forms of exercise were now exacting their toll? Freddy could not see Phil *in extremis*. For him dying was what other people did, folk who were too lazy and indulgent to bother prolonging their lives with good dietary habits and exercise. And he had raised his lifestyle and ambition far beyond all that, even. His was a serious mission to try and hang around, via cryogenics, until the immortality pill came on the market, or the chap with the stem cells had something to offer. Dying, to him, would be a tragedy. Freddy started to chuckle. It was funny, if you thought about it.

* * * * *

For Freddy the next six days passed pleasantly. He took his camera into the local woods and strolled among the filtered sunlight, straight into a moment of magic as the rays struck an oak tree, imbuing its leaves with a purple glow and, nearby, illuminating the not fallen leaves of a chestnut, a cloud of yellow and orange. The stillness was broken by a mistle thrush bursting into song, only for it to abruptly stop in mid flow. Then it started up again with another challenging call. Further on, Freddy stopped to watch a small flock of chaffinches feeding under a tree, their drab, greyish plumage making them hard to pick out in the shadows cast by the wood.

As he left the woods Freddy's spirits declined. He had reminded himself that it was St Martin's Day, a predictor of the winter to come. Legend had it that 'if the geese at St Martin's Day stand on ice, they will walk in mud at Christmas.' The geese were not standing on ice anywhere in the Peak, but the old saw continued: 'If the leaves do not fall before that day, then a cold winter we will see.' The country saying was backed this year by the Met Office predicting that a wintry chill was in the offing.

It irked Freddy to think of Phil's behaviour in bad weather, glorying in the deep freeze, striding ahead, bellowing out how marvellous the awful thing was. Freddy had lost count of the times he had been left gasping for breath or abandoned to his fate as he struggled and slipped on icy hillsides or dales.

Freddy felt even blacker when he dwelt on the ultimate indignity. Jean, his own wife, had baked his tormentor a cake. A sticky ginger cake no less, Freddy's favourite.

Jean only baked him a 'sticky' on his birthday. It was too much.

Freddy had reached the blacksmith's forge when he stopped and hesitated before turning back, making the short cut across the fields towards Phil's house. He had reason to call. He would like the forthcoming evening to be happily spent in the knowledge that tomorrow's hike would be cancelled, should Phil's illness have continued. Freddy had grounds for optimism, not having seen him since his withdrawal from the previous hike. Nor had Phil been seen at our weekly get-together in the Red Lion.

As he clonked the ancient iron knocker against the faded oak door, Freddy told himself not to be lured into the house. Of late he was convinced that Ruth was now as batty as Phil, since she screeched with laughter at almost everything he did or said. Freddy knocked again and waited. The house was empty. Freddy turned away, resigning himself to an evening of wait-and-see. He didn't want Phil to suffer greatly, but just hoped that whatever malady he was suffering from could stretch over into the following day.

Next morning, hike day, Freddy bit into his waffle drenched in honey while looking at his watch resting at the side of the plate. He sipped some coffee and vaguely heard Jean say something about how nice the day looked for hiking. Freddy paid no attention. Now! It was eight o'clock. He stared at his watch, hoping for the phone to ring. Oh, please, please ring. He waited, his chewing paused, his breathing stopped.

The phone in the hallway rang. Freddy slipped from his chair, flung open the tall pine door and raced to the phone. 'Hello?'

'Hi Freddy. Bad news. I can't hike again.'

'Oh that's awful. What's wrong, Phil?' Freddy sounded concerned.

'Still not too good. Got to see the quack later.'

'Oh, what a pity. It's a nice sunny day out there.'

After he'd replaced the receiver a sobering thought muted his whoop of joy; Phil had made no mention of the importance of the hike being kept up, as he had the previous week. Freddy felt a black mantle of unease descend upon him, his elation dying. He phoned me and said that we should get together to 'discuss Phil', and maybe we should do this on an easy 'talking' hike.

'Fine by me,' I said. 'We'll go at your pace.' The hike would be our standard fall-back, Ilam to Alstonefield, then Milldale, back through Dovedale to base. He had made me promise that I would not complain if he stopped for wild flower, bird or anything that might prove interesting. 'It would make up for all the route marches we've had to suffer,' he said.

We talked about Phil on the way to Ashbourne. 'I'm sure he's covering something up,' Freddy said. 'He can't be dying because that wouldn't stop him hiking. It's got to be something far worse. Or it might be his doll that I stuck pins in last week.'

'His legs might have gone,' I said. 'They did a couple of years ago, remember? He always has to be out in front. Maybe it's happened again.'

Freddy tried not to sound elated at the turn of events, but it gave him some pleasure to think that Phil had now, at last, admitted he was human after all. Maybe when he returned he would show a little humility.

An hour and a half later we reached the high ridge above the Manifold and stopped for coffee. The local phenomenon, a thin mist, rushed up over our heads from the steep-sided valley below. As usual Freddy polished off his banana in a trice, after which he struck up the subject of Phil once again. 'I think we should both go round to see him when we get back.'

I agreed. 'We could say we've come to report on the hike. You know he writes it up in his log book.'

Lunch, by common consent, was extended outside the George by half an hour, during which we sank a pint each of Boddingtons and enjoyed the sunlit day, uncommon in November. Freddy scanned the faces of fellow hikers, including a gaggle of cyclists, but then he frowned, looking around. 'Do you know what's missing here? The two ducks. They've never failed to turn up.' The thought bothered him. Recently, he said, there had been the incidents with the jackdaws as well as the MGB roadster, number plate YAN 578G, which had recently disappeared from its usual place in Ashbourne. It had been Freddy's idea that if it vanished it betokened tragedy, similar to the fate of England should the ravens flee from their home, the Tower of London. I smiled, but said little. Was he relating these incidents as part of a general build-up to some grand wheeze or other? You could never be quite sure with Freddy.

On our return home we called at Phil's house. Again, no one answered and so I drove Freddy home. As we passed the church I saw Phil running towards us, arms pumping, a determined look on his face. He wore blue tracksuit bottoms and his beloved red 'para' t-shirt. I stopped the car and wound down the window. Phil slowed down to address us. 'Can't stop,' he panted. 'I'm on a time, explain later.' He picked up speed, then turned to jog backwards. 'Glad to see you've done the hike!' he called out. He waved an arm then turned round to run away with a burst of speed. We looked at each other, shaking our heads quickly as if to dispel our bewilderment.

Later, Phil rang us both to ask that we join him in the Red Lion that evening. He turned up in great spirits; the transformation from the Phil of the previous week was Scrooge-like. He would have gone out and bought the biggest and juiciest goose at the market. He threatened to buy Freddy a bum warmer for Christmas. The weather, he said, was set for the next week, a high pressure area centred to the north bringing down cold winds but guaranteeing sunshine. He had a new hike that he'd planned. He was still gabbling away when Freddy put up a hand. 'Just a minute.'

As Phil shut his mouth Freddy spoke slowly and deliberately. 'You have not hiked for two weeks, because you've been ill. Suddenly all's well. So, what happened?'

'Ah,' said Phil. 'It's a long story.'

'Well, tell it us. We're not going anywhere.'

The explanation, as it came out, was unsatisfactory. He wanted us to believe that he'd suffered from a mystery bug that caused his arms and legs to hurt so much that he couldn't walk, let alone run.

'Not legorophilia. You don't believe in it,' said Freddy, warily. 'I hope this isn't an excuse for a 50-mile hike next week? A dash up Kinder Scout, possibly? A quick trip to Banff for a bear hunt at 10,000 feet?' He took a sip of Boddingtons. 'There's something you're not telling us. Something odd about this. Stevens, come on, what is it?'

Phil grinned easily. 'Nothing. I've told you what happened.'

* * * * *

It was the last hike of the month and Phil's turn to drive, his destination undisclosed. It was to be a 'mystery hike', he said. I dwelt on the irony of its description. The reason for Phil's absence from successive hikes was still unknown. That remained a real mystery and, it seemed, would remain so for ever. I sat alone in the rear seat of the car. As Phil drove away I noticed a blue printed document lying under the driver's seat. I leant forward to pick it up, and was about to place it beside me when I caught a phrase, 'PSA level monitoring'. It could have been a gas safety brief or a gardening document about testing the quality of garden soil. Idly, I turned it over.

A hand-stamped date of November, the same year, partially hid the capital letter 'P'. Printed in large white letters, on a deep blue background, was the caption: 'PSA TESTING FOR PROSTATE CANCER'. I checked that Phil was not looking at me in the driving mirror. I lowered the leaflet and read scraps and passages. 'The blood test can give an early indication that prostate cancer may be present…further tests may be needed…experts disagree on the usefulness of the test…second most common cause of cancer deaths in men…slow growing cancers may not cause any symptoms or even shorten life.'

233

I put the paper back where I had found it and sat back to do some thinking. Whatever had scared Phil had clearly vanished. Had he visited a specialist to be given the good news on the day of the second hike that he had missed? That would account for his transition, in the space of a few hours, from a reclusive, uncommunicative Phil back to his old extrovert, ebullient self.

The hike started at Hartington. As soon as we reached the first hillside beyond the cheese factory, Phil started to charge up it, stopwatch in hand. On this occasion Freddy shrugged his shoulders and gave up, plodding his weary way up the steep slope. It was my opportunity. Making sure that Phil was out of earshot I allowed Freddy to draw level. I told him about the leaflet I'd found in the car. Freddy listened then looked up to see Phil cresting the summit. When we arrived at the hilltop he was waiting, having regained his breath. 'Broken it by two seconds,' he declared.

'Well done,' I said, meaning it.

Freddy nodded and gave a little smile. 'Yes, well done.'

'Eh!' exclaimed Phil, grinning in amazement. 'Acknowledgement at last Freddy! Thank you! I think I'll have a go at K7 next week. Strike while the iron's hot. Come on, let's go.'

The last of the November hikes passed peacefully. There was a momentary scare when Phil thought he saw 'motor mouth' Clifford approaching us, our constant threat who, once his limpet grip had fastened, never stopped talking to his victim about anything and everything, from indigestion pills to imperilled birds. But it turned out to be someone quite different, a man who nodded, smiled and said, with a Dutch accent, 'Nice day.'

The homeward journey was spent in silence, Freddy quickly falling asleep and me drifting off a few minutes later. But before oblivion I caught Phil smiling to himself as he drove. It was a fixed smile, his eyes bright as he contemplated his victory. Was it *two* victories?

DECEMBER

Each Advent Freddy takes his grandchildren to Santa's Grotto at Castleton. He looks forward to this as much as he does the arrival of tuneless carollers at the front door. The countdown through the darkening days to Christmas Eve is a normally a matter for quiet rejoicing.

Christmas this year, however, was a dubious prospect. Aunt Cynthia and Max were expected on Christmas Eve, albeit for only a few hours. As it was Freddy's favourite day of the year, the very thought of the diabolical duo sliding across his Minton-tiled hallway filled him with dread. Further dark thoughts threatening Freddy's seasonal happiness emanated from suspicions that Phil, whose turn it was to provide the annual 'treat', would use it as an excuse to lure him into the skies. It was one thing to be taken up smoothly by a nubile and sane lady instructor, another to be strapped down in a tatty ex-RAF Bulldog and hurtled about by a dangerous madman. Freddy's nightmare, he told me over a pint in the Nag's Head, had Phil launching him into a weather window of only 15 minutes and then having to land in a force eight gale. And there was Jean, standing at the runway edge, cheering him on. If only he could make her see sense. Her baking Phil a cake, he told her, had far-reaching, sinister implications.

'Oh don't be silly, Freddy. It's a job. That's all.'

'Oh no,' Freddy said. 'If Ruth asked you to bake Phil a cake there's bound to be something lurking.'

On the morning of the first hike of the month Freddy stood in the back kitchen, coffee in hand, staring out at the bleak garden, the shed blurred by a white mist. He would so much like to be down at the village library, sitting in his favourite place by the radiator, scanning the new books, looking for something to explain his existence on earth. When the hike first began he had enjoyed discussing his quest with me. While Phil was busy leaping up hillsides he and I would debate the matter at length. In recent times he had given up the discussion as he found I had no more insight into the matter than had Montague, his dog.

'Not much chance of seeing into anything,' he murmured.

'See into what Freddy?' Jean was packing his lunch box.

'The fog. It's down to 50 yards in places. And it's going to last all day. There'll be multiple pile-ups everywhere.'

He glanced at the round, wooden-cased clock on the kitchen wall, watching the long second hand tick slowly, but relentlessly. It was like a replay of *High Noon*. In one hour and two minutes the train would arrive in town bearing the man who'd come to do him harm. For the 'gunslinger' read Phil, for the 'train' substitute car. The deadline for hike cancellation was eight o'clock, two minutes to go.

'The Ashbourne road is a death trap,' he announced. 'Rule 2 says the hike can be cancelled in bad visibility. I can cancel it. Any one of us can cancel it.'

'Well ring Phil and tell him,' said Jean. 'He doesn't want to kill himself any more than you do. If he thinks it dangerous he won't go, will he?'

'What! Sheer insanity. Do you know nothing of your cake eater? How can you possibly say that? I've spent my retirement escaping death at his hands! Don't you realise Phil was sent here by the same cult that produced Aunt Cynthia and Max? I was selected for special treatment. My fate is in his hands, nobody else's.'

'Oh Freddy, you are funny,' Jean laughed, stuffing his boots into a large white plastic bag. 'If you're so worried, ring Phil. Go on. See what he says.'

'You know what he'll say.' Freddy stared out gloomily at the shrouded garden. He knew that quoting the fog rule at Phil would have no effect. Phil would only counter it by quoting 'Appendix B,' a fascist device which negated all rules at his discretion. As they were nearly all his rules, anyway, it made no difference.

'That's how the Nazis got in power,' Freddy nodded sagely.

'What? Because of fog?'

Freddy shook his head in tired fashion. Jean simply had no idea of the dangers in which she placed her husband, so respectful was she of Phil's special achievements in the world of physical endeavour, anathema to Freddy.

Jean produced Freddy's anorak from its hiding place behind the door leading to the cellar steps, then folded it neatly and stuffed it into Freddy's rucksack. 'Hiking socks, boots, stick, lunch, water bottle – and don't forget to drink water.' She placed the rucksack by the front door.

'It keeps you hydrated. Even in winter you need water. Freddy? Are you listening?'

'I'm ringing him.' Freddy said decisively and picked up the phone in a commanding manner.

Since the call was made dead on eight o'clock, Phil knew who it was. He sat in his conservatory licking the dribbly bits from his syrup-coated waffle. 'Freddy. No. The fog will lift. Anyway...'

'Stevens?' Freddy cut in, using clipped Germanic tones. 'This is a special weather report for all Gruppenführers. Fog in the Peak District will persist all day at nil visibility. All hikers intending to enter this area should carry an emergency locator beacon and Kendal Mint Cake. Better still to stay at home by the fire and keep warm...'

'Freddy,' Phil interrupted. 'The fog is on the hills. We're going into the dales. It's good visibility down there.'

'My niece in Youlgreave doesn't think so. She takes her dog down Lathkill Dale every morning and it's terrible. She almost fell into the river. She says you'd need balls of string to find your way back. She just rang to tell me.'

'One day I'll meet all your nieces and aunts,' said Phil. 'They'd fill a football stadium.'

The hike began at Dovedale, scene of my childhood adventures. Two or three times a year we would catch the trolley bus from Chaddesden into Derby and then take the Trent bus to Ashbourne, from where we would walk to Dovedale. The names of my pals are still sharp in memory: Alan and Trevor Hill, George Howe, Bert Lowe, Phil Lawrenson...

Dovedale was our adventure playground. Rarely did we see other children. And definitely no adults. There was no car park near the entrance, not that anybody below the rank of doctor owned a car in those days of childhood freedom. We would climb the hillsides to slide down the rock screes on our haunches, wearing out our black Co-op utility shoes, risking our necks. For 'snap' I always had leaky jam sandwiches washed down with lemonade. After three hours of roistering around we would trudge back to Ashbourne for the journey home. Visitors to Dovedale before the world wars were few. In the early part of the 19th century it was the toffs who had arrived in their carriages.

'No fairer or finer view exists in the whole of Italy or Greece,' wrote Byron after his visit, guided through the Dale on horseback.

Today, only a few cars were found in the car park. But Phil was right. The fog in Dovedale was nowhere near as thick as it had been before the descent from Thorpe village. We began the trek, keeping to the left-hand side of the river, where a hard surfaced path provided easy walking. We had not gone 100 yards when we encountered something that surprised us all.

A gathering of monks. What would you call it? A monastery of monks? A meditation of monks? A memoriam of monks? They were 12 in number, brown and gold robed, with shaven heads and wearing sandals. They stood at the side of the river, staring down into the water.

Asian monks, by their appearance.

Ever since our visit to the Tara Buddhist Centre at Etwall we had tried to steer clear of monks. Freddy's prize fart in the group silence led by one of their number had brought that about. We had invented fanciful scenarios in which Freddy had a monk sweeper built on to the front of his car in case any of them tried to block his path to remonstrate with him.

None of the monks acknowledged our presence, each quietly contemplating whatever it was that needed contemplating. It was very odd because we had encountered another group of religious men at exactly the same place once before.

They had been Orthodox Jews, wearing black hats and sporting dreadlocks, each of them reading from a small book of prayer. What was it about this spot?

We passed by unnoticed.

Once out of earshot it was Freddy who spoke first. 'Far better than the Wailing Wall if it brings together different religions. All we need now are the Muslims and we've got the first step to world peace. Bingo.'

Further on up the Dale we came to stone steps, placed there by the National Trust to prevent further erosion of the footpath.

Many of these stones were covered in very light coloured crinoid and brachiopod fossils. The White Peak limestone was formed around 350 million years ago. At this time Derbyshire was covered by a shallow tropical sea, quite close to the equator. The bodies of dead shellfish, corals, sea lilies (crinoids) and other sea plants gradually built up on the sea floor and fossilised over time to become limestone. Thorpe Cloud hill was itself part of a reef of pure calcium carbonate. How did I come by this knowledge? It was not taught at school. I could say Google, but it wasn't. It was Freddy, of course. He may not be the world's best hiker – that title belongs to Phil – but he loves the plants and birds as well as the beauty of the skies and colours of the landscape in the changing seasons. For all his protestations I suspect it's not merely pressure from Phil and Jean that keeps him on the hike.

* * * * *

On the second hike of the month Phil spoke little, preoccupied with his own thoughts.

'Gruppenführer. What ailest thou?'

'What?' Phil came out of his reverie.

'What is it this time? Personal best times slipping?' Freddy's teasing and Phil baiting was another way of combating the stress and pain of hiking. 'Your dark angel deserted you?'

'No...nothing,' said Phil and continued walking.

As the days wore on, Freddy became less anxious. Our leader had stopped dropping hints or boasting about the joys of aviation. Clearly, he had other things on his mind. We had gone through periods like this before, of course. Phil had once fallen into silence for a whole fortnight, the time when he had found it painful climbing hills due to the anti-insomnia pills he took each night. And last month there had been the fear of something much worse. Phil always kept quiet about his weaknesses, as it would affect his reputation and self-regard as a superman, undermining his battle to achieve immortality. Whenever he beat his 'personal best' racing up hillsides he convinced himself he was growing younger, or at least standing still. Anything else was going backwards in time. No doubt the current problem would be something akin to the latter.

Freddy decided the time was ripe for an open challenge.

'Gruppenführer. What's the problem?' Freddy stopped walking. 'Come on. What is it? If it's nothing trivial we could all go home.'

'It's...' Phil shook his head irritably, signalling it was a minor thing.

'No. Tell us. That's why we're here, Don and me. To delight in your troubles. It gives us hope that one day the hike will be ended and our travails eased. So what is it?'

239

Phil sighed. 'Okay.' He confessed his problem. He was in the process of trying to wrest a bond from the Sun Life insurance company. Time was critical in the process of taking the money out, he told us, all to do with avoiding a hefty income tax liability. He was in daily conversation with a 'Mr Gupta' in Bangalore or Bombay, but whose lilt of voice made him difficult to understand.

'I just want to talk to somebody in Bristol, their HQ. All I want is a withdrawal form. A form that you fill in, sign and return. Nothing difficult.' He said that Gupta had assured him in five telephone calls that all necessary steps were being taken. That was a week ago.

'All I want is a piece of paper. They must have thousands of withdrawal forms!' exclaimed a peeved Phil, devouring his Cornish pasty as we sat in the hikers' shelter at Milldale.

'He keeps telling me it's been sent from their Bristol place, but it hasn't. And it's Ruth's money and if she can't draw the money out before Christmas she has to pay two grand in tax.'

On today's hike, from Ilam through Dovedale into Mill Dale, Freddy had brought a friend along, David from Buxton. A new rule (123b), introduced by Freddy, gave us individual freedom to bring along a guest on a one-off hike, the notion being that as we grew older one of us would either 'pop his clogs' or fall ill, the novice taking his place in seamless fashion – subject of course to the common will. Phil found it difficult to reject the idea as, on the face of it, its logic was undeniable. But he knew Freddy and his wiles. As soon as David had hiked a couple of times and the weather was bad Freddy would go down with some incurable malady, probably an aching lower back, a difficult problem to diagnose and therefore dispute. David would take his place.

'Why talk to somebody in India?' David spoke in the calm and measured voice of a retired lecturer at the London School of Oriental Studies and, later, Oxford University, where he'd been Reader in Persian Studies. Such is the measure of his intellectual range that one of his numerous hobbies is knowing everything about the aeroplane engines of the Rolls-Royce dynasty. He'd been on the *Brain of Britain* show. He was not only fluent in Arabic and Japanese, but was also a solver of Killer Su Doku. Above all, in Freddy's regard, he had elite status as a connoisseur of the Cornish pasty, the sole reason that Freddy had brought him along. Jean had banned Freddy from the delicacy due to its cholesterol count. Tucked away in his rucksack, still warm from the baking, was the forbidden delight. David was undetectable as Freddy's smuggler.

'Why not talk to head office here and say you need to speak to Bristol? They must have a customer services there?' David put the point to Phil.

'I do! But when they put me through I get Gupta!' Phil wrinkled his nose.

'Every time an English voice answers I've no problem with it. I can understand. But when I get Gupta I don't. I know what'll happen. If I complain too much they'll take me to court on a racist charge!'

'Oh,' David mused. 'Yes. You do have a problem.'

'I have,' exclaimed Phil. 'I talk to Gupta. Or I don't because he's always on a lunch break. I once got a Jane from Bristol headquarters. That was brilliant. I explained everything and she said she had the right person to talk to. Told me to hang on, putting me through – guess who I got?'

'Don't tell me,' said David.

'Absolutely,' said Phil.

'Gupta,' Freddy said.

David then talked about Kafka, bureaucracy and the submission of the individual to the workings of the state. Was there anything this man didn't know or have an erudite opinion about? The good thing was that David never sported his knowledge as had George. He was tolerable, dryly witty, and helped Freddy, this day at least, to pass the time as something less than a curmudgeonly backslider.

Phil waved his hiking pole in frustration. 'He said it will arrive tomorrow. But it never does.'

'Hmm.' David meditated a moment. 'Well, I'd call customer services at Bristol and tell them you're going down to pick up the form. Just tell them that. Pick your day. Go down and wait until you get it.'

Phil grunted his thanks. As he thought about it his voice became lighter, saying he would give it a try.

As we stumbled up Mill Dale – Phil choosing the foggy hike because we knew it by instinct – Freddy was peculiarly cheerful. In a secretive moment, later in the hike, he gave me his reason: it was now obvious that Phil would not go flying – and therefore not be a 'Freddy threat' –

until he had secured his blessed bond. Freddy wondered if he could pose as 'Gupta' on the phone and prolong the delay, but gave it up when I pointed out it would be a criminal offence. Not that Freddy minded being cast in chains, he said, anything was preferable to enduring Phil's enemy action. He was sure that Jean was colluding with him in some 'diabolical scheme'.

'How do you know that?' I asked.

'The cake! The cake! My cake. My own lovely cake baked for Phil! Jean hardly ever makes me one, always going on about cholesterol. But why deliberately make something I really like for *him*? It can't be his wedding anniversary. It's got to be something devious.'

I gestured at the mist-shrouded figures of David and Phil a hundred yards in front, threatening to disappear into the fog. 'Best keep up,' I said. 'We don't want to end up as bleached bones.'

'I don't know,' said Freddy. 'Better than dying in a plane crash.'

* * * * *

Phil's withdrawal form still had not materialised and so he followed David's advice and booked a seat on the following day's 10 o'clock InterCity train from Derby to Bristol, having notified Sun Life HQ that he was on his way. In the Red Lion that night he said it would be a lightning strike, SAS style. He had planned it like a military operation. Aim: to secure the withdrawal form. Method: by train and foot. He had made his recce via the internet. Alighting at Bristol station it would be a 10-minute walk to the huge modern building surrounded by parkland and water features.

Sun Life is the 21st century's temple to Mammon. Three thousand staff work at HQ. The mission would entail Phil picking up the form in reception (the receptionist would have it at her side) then a quick march back to the station to catch the next train back to Derby. In case of any hold up at Sun Life he had not booked the return journey. This proved a wise decision.

The next night we assembled once more in the Red Lion, this time to be debriefed. Phil said that the train to Bristol had kept to time. It had taken 11 minutes and 30 seconds to walk from the train station to the imposing entrance of Sun Life. He had walked across a moat-like entrance into its vast entrance hall. There, a young man at the large desk had asked Phil his business. It was a mark of how few customers were expected at Sun Life that it had only one receptionist.

'You have a withdrawal form for my wife's Deferred Distribution bond. I rang yesterday and you said it would be waiting for me in reception. Stevens. Phil Stevens. I told you I was coming.'

The young man hesitantly declared himself a temp, who had been recruited that day. He consulted a sheet of paper and told Phil that there was no note about it. Phil had told him to keep looking. But no. The man searched and found nothing. Phil would have to present his request anew. Bristling with outrage at such inefficiency and ineptitude, he repeated his long-standing call for a withdrawal form. 'I just need a bond withdrawal form. It's standard issue. You must have millions. I want one now. Please.'

The temp said that he would speak to the department most likely to provide such a facility. Would Phil please care to sit down while he made his enquiries? Phil had reluctantly retired to the window seat to watch the smartly dressed staff pass to and fro through the chrome turnstiles by inserting their security cards. Minutes passed by. Finally the temp summoned Phil back to the desk to tell him that the matter was in hand and would be dealt with shortly. Phil stressed the actual words spoken:

'It's in hand. People are on to it.' Phil went back to his seat, where he picked up a glossy magazine extolling the magnificence of the new building. It boasted 46,600 square metres of floor space. It had seven office modules accommodating seven operational teams on one or half a floor of a module. A 'sinusoidal wave form fabric roof covered walkway' provided the means for communication between modules and floors and contributed to informal meetings away from the work space. The engineering services were designed to provide a high level of flexibility and system resilience. There was a remote Energy Centre, Kitchen, Restaurants, Gym Facility, Printing, Training and Management Suites together with a 150-seat Auditorium with full AV and translator facilities...'

'Sir?'

The temp beckoned Phil back to the desk to inform him that the matter was proving more difficult than had first been imagined, but it would be solved soon as departments 'were talking to each other about it.' A further

10 minutes elapsed after which the temp, cautious now in the face of Phil's reddening face, admitted that the required form was not kept in that building but elsewhere and a messenger had been despatched to find it. Phil went back to his window seat. It was now lunch time and he had sat watching the employees of the 21st century palace of financial efficiency surge out through the main doors, no doubt going out for a walk around their splendid grounds. Bought with Ruth's money, noted Phil. It had occurred to him that he was now caught up in some Kafkaesque (not his word, of course, but Freddy's) nightmare. The masters in their modules would have discounted the idea of anybody ever wanting to visit headquarters when they could do it by fax, e-mail or phone.

A human being entering their inner sanctum had thrown the whole place into chaos. There was not a procedure for it. Phil repeated this. 'No procedure.' The log fire spat out a spark which died on the grey-black flagstones. Phil paused to raise his glass.

We were all on our second pints, warming ourselves by the huge log fire, allowing Phil a swig of Boddingtons before carrying on with his story.

Phil recommenced with the confession that he was at the point of launching himself across the desk, clutching the temp by the throat, dragging him over the chrome turnstiles and screaming his demand. But he brought himself back from the abyss. A night in a police cell would not have secured him his withdrawal form.

Phil had looked at his watch. Fifty minutes had passed since his arrival. Suddenly, eureka! The temp, now caught up in the thrill of the chase, had excitedly waved him over, telephone in hand.

'Sir. The person you need is here. He knows who you are. It's all been explained to him. He deals with all the forms and he'll see it right.'

Phil said he had taken the phone in sheer relief. It had never occurred to him to ask why he should have to speak to somebody on the phone when that 'somebody' in the building obviously knew he was present in reception.

Phil had taken the phone in a relaxed manner, exhaling softly.

'Hello?'

'Mr Stevens? This is Gupta. If you go home now I'll send you the form by first-class post.'

We roared with laughter. I spilt my drink on my trousers. Other locals, drawn by the hilarity, came over to enquire. The story spread like wildfire.

'But what happened then?' I was the first to regain my breath. 'Did you get the form or not?'

'I did,' said Phil. 'I told Gupta I was not leaving the building until I got the form. And I damned well meant it!'

'And?'

'Five minutes later a woman came to see me. She said she was from customer services. She took me through the turnstile and to a restaurant, insisted she bought me a meal. I asked her how it was that it had taken her all that time to see me? She said no one had told her I was there. She had the form with her. She would help me complete it. But she saw a snag. It couldn't be done there and then.'

'Oh no.' I said.

'Since it was Ruth drawing the money she had to sign the form.'

More laughter.

'So you took it home,' said Phil.

'Yes. I posted it this morning by guaranteed delivery.'

'They should have refunded your train fare,' I said. 'Bet they didn't.'

'No. Doesn't matter. It's over.'

'They should have sent the form by e-mail attachment,' I said.

'Good God, no. They couldn't do that. Far too hi-tech,' said Freddy.

*****

Christmas was coming and – global warming or no – a period of intense cold set in, with a zone of high pressure over the British Isles heralding blue skies and brisk hikes. Phil rose each morning to the task of extending his life. The morning jog was followed by a 20-minute meditation session of Autogenics, to which benefit he'd been directed by the man in the bus shelter at Parwich. In the late afternoon another running session of two and a half miles was followed by stretches, crunches, press ups and balancing exercises. The latter involved standing on his left leg, closing his eyes and seeing how long he could remain like a one-legged parrot on a perch.

Freddy was in another element, purely spiritual. He had heard the first carollers, tuneless though they may have been. And he had won – at long last – a dispensation from the Gruppenführer allowing Freddy and me to take it in turns to choose a pre-Christmas hike. This had nothing to do with the 'treat', which was in Phil's hands and loomed larger over Freddy each day like a thunder cloud.

Freddy chose – and I could not believe it, let alone Phil – a route starting at Castleton.

It had been Phil's turn, two years back, to take us on a 'treat' hike and he had chosen the same place. Why Freddy should want to choose Castleton as a hiking start was a mystery. For the three of us living in the south of the county it's almost foreign country. Castleton is nearer to Manchester and Sheffield than it is to our local city of Derby. Visits to the area are special and Freddy's memories of them are not of the best. There had been the nightmarish overnight camp after the first Kinder expedition in which Freddy had slept little, kept awake by Phil's snoring. Then, shortly afterwards, this had been followed by an even more alarming hike, across the centre of Kinder's cratered and ribbed surface, during which our sterling leader had allowed his navigational skills to be usurped by a lady Amazon bearing a sat nav.

So why had Freddy chosen a hike in that area, a place of bitter memory?

'Castleton? Freddy? You amaze me.' Phil stood grinning in his conservatory, the phone to his ear. The big country around the Hope valley was his kind of territory. But he knew Freddy. There had to be something...

'Freddy? Have you got a philosopher up there? Or a pub en route you'd make us go in?'

'No.'

'Not an aunt or a niece who just happens to have a café or a personal chocolate shop?'

'No.'

'There's got to be something. You don't just go all that way when you can get from Etwall to Ashbourne in 20 minutes. Come on, what is it?'

'No. I just like the walk around the Castleton area.'

'No you don't. You said you'd never go further north than Buxton. You said it froze your hands. You couldn't hold your stick. You'd fall down.'

'Do you deny me my choice of hike, leader? My statutory right to guide us this one day of the year?'

'I don't. But we need to know if there's to be any, you know, Freddy wheezes, like watching the sun go down and up again in the wrong place? Or watching birds creep down trees? Flower spotting perchance?'

'What? In December?'

'Okay. But there's something fishy going on. So watch it. Hold on. Wait a minute. I know. It's your Land Rover, isn't it. It's to get out of driving that far, isn't it? Even your bum gets sore.'

'No. But if we can go in your car I'll drive for the next two hikes.'

'Hmm.' Phil was unconvinced. 'Alright. But don't forget. I'll be watching.'

* * * * *

We assembled as per ritual at nine o'clock to set off in Phil's Volvo estate car. The journey north was remarkable in that visibility in the cold air and the cloudless blue sky gave views of distant hills that are often shrouded in haze.

Phil drove in silence, his mind ticking over the 'Freddies' – as he termed them – that might be deployed by his duplicitous, unpredictable and totally unreliable charge. His view of Freddy had been coloured when he'd learnt that he'd 'got out' of doing his National Service by working up some devious medical ploy. Evading one's duty to Queen and country had put many a man in the social dock. Phil had even played a part in the downfall of Terry Dene, a good rock and roll singer in the 1950s and whose promising career was to be short-lived, due to Phil and his coterie of warriors. Believing that Dene had escaped his military duty to exploit his talent, Phil and his military mates had ruined his comeback performance at the Majestic Cinema in Chaddesden, Derby, by barracking him from the first guitar chord. After that Dene had disappeared from public view. In Phil's eyes Freddy was in the Dene mould, a backslider who would come up with all sorts of ailments to escape his obligations.

Phil remained sceptical as we drove along the road from Hope to Castleton. It was an hour and a half since we'd set off, during which time he'd monitored Freddy's mannerisms and voice. On the hike Freddy usually modulates between 'moaning high pitched' and 'apathetic'. But when he's about to initiate a wheeze his voice becomes lighter and slower, dwelling on words for effect. Freddy never uses bludgeons. His weapons are like stilettos, inserted in Phil's brain to make him feel uncomfortable and uncertain.

But as we arrived in Castleton Phil had not yet seen any warning sign of an imminent 'Freddy'. The routine of putting boots put on, slipping on rucksacks, gathering sticks in hand, was all perfectly normal. However, as Phil broke away to stamp his boots and limber up Freddy, the last to tie up his bootlaces, stood up to give me a smile. I recognised it for what it signified: a wheeze was on.

We had gone no more than 100 yards when Freddy spoke out in a tour guide voice. 'Castleton lies between the Dark and the White Peak areas of the Peak District.'

'What?' Phil looked at Freddy.

'It has dramatic scenery, ideal for hiking or walking. Created for you specially, leader.'

'Oh yes.' Phil eyed Freddy heavily.

Freddy gave a light laugh. 'A little knowledge makes the day pass quicker.' Then added, 'or better.'

'Hmm,' murmured Phil.

We walked past the church into the main square behind, then took the narrow road out of the south-west corner of the square. As we left Castleton and trekked in a south-westerly direction we came to the entrance to Peak Cavern, the largest natural cave opening in the British Isles. We stood for a moment, gazing at it.

'Also called the Devil's Arse,' said Freddy. 'As it's known by the potholing fraternity.'

'Yes,' said Phil, eyeing Freddy for any deviation from the hike. 'We're not going in.'

'Of course not. But important to know that inside are unusual rock formations.'

'Yes. I know. I've been in,' said Phil.

'Ah, then you've experienced the eerie sound of running water and echoes of a dark past.'

'Not really.'

'There you are, you see. I try to bring knowledge to the hike and what do I get? Philistinism. *Phil – istinism.*' Freddy stressed, giving me a quick smile. 'Now then,' he said dramatically. 'We head north.'

Later we climbed up the eastern side of Mam Tor, the shivering mountain, which stands guard at the western end of the Hope Valley. Freddy began to inform us of its history of geological problems. He waved his stick to reinforce his comments. Mam Tor means 'mother hill', he said. 'Is that why Derbyshire kids call their mothers "mam" do you think Gruppenführer?'

Phil glanced at Freddy. 'That is interesting. Give you that.'

'The road was closed in 1979,' said Freddy. 'It refused to stop sliding down the hill. As I like to do.' He shot a smile at Phil.

'What's all this about Freddy? There's something going on, isn't there?' He gave Freddy a warning look. '*Isn't* there?'

'Of course there is!' cried out Freddy, brandishing his stick. 'This is mother nature Gruppenführer! Or "mam" nature! Things are going on. Things fall apart, the centre cannot hold! Like your hard-tempered body. Ashes to ashes...'

'Okay.' Phil stopped walking. 'How does all this end up?'

'End up?'

'You know what I mean. What wheeze are we on to? I need to know.'

'Wheeze? No wheeze, leader. All I'm doing is entertaining you and Don while helping myself to endure the pain of hiking. You should be pleased. I bring you knowledge, of which you are in a significant minus mode. Physical health is one thing but education and...'

'Freddy,' said Phil ponderously. 'I know you're up to...'

'Do you realise,' interrupted Freddy, pointing at the landslip, 'all these sedimentary bands of shale and gritstone were laid down 350 million years ago? What happens is that the ground moves after heavy rainfall. The water lubricates the joints.' He looked at Phil. 'Hiking doesn't.'

Phil looked at his watch. 'I see. You've been talking for 40 minutes...'

Freddy continued to annoy him. 'Do you know it will keep moving for another 1,500 years? Imagine that. How old will you be then Gruppenführer? Will you still be in some cryogenic hide-out, or will you have been stem-celled a hundred times to remain the same old hiking leader? Just a thought.'

Phil gave a grunt. 'How did you learn all this? Off Google?'

'Yes. Partly. And what is wrong with that if it lubricates the rusting hinges of the mind? Now then, up there...' Freddy pointed uphill. 'On the top, up there, are the remains on an old Iron Age fort, a ditch and a rampart.'

'I don't wish to know that,' said Phil. 'We've had enough now. Can we enjoy the hike?'

'Did you really learn all this from Google?' I asked Freddy.

'No. I've got a cousin who lives here. She keeps sending me stuff, always asking me to come up.'

'That's it.' Phil stopped. 'Another relative. You only ever mention an aunt or a nephew when something's up. Go on then. Let's hear it. Go on. Whatever it is, let's have it.'

'I give you my word. I have a cousin in Castleton.'

'Address?'

Freddy hesitated.

'You see!' said Phil triumphantly.

'Leader…'

'No Freddy. I've got you and you won't admit it!'

Freddy gave out a long sigh. 'Cynicism will destroy you, leader. I give you my word we're not going to see her. She's in Greenland on a musical expedition. She moves about. A peripatetic teacher of the violin.'

Phil remained rooted, shaking his head. Finally he set off again behind Freddy.

'Now then, party.' Freddy pointed to the hilltop. 'The earliest remaining features on Mam Tor are two Bronze Age burial mounds. They contain the remains of our ancestors. Even yours, leader. At a later stage in the Bronze Age, probably between 1000 and 2000BC, there were lots of small level platforms scraped into the hill near the summit. Celtic folk probably, connected with a tribe in south Yorkshire. Now…'

'No Freddy. That's it.' Phil stopped walking, bringing Freddy to an enquiring halt. 'Come on. Stop pratting about.'

'In a moment, Gruppenführer. The tour hasn't finished. Do you realise that on the top, up there, is the earliest hill fort in the land? And it's the second highest at 1,700 feet?'

'Freddy. Navigation rule 66d. "Should there be any deliberate departure from a minimum of an eight-mile hike while being led by a hike member, not the navigator, then that member shall receive a warning." And 66d(i) "In accordance with rule 66d should this person fail to observe proper procedure then the official navigator can, if he or she so wishes, take over."'

'You shall have your eight-mile hike. Coffee break.'

We had arrived at a point between the Speedwell Cavern and the world-famous Blue John Cavern. Freddy sat down near the roadside and opened his rucksack. Phil, about to say something, decided against it and joined him.

Freddy stared ahead, eating his banana and sipping coffee in silence. Phil, after flashing him a few glances, looked – for the moment at least – satisfied. He too ate and drank in the peaceful quiet.

We headed for lunch at Losehill, at 1,570 feet giving great views down the Hope Valley. The footpath along the ridge from Mam Tor is one of the most popular in the Peak District, providing breathtaking scenery in every direction, including the Edale Valley, Kinder, the Derwent Moors, Stanage Edge and the limestone plateau to the south. But, being popular, 'the ground underneath boots' (Freddy's phrase) was badly worn by the tramping of many hikers.

'Look at it, Stevens. You and your mad cohorts have done this. Hiking is the most un-green activity! Hikers should be arrested.'

I laughed. Phil smiled bleakly. But Freddy had a point. Ground erosion caused by the sheer number of visitors has resulted in some routes to the summit being closed and hikers being encouraged to use surfaced paths constructed over the last 10 years. Flagstones have been laid along the ridge route to protect any archaeology underneath.

Freddy jabbed his stick at Phil. 'What we're doing is ecological vandalism. The countryside should be left to itself while we sit at home nice and warm.'

Phil scoffed. 'What's the point of hills and mountains if you can't climb them to look at them!' He grunted and gave up. His fears of a 'Freddy' had all but disappeared. We were at the mid-point of the hike. Whatever happened, Freddy, as hike navigator, had to get us home and that meant another four miles of hiking. Phil could relax.

Just then Freddy exclaimed sharply, clutching his knee. 'Hell's teeth!' he gasped.

'What is it?' I asked.

'The old injury. Bit of gyp.'

'Not legorophilia?' Phil sighed, his relief cut short, knowing that in its place would arrive the usual boredom and frustration in the face of a 'Freddy'. It was all too much.

'My leg just went,' Freddy muttered.

'Wish you'd go with it,' Phil said.

Freddy sat down, still holding his knee. 'Feels as though I've been shot.'

'You should be.' Phil cackled briefly. 'Freddy? What is it? What's the wheeze?'

'You doubt my pain receptors? Oh…' Freddy closed his eyes, the pain of rebuff equal to that stemming from his injury.

Phil sat down. 'Okay. I sit here until you're ready. We are not fetching the air ambulance. We are walking back. Rule 4.'

'Afflicted by a cold-hearted Hun as well as this. Too much.' Freddy made a pillow out of his rucksack and lay his head on it. He made himself as comfortable as possible. 'That's a bit better. What usually happens is that after half an hour it goes.'

Phil blew out his cheeks and gave a great sigh.

* * * * *

We could see the Christmas lights as we descended towards Castleton, taking care in the fading light. It was pitch dark before we entered the village, yet Freddy's eyes shone with expectation. I noticed that his limp, so pronounced when we had resumed walking, had now vanished.

We entered the village by way of a narrow lane, its cluster of old stone cottages festooned with bright decorations. Santa's Grotto was in full swing, with mothers and children queueing outside. The sparkling stream leading to the Peak Cavern through the oldest part of the village was lit along its length by strings of coloured bulbs. Each of the gift shops, cafés and restaurants had 'light pictures', a sleigh here, a fantasy there…

Freddy loved it all. We had difficulty getting him back to the car park.

On the journey home he fell asleep after murmuring something about the hike party that we held each Christmas. Something about 'the wives…'

Phil drove for a time before speaking. 'Knee hurt?' he said disparagingly, then looked at me. 'He didn't want us to get back too early. He was waiting for it to get dark. So he could see the lights.'

Later, with Freddy snoozing, Phil spoke again. 'You know we've done 5,250 miles since we began the hike? I did a count last night.' He glanced at Freddy, slumped beside him, snoozing gently. 'If it hadn't been for him we'd have done it in half the time.'

We passed through Bakewell.

Overhead and all around the lights, flags and the Pudding Shop sang of Christmas.

* * * * *

It was Freddy who had come up with the idea of an annual 'treat'. It would be a 'surprise' he said, lightening at least one of the grim hikes of winter. As he gazed out at the frosty December morning, he regretted his impulse. There was little wind and a perfectly blue sky. Phil waxed lyrical about such days. Flying in cold, still air, he always said, was 'like skating on ice'. Once altitude, speed and course had been established, the pilot's hands, literally, could be taken off the controls. It was like 'flying on autopilot,' he maintained, giving Freddy one of his infuriating smiles of encouragement.

Freddy said that Phil with no hands was a greater threat than Phil with two hands clapped firmly on the tiller. He would have none of it. He sipped his coffee, looked at the clock – a minute to eight – and made up his mind.

'That you leader?' It was 8am, of course, last time for cancellations.

'Hello Freddy. What a beautiful day, eh?'

'Yes. Perfect for flying.' Freddy closed his eyes as he awaited the response.

'Hah.'

'Hah what?' said Freddy, dreading the worst.

'It's a pity.'

'What is so pitiful about taking me up to my death?'

'No. Pity me because I can't fly today. I've had a hold up on my annual medical.'

Freddy's heart leapt. 'You mean at last you're dying? I'm not to be taken into the skies? I'm not going to be subjected to G-forces that rip out my teeth?'

'No. Just a bit of a set-back. A medical thing.'

'Nothing trivial, I hope?'

'Yes. It is, actually. Some of the pills I've been taking are banned by the CAA. I was told that by the doc yesterday. I have to wait a fortnight to get them out of my system.'

'Oh, that's great news. So what's the fall back? A blast off to Mars? A trip round the Moon en route?'

'No. Afraid not. Usual time.'

Phil took us to Brassington, an old lead-mining village lying in a steep north-south valley running down from the edge of the White Peak. To the north is the plateau of Brassington Moor, to the east the high rough ground of Carsington Pasture and to the south the South Derbyshire plain. The name is Anglo-Saxon – meaning 'Brand's people's place' – and the Saxon settlement was probably founded in the fifth or sixth century, after the departure of the Romans.

Phil, who knew none of these things, had only one thing in mind. A fast morning's hike and then the treat.

Freddy put his hands on his hips. 'A fast morning's hike? I don't do fast mornings. And I certainly don't do fast afternoons, especially after my Cornish pasty.'

'Freddy. I don't mean charging. I mean brisk. You can do that.' Phil pulled on his boots as we sat on a bench seat close to the centre of the village.

Freddy sat down. 'I am not taking part in record breaking. You can do your personal bests entirely on your own.'

Phil paused. 'Alright. A carrot for the donkey. If I tell you what the surprise is and you like it will you promise to walk fairly quickly this morning?'

Freddy thought about it. 'Only if I genuinely like it. What is it?'

Phil pointed in the direction of Well Street. 'There, Freddy, is the Olde Hanging Gate. You spend your hikes trying to get me into pubs. Well, you have. We're going to have lunch in there, at my expense. And you can sample the brew.'

'Gruppenführer. You always lie when you tell me I'll like anything. Don? Did you hear that?'

'I certainly did,' I said.

Freddy was the first to put on his rucksack. 'Right. I shall sue for £4.5 million if it's a con. Come on. Let's go.'

The 'carrot' was very enticing and Freddy stayed with Phil for the two and a half hours it took to march a circular route, first approaching Carsington Water and then turning west towards Bradbourne before turning north, back to Brassington.

The Olde Hanging Gate Inn was first opened in 1616 and has a reputation for being haunted. It has two pub signs, one conventional, the other an actual gate, which is painted white and hangs from the side of an upstairs window.

Freddy was less concerned with the history of the place than its food and drink. Once established at the fireside, he tucked into the generous menu of roast duck, salad and chips with relish, washed down with a pint of Banks' Top General.

'Gruppenführer. I have never praised you, have I?'

'Only when I had to ring up and cancel. You were always ecstatic then.'

'True. When you were dying they were good times. Oh…' Freddy stopped eating, his glass mug poised. 'What do we do this afternoon? There has to be some payback. Some cruelty. How far? I'm not doing any more than two miles.'

'You won't even do that. We're going home. It's your treat. No more hiking today.'

'Oh joys.' Freddy's eyes shone in the firelight, reflecting the glow from the copper utensils around the hearth. 'I cannot tell you how happy…'

'Shut up, Freddy, and eat.'

An hour and a half spent in front of a hot fire with a meal and a pint of beer tucked away is a recipe for soporific inertia. Neither Freddy nor I was an exception to the rule and we were both asleep within minutes on the homeward journey.

It wasn't until we reached Ashbourne that I woke up to find Freddy examining the contents of a plastic bag that he'd removed from his rucksack. Conkers. Beautiful, polished conkers, collected in November.

'Now then,' he announced. 'Tomorrow is my treat. A conker match. I challenge you, Gruppenführer, to a duel to the death. The loser buys the round.'

Phil pursed his lips, thought of saying something, then changed his mind. It was Christmas, after all. And if it would keep Freddy happy and on the hike it was a small price to pay. And he was competitive, after all. Freddy had banked on that.

What Phil didn't know was that Freddy had secreted in his pocket a 'special', which had been soaked in vinegar, baked in the oven and then coated with clear varnish. It was cheating, of course, but done as a wheeze.

We met in Freddy's garden. He handed Phil a personal chocolate taken from his cache in the shed, plus six conkers. It took no more than five minutes for Freddy's cannonball to destroy Phil's collection. As the last one splintered Phil grabbed hold of Freddy's 'sixer' and with his fingernail scratched its surface.

'Ha ha! Varnished. And I bet pickled in vinegar!'

'Not at all,' Freddy said loftily. 'You can't bear losing, that's your trouble. Am I the winner or not?'

'Hmm.' Phil grimaced. He reminded himself that the hike, his great hike and one means of living to a time when technology could have him pickled and kept alive for 1,000 years, depended to a degree on the willingness of his foot soldiers.

'Okay, you win,' he grunted. Then he smiled in encouragement. 'By the way, meant to tell you both. It was in the paper this morning. The NASA people are now saying that...'

'No!' shouted Freddy, backing away and making for the Red Lion. 'I don't wish to know anything about that!'

'But Freddy it's...'

'No. And mine's a Boddington's.'

Printed in Great Britain
by Amazon

66172653R00147